THE KING

THE
KING

DENIS LAW

WITH BOB HARRIS

TED SMART

TRANSWORLD PUBLISHERS
61–63 Uxbridge Road, London W5 5SA
a division of The Random House Group Ltd

RANDOM HOUSE AUSTRALIA (PTY) LTD
20 Alfred Street, Milsons Point, Sydney,
New South Wales 2061, Australia

RANDOM HOUSE NEW ZEALAND LTD
18 Poland Road, Glenfield, Auckland 10, New Zealand

RANDOM HOUSE SOUTH AFRICA (PTY) LTD
Endulini, 5a Jubilee Road, Parktown 2193, South Africa

Published 2003 by Bantam Press
a division of Transworld Publishers

A catalogue record for this book is available from the British Library.
ISBN 0593 051408

Typeset in 12/16pt Granjon by
Falcon Oast Graphic Art Ltd.

Printed in Great Britain by
Mackays of Chatham plc, Chatham, Kent

1 3 5 7 9 10 8 6 4 2

Papers used by Transworld Publishers are natural, recyclable products made from wood grown
in sustainable forests. The manufacturing processes conform to the environmental regulations of
the country of origin.

To my family, past, present and future

CONTENTS

ACKNOWLEDGEMENTS

Denis Law and Bob Harris would like to thank their families for their support; Sir Richard Branson and Paul Clark for their help; Jackie White at Sandy Beach Hotel in Barbados for her hospitality; John D. Taylor of Football Italia; literary agent Jonathan Harris; and editor Daniel Balado and publisher Doug Young for their patient efforts.

FOREWORD

By Sir Bobby Robson

I GO BACK A LONG WAY WITH DENIS LAW, AND, LIKE HIM, I WILL never forget the day in April 1961 when we clashed in front of Her Majesty Queen Elizabeth II at Wembley. In this, his long-awaited autobiography, he blames me for the incident, but I still have the bruises. Kick Denis first? I should be so lucky! He was a real will-o'-the-wisp player, as sharp as a needle and lightning fast in his movements, with a brain to match.

Denis lived to score goals, and did so with consummate ease because he perfected the art of getting in behind the defender, the hallmark of any great striker. I wonder how many goals he would score a season these days, and what he would be worth on the transfer market. And he was brave with it, too. If you weren't brave in those days you never got there at all, never mind managed a strike on goal. Courage was a key quality for any striker in those rough, tough days because the defenders would kick you as soon as look at you, and a player like Denis was earmarked before the players ran out of the dressing-room. That was a compliment to him; he was such a wonderful player and an exceptional finisher. He was rarely even aware of his opponent in the penalty area because he only ever saw the ball and the goal in front of him.

Scotland have, over the years, boasted some truly great players, men of the calibre of Kenny Dalglish and Jimmy Baxter, but Denis is right up there with the very best the country has ever produced. A truly great player, fabulous in every sense of the word. Speaking personally, I found him the very devil to mark because he was always on the move; he was always feinting, dropping a shoulder, wriggling his hips to throw you off the scent and lose you. He was incredibly elusive, and once he had left his marker you knew you were in trouble. The advice I always used to give to anyone who had to mark him was track, mark and tackle . . . and wear your shin pads! But he knew too well what those instructions would be, and he made sure he was always on the move and hard to catch. If those knee injuries could not slow him down, then there weren't many defenders who were going to do so. Denis was also fabulous in the air. He had the ability and agility to outjump defenders and hang in the air. When the ball came over he didn't let the ball just hit his head, he put his head to the ball and generated terrific power.

Who can forget that shock of blond hair, that slender, wiry body, the right sleeve grasped in his hand before raising it to celebrate another goal? He was a player you loved to watch and hated to mark, as he demonstrated on that spring day more than forty years ago. I haven't forgotten that – nor the score!

As a bloke he was always friendly, always had time for you. I got to know him better in his BBC days when he followed club and international teams around the world. He was always good company and easy to mix with, a real football man. We always got on well when we met, so I needed no persuasion to salute with this foreword one of the greatest strikers these islands have ever produced. In fact, it is a privilege.

Bobby Robson
July 2003

1 THE NORTHERN LIGHTS OF OLD ABERDEEN

AS A GROWING YOUNGSTER IN SCOTLAND, I LOOKED ANYTHING but a future professional sportsman. Small, skinny and be-spectacled with a dreadful squint, it is a wonder my fisherman father did not throw me straight back into the North Sea.

I was a war baby, born in the north of Scotland, in Aberdeen, on 24 February 1940, one of a sizeable brood of seven. I was the youngest by far, the last in line, and by the time I arrived my father, George, who had already served his country during the First World War in the army, had been called up to do so again in Britain's hour of need, but this time in the navy. It was a fairly logical step as he earned his meagre living fighting the elements as a fisherman. I still find it hard to imagine that such a young man should have fought in such a bitter war as the 1914–18 conflict. He was very, very young at the time – we worked out that he couldn't have been any older than seventeen. That seemed like madness to us kids, but then we discovered some of the soldiers were fighting at fourteen and fifteen. He did not come through unscathed, either, as an Italian sniper shot him. Fortunately, the bullet went right through his thigh and no bone was damaged. (Some years later, of course, one or two Italians tried to gun me down in a different way during my short stay in Italian football, and I, too, managed to escape with no broken bones.)

You would have thought the injury would have excused him second time round, but not a bit of it. It was all hands to the pumps again, this time with the Royal Navy, serving on the flotillas that went to Murmansk in big convoys. The U-boats patrolled the waters at that time, posing a constant threat to every sailor in every ship. My father never talked about it, and I was only five when he was demobbed, so consequently it meant little to me. Even during peacetime the only time I saw him was at the weekend. Every Saturday night he would be in the pub, getting bladdered, and then he'd sleep all day Sunday before getting up and going back to sea on Monday. I used to think my old man was an alcoholic, but I didn't realize at the time that he didn't drink beer or whisky at all at sea, and would only have a drink on a Saturday night. I doubt as well he could afford to do it for more than one night a week. I can understand his bingeing now; in fact, I'd have probably done the same, even if only to blot out the thought of what lay ahead each week in those giant, icy cold waves.

Some of the stories I later heard about life at sea were truly horrific. Ice sheets would sometimes close in on the ship, and heavy layers of ice would encrust it; the fishermen would have to knock it off with axes to stop the ship capsizing. At the time I never worried about my dad being in similar situations, because I was unaware of all these hardships; and it was only later when I watched some old black and white films that I realized what he and the other guys had gone through for that ten-pound note. I do remember him telling me that some days, when the fish catch was not so good, they would have to go to the Faeroe Islands and would be away for three weeks. What problems that must have brought, not only for him but for my mother. As far as I can gather, there was little or no radio contact in those days, other than to the guy back in the office, probably in Aberdeen. It meant the fishermen's families were left without money for all the time the men were absent. The women would have to go down to the office and get what they called a 'pay slip', then change it for cash or an advance at the Fisherman's Union.

As a result of his lifestyle, I didn't really get to know my father until much later on. I certainly don't have any memories of him from those early years because, quite simply, I never saw him. It was left to my mother Robina to bring up the seven Law children.

My eldest sister was also called Robina, an unusual name you don't hear a lot these days – even more unusual for a family to have two of them! Fortunately, however, my sister was referred to as Ruby. It's strange how Christian names change in terms of popularity over the years. Another of my sisters was called Georgina, a name that seems to be coming back into favour now, as is Frances. In family order, the Law siblings were Robina (fifteen years older than me), Frances (thirteen) and Georgina (eleven) followed by John (nine), Joseph (seven), George (five) and me. The first three girls, the next four boys – surely that's unusual too? But there was nothing unusual about the size of the family in those days. Seven wasn't at all over the top, especially in our family tree: my mother was one of twelve, my father one of fourteen. How such large families managed to survive through two world wars and all the deprivation and poverty they brought, God only knows.

Certainly during those dark days of war things must have been very tough for my mother, and rationing continued after the war when we were all brought up on less than ten pounds a week, which was my father's wage when he returned to Scotland and resumed trawling. How we got by day to day I don't know, but everyone else in our neighbourhood was in the same situation so we hardly noticed. There were compensations, of course, one of them being the fantastic Northern Lights – wonderful colours playing about in the night sky. With so little light pollution in our part of the country they were a yearly and much appreciated event, as were the short nights during the summer with little more than a couple of hours of darkness. They were one of nature's most beautiful spectacles, and I wish I'd taken more notice of the 'Northern Lights of Old Aberdeen', as the song went.

But there wasn't a great deal else to feel joyous about. We couldn't afford shoes, for a start, and instead wore black canvas plimsolls. They were fine in the summer, good for running home after school, but when it was snowy I would arrive at school with wet feet which stayed wet for most of the morning as we sat in the classroom quietly steaming. And in the post-war years we had real winters. The southern softies wouldn't appreciate just how bad it could get up there in the distant north with snow, but for us it was very much the same for everyone and we hardly noticed because we had no comparisons. Eventually I was given a pair of second-hand wellies, though we weren't allowed to wear them in school. We had to put the gym shoes back on, but at least they were dry.

It wasn't just our family that had to make do like this; everyone at school was in the same boat. We lived in a tenement council house, 6 Printfield Terrace, Woodside. There were ten of these council-owned granite houses on either side of the street, each of them three storeys high. They're still standing today. Then, they must have housed some twenty families. I think we were one of the biggest in the street, but there would certainly have been up to five children in many of the apartments. Whenever I go back I drive around just to have a look and remind myself of the good fortune I have enjoyed since. The guy next door, George Geddis, was a little bit better off than most of us in the neighbourhood. His father had a good job and theirs was a smaller family with not so many mouths to feed. It was George who gave me my first pair of football boots, his cast-offs. I was so proud of them, even though it used to take me half an hour to get the laces undone. It was also my first experience of dubbin, which I rubbed on energetically to stop the boots from falling apart. My mother then bought me a pair of football socks on tick (hire purchase). That was another treat, and it was outside my mother's budget. I remember that when my father came home we had to hide them because he would have been cross with her for wasting the money.

Every penny spent had to be judged carefully and weighed up against whatever else was needed. When my father went to sea on Monday his suit would go straight to the pawnbroker's. Come Friday, my mother would put together the money to buy it back for Dad to wear down the pub on Saturday. He never knew that it disappeared as soon as he was out of the door. It was only pennies, but she had to get it all back together by Friday to redeem it.

I didn't own my first pair of shoes until the age of fourteen. I could have had free shoes, but they were like big tackety boots and we were too proud to have them because everyone would know they were handouts. Thankfully, there was no regulation school uniform, just shorts, a shirt and a short-sleeved jumper. They would be bought on tick when new ones were needed, but they were usually hand-me-downs. I remember Mum buying me a brand-new jerkin, probably in a sale, complete with buttons and pockets. It was grey, and it lasted for years. I thought I was the bee's knees whenever I wore it, and it kept me lovely and warm when we had three or four feet of snow. Small things like that made you stand out from the crowd, though George, who had a school uniform for grammar school, was never a part of that particular throng. That could have set him apart and made him unpopular, but it didn't. No-one took any notice, and he remained one of the lads, which showed what a good bloke he must have been.

Whenever I look back at how life was lived when I was a child, it's all quite amazing, and difficult to explain to the modern generation. Our house had no carpet, no central heating and no TV. There was a pantry instead of a fridge, and I have difficulty recalling eating any food during the week other than soup and a bit of pudding. Mum was too proud for us to have school dinners, which were provided for nothing to the poor children, so we went home at lunchtime for soup and sago pudding, which looked like frogspawn. I had to close my eyes to force it into my mouth, and I have never eaten it since. It's not that tricky to avoid, of course, since you rarely come across it in everyday life, but I was in a restaurant recently and there it was on the menu, sago pudding with strawberry jam! Talk about nostalgia, but I couldn't face it, even with the jam. We certainly never had strawberry jam when I was at school. Had we done so, it might have changed my opinion.

We had our hot Aberdeen roll with margarine and a mug of tea at breakfast, of course. Lovely. When I go up to Aberdeen I bring a few dozen of these special bread rolls back with me. They are hard and flat, like soda bread. You can't get them anywhere else, at least not to my knowledge. I even ask friends to bring them back for me when they travel to Aberdeen. I love them, and I always looked forward to that first meal of the day. If I ever had a sandwich later on in the day, it was just bread pasted with margarine and dipped into the sugar bowl. Some of the boys had dripping sandwiches – the solidified juices from the Sunday roasting tray, spread like butter on the bread – but we didn't have them because we rarely had any meat to eat. Dad would have meat on Sunday to keep up his strength, but there wasn't enough to go around for us children. But again, we didn't worry because we didn't know any different, and we could always look forward to the Monday highlight – 'stovies'. If Dad had left a bit of meat it would be chopped up into little squares and fried with potatoes like a corned beef hash – stovies. Delicious. For a real treat, which happened only every now and then, we would have Scottish pies with a bit of gravy and mince.

So food was fairly basic, but none of us was going to starve as there was always plenty of fish in the sea, though even then the fish was only brought in when the boats came back on a Saturday. They used to go to sea on Monday morning and come back Saturday morning. It was afternoon by the time they had unloaded their catch, but if they'd enjoyed a decent week in those cold North Sea waters, that was when we ate quite well. We usually had deep-fried haddock and chips on those occasions. Sometimes we would have fish and chips during the week, too, but then it was ninepence for the fish and threepence for the chips in old money – a big lay-out if all the children were around for dinner.

My kids used to laugh at stories such as these in their nice, warm, centrally heated house in Manchester, but it wasn't so funny at the time. It was cold, and there was no such thing as an electric blanket. Instead, we had a big, solid water bottle with a cork to keep the hot water in. Of course, it was great when it was warm, but not so good halfway through the night when it had cooled off. I never had any proper pyjamas either, and there would often be three in a bed. We were usually packed off to bed early, but there were few complaints during the winter when bed was the best place to be, especially as I was fortunate enough to have 'borrowed' a wee battery-powered torch from a friend of mine, Big Jan, which cast a light strong enough to enable me to read my comics under the blankets.

There was just one bathroom for the entire family, too. We would have a bath every Sunday night, because that was the only time there was hot water, but none during the week. We washed and bathed in the sink most of the time. I was, however, very fortunate to have the use of an inside toilet and bath; most of my pals had to go outside to go to the toilet, rain, sun or snow, and their bath was a big zinc thing in front of the living-room fire. My brothers and sisters had all experienced the outside toilet and the tin bath in the house, but by the time I was born we had moved, so I managed to avoid that particular problem.

At that time, all mining and fishing families lived in similar straitened circumstances, and partly as a result I've always thought they must be the two hardest jobs in the world. It wasn't just the immense hard work and the long hours involved, but the fact that every day these men went to work down the pits or out to sea they were risking their lives to earn a barely adequate living for their families. As a child, I went out to sea with my father just the once. Every six months the trawlers would sail out a couple of miles or so to adjust the compass, as it would have lost a couple of points during the weekly fishing trips. It was a beautiful sunlit day when I joined them, but even then the little boat was going up and down the further out we steamed. As I struggled to keep down my breakfast, I remember thinking, 'This is not for me.' In those days, they fished when the fish were running, not like nowadays when sonar can tell them exactly when the shoal is coming up. In Dad's day they fished any time; it could be three a.m. or it could be five a.m., but rarely, it seemed, was it at a sociable hour. I went downstairs to explore the cabin where they slept for five nights a week. It was just small, cramped bunks on either side of the boat, and after laying their nets there they rested in the huge sea swells, waiting for the call. They would trawl a few hundred yards, feel the drag as they caught the fish, and use the second nature they all seemed to possess in those days. In his spare time he probably also manned the lifeboats, because most fishermen did in those days. Since the advent of oil exploration, the Scottish fishing industry has changed drastically. It has moved from its traditional home in Aberdeen to Peterhead, and the boats are obviously much improved – though, let me tell you, the North Sea hasn't changed at all. It was a hard life in the 1940s and 1950s, especially as my father was carrying a wartime injury.

His whole life at home was spent within a radius of a couple of miles. I didn't realize what a tough life it was until I was a lot older. Even when I was twenty and living in comparative luxury I was still taking it all for granted. Many of the people living in the area were fishermen, and the rest of the community was made up of tradesmen: joiners, plumbers and the like. In those days you served your apprenticeship in one of the trades, and in truth there was nothing else for people to do. They didn't have the money to do anything else, nor the opportunity of further education. The thought of going to university didn't even cross most people's mind then.

I do wish I had got to know my dad better than I did. I did manage to improve our relationship later on, but by then I was living away from Aberdeen so we still didn't see a lot of each other except when I returned home in the close season. A pal of mine once gave me some sound advice. Though it sounds so simple and obvious, it bears repeating, and it's something I'd pass on to every ambitious young man and woman: he told me always to look after your mum and dad, because when they're gone it's too late. They were wise words. You hear of so many people, me included, who regret so much after their parents have gone, wishing they had enjoyed more contact and done more things together.

Still, I was very close to my mother, with Dad being away so much and my brothers and sisters all being so much older than me. Even then, as the youngest, my brothers and sisters looked after me, especially during the war years. Mum was already forty-one when I put in an appearance during the middle of a really cold winter, but the girls were old enough to help, taking over the cooking and the cleaning for the few days Mum had to spend in bed. We were a close-knit unit.

I remember very little about the war. Perhaps the strongest memory I have from those dark days was the sound of the sirens. They were very frightening, and we used to scramble into the air-raid shelter worrying about what we might be in for (fortunately for the Law family, nothing traumatic happened and we survived unscathed). The Germans were after the big RAF airport near the city, but they never found it. It was cleverly tucked away in a valley, and although the enemy had an idea where it was, they never actually struck home. Aberdeen was also an important port for the convoys across the North Atlantic, which constituted an important part of the war effort. Add crucial staging post to the fact that the RAF had a couple of bases over that way, and we were a bit like a dartboard for the Luftwaffe. I can vividly recall my eldest sister Ruby being in an air-raid shelter with me one night when the Luftwaffe was bombing Aberdeen. Those shelters were around for years and years. I remember them being knocked down many years later, and thinking that it was about time. They were left to become dumps after the war, though for kids they were exciting places, and we used to make campfires in them. We even formed a little club and sat around a flickering candle talking.

I remember, too, my dad coming home from the war. I thought

he was captain of the ship because he had on the full uniform, but it transpired he was only a petty officer. A photograph was taken of him on his homecoming, and it stood on the mantelpiece in pride of place for as long as I can remember.

My other memories from the first decade of my life revolve around football. As early as I can remember I was kicking a football about, and with three older brothers there was usually someone to play with. George was an excellent footballer, and he might have made it in the professional game with a little perseverance, not to mention luck, for when he was eighteen he broke his leg badly and that was that. It was a shame, because I remember him being a fantastic player. Strangely, at this time only George was passionately inclined towards football. Part, at least, of the reason for this was that there was no football heritage in the family at all. Certainly my father had no interest in watching or playing, mainly because he was always away at sea. In those days in Aberdeen, youngsters just didn't dream of becoming a footballer, unlike today, when every boy, it seems, wants to become a professional. That destiny was for another band of people altogether during my childhood.

Like most places throughout Britain in the 1940s and 1950s, we satisfied ourselves by supporting our local team. There was no television then on which to watch the bigger teams like Rangers or Celtic, or even teams from across the border; the first game I ever saw on television was the 1955 FA Cup final between Manchester City and Newcastle when I was fifteen (the Geordies won 3–1). There was little transport, too, so you couldn't easily travel anywhere to watch another team. The team we watched and supported was Aberdeen; Pittodrie was only a walk away, or a short bus ride, though we usually walked to save the money. Generally, though, we couldn't afford to go to Pittodrie; instead, we used to go down and watch the local non-League football in competitions like the Highland League, which produced many good players. We just climbed over the wall, and we didn't even get into trouble for doing it because no-one had to pay to get in. That was just the way it was then: people went to see their local teams playing. It was only when people began to find themselves with more disposable income that they started to watch other teams on television, or listened to matches on the radio. Many teams suffered over the years because of this growth in media coverage, allied to the increasing ease with which people could travel. It was especially noticeable in the big conurbations. In Manchester, I remember particularly the detrimental effect on local teams like Stockport, Bury and Rochdale when, suddenly, their local fans became Manchester City, Manchester United and Liverpool fans. I remember going home a year or two ago and visiting a little place north of Aberdeen where all the kids were wearing Manchester United shirts. They had a good local team down the road, but they were supporting an English team hundreds of miles away. This was solely due to the power of television. Without it, they wouldn't worship the Beckhams and Giggses of this world, they would be ardent fans of their own team's best players.

A classic example is John Charles, who moved to Juventus in 1957. One of the finest Welsh players of the post-war era, Charles became a big star in Italian football, but this was in the early days of television, and though he was worshipped over there and called 'The King' his skills were hardly acknowledged in Britain because nobody ever saw him play, except on occasional excursions home to play for Wales or the League of Italy. Who were Juventus anyway? What was Italian football like? People forget now that it wasn't until 1960, when the fabulous Real Madrid came to Hampden Park and thrashed Eintracht Frankfurt to win their fifth consecutive European Cup, that football on a wider scale really hit home. It was one of the greatest games I've ever seen, the Spanish side winning 7–3; Ferenc Puskas scored no fewer than four goals, and the great Alfredo Di Stefano also weighed in with a hat-trick. Scotland had played England a week before in the same stadium, and the game had been garbage as a spectacle. The Madrid game was on a different planet altogether. I had, of course, heard of the Hungarian Puskas when I was a boy in 1954, not to mention the mercurial Di Stefano, but I'd never seen them play before. I watched the game on TV at home in Scotland in awe, marvelling at the skills and qualities of the two teams, little realizing that a few years later I would be playing with some of them in a Rest of the World side.

My heroes until that point had been the local boys, players like centre-forward George Hamilton, Paddy Buckley, Harry Yorston, goalkeeper Fred Martin, and Graham Leggat, who went on to Fulham and Birmingham. When we could afford it, we went to Pittodrie to watch Aberdeen; for afternoon cup games during this pre-floodlights era, they'd let us in for a fraction of the normal price. The ground held about 41,000 in those days, and although it's now a well-worn cliché, there was never any trouble. The youngsters would be handed down over the heads of the fans to the front of the ground so that we could watch uninterrupted. They were good days, and Aberdeen was my team. Aberdeen's are still the first results I look for, along with my first club Huddersfield. But because of the money situation I was by no means a regular at Pittodrie. I only ever went as a special treat, and mainly midweek when, as I said, they let the schools in at a reduced price. For any other games, my mother would have to pay.

She worked in my school as a cleaner, earning some vital extra money to supplement the wages Dad brought home after working hard at sea. I felt no embarrassment at the fact that my mother worked at my school; in fact, I thought it was great because she would occasionally bring home the odd rubber or pencil. It doesn't sound much now, but in those days gifts such as these were like gold dust. Kids just wouldn't understand now, but to be given a coloured pencil was something very special. It was treasured, and used only sparingly.

I wasn't a total waster at school. I was good at English, science, geography and technical drawing – in fact I was a fairly bright student. I certainly passed for grammar school, which was fairly unusual for pupils from my school, Kittybruster, where I'd gone after a stint at Hilton Primary. Then I found out that my new school didn't play football, only rugby and cricket. Well, that was no good to me. I didn't want to go to a school where I couldn't play football, which had already become an important part of my life. Mind you, we all felt the same; all we wanted to do was play football. We would play on the way to school with an old bald tennis ball – or a tin can if we didn't have a ball – knocking it off the walls as we progressed, and then back home again in the afternoon. It was good practice for control and balance, because we usually had our school bags over our shoulders. The game we played was called 'Three Lives'. We'd knock the ball against the wall and pick up the return. It was quite tricky because you had to flick it to the side and beat your opponent. It demanded close control, not to mention the ability to avoid various obstacles on the street, some of them left by the local dogs. We would play to and from home at lunchtime, get back early to play in the school yard before the bell rang, then on the way home after school. When the homework was done, it was back out to play again in the street, using lamp-posts and a grid as goals. There was grass around the roads next to the old air-raid shelters, and if you were good enough you got the ball off the street onto the grass. If a guy had a football, he was the king. He'd be the one to pick sides and be the captain.

Football dominated because we didn't have much else at home for entertainment purposes, other than one another and the radio. Our radio was in the kitchen, which was very small as you might imagine. There was only a cooker, a sink and a boiler – well, not a boiler; more of a big drum in which my mother used to do the washing. These items were contained in an area of about three feet square, and then there was the table with a pulley above it where we used to hang out the clothes to dry. We used to listen to *Dick Barton, Special Agent* and a most frightening programme called *The Man in Black*, whose presenter used to say in a deep voice, 'This is the Man in Black.' Oooh, it scared me and my sister to death, especially as we used to listen to it with all the lights turned off. Another radio programme we listened to avidly was *Quatermass*, a science fiction series about scientists and beings from outer space in the London Underground, but I must say that the one that frightened me most was that man in black. I learned later that the presenter with the booming voice was an actor by the name of Valentine Dyall. I'll never forget his sinister tones.

I remember, too, coming home at lunchtime and listening to the shipping forecast, probably because of its relevance to my dad's occupation. If you tune in to Radio Four today, they'll still leave, for instance, live commentary of a Test match for ten minutes just to do the forecast. Rockall, Fair Isle, Cromarty, Dogger, Faeroes – I found the names so intriguing. I still keep half an ear open for the shipping forecast today – what a boring life I lead! Lundy, Fastnet . . . I used to know them all. They were names to conjure with! It excited the imagination, as did the World Service, which also left a big impression on me.

When I was in Argentina with the BBC for the 1978 World Cup, we regularly listened to the World Service for news from around the globe, and especially Britain. Whenever I was working for radio at home, at some point during a game they would welcome listeners to the World Service, bringing people and families closer together. It certainly did just that for me and my family once. I remember doing a game at United when my son, Andrew, was somewhere in the Indian Ocean with the Merchant Navy, but I knew he would be listening to the game as it was the derby against Manchester City. The World Service was due to join us at around four p.m. in time for the second half, so I thought, 'Right, I'll let him know I'm thinking about him.' When the time came, I said, 'Now, I know my son, Andrew, is in the Indian Ocean somewhere. I know he will be listening because he's a City supporter and we are at Old Trafford, and he'll be happy to hear that City are drawing nil-nil at the moment.' I got a call about a week later from Andrew who said he'd heard it all on the ship. All the troops had been listening in and he'd been delighted with the mention from his dad. Yes, the World Service has always been a good thing.

We made use of everything in those days, and in that kitchen where the beloved radio sat, we used to tie a string from the pulley with a ball of wool on the end. The first thing to do was swing it round to ensure it wasn't hitting anything; then I would kick it to see where it would go. That done, I was ready to play, and I used to kick and head that ball of wool for hour after hour. Apart from the radio, that was more or less the sum total of my indoor entertainment. How many professional footballers can say they learned some of their ball skills in the kitchen?

My obsession with football back in the early 1950s meant that my mother had a hell of a job getting me out of grammar school. She was clearly disappointed, but in some ways also relieved, because had I gone there she would have had to buy uniform, books and sports equipment and we just didn't have the money to spare. On reflection, I feel sad about this time because I would like to have had a better education, but it wasn't to be, and off I went to Powers Junior Secondary School, which at least had a football team.

With my mother bringing me pencils and rubbers, I became quite good at technical drawing, and I decided I wanted to be a draughtsman or an architect or something in that line when I finally left school. I definitely did not want to go to sea! I wasn't tough enough.

Then, of course, everything changed. It was good for me that I went to Powis Junior because of the help I received with my football from Mr Durno, who ran the team, and he switched me from full-back, where I'd generally played until that time, to inside-left – quite a significant change as it proved. It is strange how such seemingly insignificant things like this can have huge consequences. The same thing in reverse happened to England's World Cup-winning full-back Ray Wilson: he started off as an inside-forward with Huddersfield, and then went to full-back. That was why he was such a good player at a time when the game was changing; he could pass the ball and he was fast. The likes of Stan Lynn, Aston Villa's outstanding right-back, were a dying breed. Players like him could still get a game and were worth their place because they could chip a winger fully fifty yards, and when the ball was wet they were among the few players who could get the heavy, sodden leather ball into the middle from a corner. On damp days, the ball used to weigh a ton. Stan Lynn could thump a ball almost as hard as he could thump a winger.

However, whenever I played representative football, it was embarrassing, for I had a terrible squint, and children were, of course, cruel and would call me names like 'Cockeye'. It was all part of the growing-up process, I suppose, learning how to handle yourself, but it was still a tough thing to go through. I was not alone, though, because most of my family had squints. It was almost normal in our house, and as a problem it didn't seem to be anything out of the ordinary. Unless, of course, you planned to become a professional sportsman.

2 THE BOY WITH THE SQUINT

ALL BUT ONE MEMBER OF THE LAW FAMILY SUFFERED FROM A squint – or strabismus, to give it its proper medical term. We weren't born with it, it was just a condition that gradually developed, though we now know it's wired into the genes. Fortunately, it seems to have skipped a generation, for my own family has not suffered with the problem. Having said that, whenever my children, especially my daughter little Di, were unwell as youngsters, one eye tended to turn inwards a bit. That had happened with my brothers and sisters, too. Whenever any one of them was a bit down physically or mentally, or if they had a cold, the eye started to come in a bit. I could tell just by looking at them that they were under the weather; 'You're just off centre a little bit,' I'd say. We called it a 'glai'. Thank goodness, though, none of my children seem to have inherited the dreaded squint. I have nephews and nieces with squints, but my direct line has stayed clear.

As a child, I sported corrective eyewear, but I'd have to take my glasses off in the dressing-room before a game, and then, all of a sudden, my eye would be all over the place. To compensate, whenever I played I did so with one eye closed. Despite this handicap, my footballing education went from strength to strength. Basically, school was at the heart of my life because it was centred on football. John, Joseph, George and I were all members of the Aberdeen Lads Club, which is still going today. The club didn't just play football – there were facilities for table tennis, handball and other indoor sports – but on Saturdays it was for the Aberdeen Lads Club football team that we played, after representing the school in the morning. Actually, the club hadn't had a youth team when we arrived on the scene, so, along with a next-door neighbour, Sid Thompson, we formed our own and called it the ALC Colts. It was an under-16 team and, needless to say, we had very little money. We used to go round the houses selling raffle tickets to raise funds just to buy some shirts and socks. Then we became more ambitious and set up a league with a few other teams. The ALC Colts lasted quite a few years after I left, so we'd clearly built it on firm foundations.

Talent abounded in our area, and there were some interesting characters at the club. John 'Tubby' Ogsden, a goalkeeper, was one of the Lads Club who went on to have a career in professional football, with Aberdeen, and there was another fine goalkeeper, Adam Blacklaw, who kept Tubby out of the Aberdeen Schoolboys side. Adam went on to have a very good career with Burnley having also started his career with Aberdeen. I got on particularly well with Gordon Low, another impressive player. Several years later he was picked for the Scotland under-23s against England at Ibrox Park, only for the game to be called off because of heavy snow. When the game was rearranged he wasn't selected and was never picked again. What a shame that was, because once you have forced your way into an international inner circle you're in the chosen group and automatically come into consideration for selection every time. It was just unfortunate that Gordon wasn't given another chance because he might easily have gone on to play for Scotland at full international level. There was also Joe Fleming, an outside-right who went to Spurs and also played for Cardiff City, and a few others who went on to make careers as professionals.

With so many good players around, it was no wonder that Aberdeen Schoolboys and the Lads Club did so well. Even as young as under-12s we were doing well, reaching the final of the Scottish national competition and playing the first leg at Motherwell's Fir Park Stadium – my first experience of being away from home and playing on such a big ground. We lost, but the memories are good. The success continued, and we also reached the under-15s final. In that match, I played with Alex Dawson, who went on to earn a name with Manchester United. At the time, Alex was the greatest thing on two feet; he was playing for the Aberdeen Schoolboys under-15 side when he was thirteen. He was a big talent, and no-one was surprised when he went off to Old Trafford. He was a tank of a centre-forward who only had eyes for the ball, no matter what lay in his path. He actually broke into the team after the Munich disaster in 1958, and helped United reach Wembley that year with three goals in two FA Cup semi-final clashes with Fulham. After that, he moved on to Preston, where he scored masses of goals and became known as the Black Prince of Deepdale.

I, too, tasted some success. I was selected for the Scotland Schoolboys squad and went on my first trip abroad, to Ireland, though I didn't play. I was back there again not long ago at the Giant's Causeway to start the Meningitis Walk. The memories flooded back, and I told the charity organizers that I was making a return journey after forty-seven years, observing, 'It ain't changed any.' And it hadn't. Then, during the 1954/55 season, I was spotted by a scout from the Division One side Huddersfield Town. Their Scottish manager, Andy Beattie, had a brother called Archie who lived a mile or so up the road from us and from time to time watched our junior games.

In those days, there were few talent scouts in Scottish football; there just wasn't the money available to set up sophisticated networks. It was mainly schoolteachers who ran local football clubs and schoolboy teams; they and a few other interested parties were the ones who had their fingers vaguely on the pulse of the game, and if they had a friend at Spurs, say, or some other club, they might occasionally comment, 'We've got a kid up here.' That's why an approach could come completely out of the blue. It was all down to word of mouth, whispered recommendations from ex-players, schoolteachers and a few others with contacts in the game on either side of the border. Archie Beattie was one of these scouts who followed the local clubs and school teams; he would keep a close eye on up-and-coming players in Aberdeen and then send the promising ones down to his brother to have a look at. Archie had a decent eye, too: another player he spotted for Huddersfield was centre-forward Les Massie, a good player who scored plenty of goals and was a professional for a long time.

I have to admit I was surprised I caught anyone's eye, for several reasons: I was only a little boy, undernourished, under-developed and weighing in at eight stone soaking wet, and I had this terrible squint. Did I have a talent for the game of football at that age? Well, that's for others to say. All I can say for myself is that at the time I played as much football as I could and enjoyed every kick of the ball, whoever I was playing for. I used to score a lot of goals, so that was probably what got me noticed. I was an inside-forward by then, of course, which meant I was up and down the field and got my fair share of goalscoring opportunities, some of which, with a bit of luck, I managed to slot home. But then I would be back defending and working hard. It was a position I liked because I was busy and involved. I suppose any football-lover enjoys watching an industrious goalscorer. Maybe had I still been a full-back with a squint and a slight frame, Archie wouldn't have been interested.

My brothers came down with me originally for the trial. I appreciated the company because, don't forget, the furthest I had travelled south on the mainland for football was Motherwell – which, to put it into context, was like travelling from Manchester to Birmingham. And the furthest south we'd ever been as a family was Stonehaven – and to put *that* into context, it was like going from Manchester to Stockport. Stonehaven was the next place down from where I was brought up, a beautiful little village along the road from Aberdeen; it's still gorgeous and unspoiled today. It was the nearest and the cheapest place for us to go to; it was our idea of the perfect day trip. We certainly couldn't have afforded to stay the night. Where I lived, there was no such concept as taking a holiday in the accepted sense of the term. So travelling into England, to Huddersfield, for the first time was a huge adventure, and something of a shock as well. Aberdeen was a lovely, beautiful city with beaches and fresh air; Huddersfield was an industrialized town, a thriving wool and engineering centre in the West Riding with chimneys and old mills, and when I arrived I immediately felt homesick. I remember standing on the station platform at Huddersfield after getting off the train and thinking, 'Wow, where is this place?' It was big and it was completely new to me, like nothing I had ever seen before. I suppose a boy of fifteen today could cope with such a change of scenery much easier, but at fifteen in the 1950s we were more like ten-year-olds nowadays.

After having taken a look at me, Andy Beattie was quoted as saying to his brother, 'The boy's a freak. Never did I see a less likely football prospect – weak, puny and bespectacled.' I was fifteen years old, stood between my older brothers George and John – who were not particularly big, but to me, and certainly next to me, they were – and as I've said, at five feet three inches with round glasses correcting a squint and a huge boil on my cheek that was an angry red and ready to burst, I was not an impressive specimen. I must have looked a miserable bag of bones that spring in 1955. Andy must have thought one of my brothers was the one he was supposed to be assessing when the three of us arrived. I think that Huddersfield's assistant secretary Eddie Brennan, who had come to meet us off the train, had thought the same (Eddie had bad eyes as well, as it turned out): when my brothers announced that it was me, he looked as though he thought we were pulling his leg. Andy thought it was a joke being perpetrated by Archie. Still, once the confusion abated, my brothers sent me outside while they had a private word with Andy. While they had a chat, I played against the office wall with a rubber ball I happened to have in my pocket.

I was down there for about a week for that trial, and most of my time was spent at the ground. The football we played was more in the form of five-a-side practices; I cannot remember ever playing in a full eleven-a-side trial game. I think the idea was just to see how I did, how comfortable I was on the ball, and whether I was as weak and fragile as I looked. There was no-one more surprised than me when, after that first week, they told me they would like me to sign for the club. Archie came to my house to see my mum, and they sent me out while they discussed my future.

There were no strong objections from my mother for two reasons: Archie assured her that the club would put me in digs and keep an eye on me, and she was fully aware that I was into football, that it was what I enjoyed doing most. Her support for and belief in me at a time when I was barely fifteen were much appreciated. I eventually signed for Huddersfield on 3 April 1955.

A story did the rounds that by leaving school to go to Huddersfield when I did, I missed out on the chance of actually playing for Scotland Schoolboys, but it was perfectly legal for me to end my education at that time. If you were born prior to April you were able to leave school around Easter time rather than the summer, and if you weren't going on to further education – and few did where I lived – you left school at fifteen. I was of the recommended age when April 1955 arrived, and I was able to accept the exciting offer Huddersfield had made. Had I been born in the May or into April, I would then have had to stay at school until the summer, but as a February child I was able to go immediately. I suppose Scotland Schoolboys might have offered me a game between the spring and the summer, but as far as I know they had no plans to do so. The only trials I was involved in were at Huddersfield, certainly not for Scotland Schoolboys, and as for being offered a place at Aberdeen Football Club, as another rumour suggested, I can state categorically that there was not a single offer from that direction. If Aberdeen had a scout, he was probably elsewhere at the time. Archie had the field to himself. It was also suggested that I eventually moved south to Huddersfield for the fame and the money, but it was for neither.

When I first went to the north of England I had no burning intention to become a professional football player. I was just very proud to have been asked to go down for a trial to Huddersfield, and I went because I loved playing football. I would have gone anywhere for a game, and I honestly didn't consider the consequences.

It was said only an offer from Rangers would have stopped me going south when Huddersfield came in for me. Who would not have liked to join Rangers in those days? Along with Celtic, then as now, they were the biggest team in the country, but they weren't the only ones, of course. You could not dismiss the two Edinburgh teams, Hibernian and Hearts, and Aberdeen were certainly knocking on the door of the top group of Scottish club sides. Hibs were the cream in the mid-1950s because they had the 'Famous Five' – Gordon Smith, Laurie Reilly, Bobby Johnstone, Eddie Turnbull and Willie Ormond, all Scottish internationals. At Hearts there were stars such as Dave Mackay and Willie Bold. These were big names, not just in their own immediate environment but to Scottish football fans in general. But none of these big Scottish clubs came in for me, not one. In fact, had I been asked at the time what team I would really prefer to play for, I would have said Real Madrid. I probably wouldn't have been alone in that sentiment either, for Real ruled the world in the 1950s. They were the biggest and the best, and they signed all the top Hungarians and South Americans as well as having the cream of the Spaniards. Having said that, had I received a Huddersfield-type offer from any of the five Scottish teams I've mentioned, I would have jumped at the chance. My ideal choice would have been Aberdeen, then I could have lived at home. At fifteen, who wouldn't want the easier option?

One of the things that attracted me to Huddersfield was the fact that they had a Scottish manager I admired. Even when Andy Beattie left the club in January 1957 he was replaced by another Scot for whom I had a great deal of respect, the legendary Bill Shankly. I have to admit that knowing a fellow Scot was going to be looking after me was an important factor in my decision to leave home, because Huddersfield seemed an awfully long way from Aberdeen: it was twelve hours on the train to Leeds, and then change there for the stopping train to Huddersfield. It was a huge wrench for an inexperienced teenager.

But it was during those early months at Huddersfield, throughout which I remained terrified by the reality of living away from home in a strange town, that I received an enormous boost to my self-confidence in the form of a telephone call informing me that I had to return to Aberdeen for an appointment with an eye specialist with a view to corrective surgery for my squint. I had been waiting two years on the NHS list for this operation, and the timing was perfect. Just the thought of someone messing around with such a delicate organ as the eye is horrible, but even then it was a very simple procedure. As far as I can recall – it was nearly fifty years ago, I have no medical training, and I was under anaesthetic at the time – they went in by the ear, manoeuvred behind the eye, tugged a sort of muscular fibre, pulled the eye back into the centre and secured it. That is the way it was explained to me anyway.

When I woke up, I had bandages all around my head. I must have looked like the Invisible Man for several days, and then it was just like being in one of those old war movies when somebody has been injured on the battle front: the nurse came in one day and gently unwound it layer by layer. I kept my eyes tight shut. Gradually I opened them, and the nurse told me to go and look in the mirror. I shuffled over, dreading what I might see. All sorts of thoughts raced through my fertile young mind. The first thing I noticed was that the eye they had operated on, the right one, was bloodshot. I immediately assumed that something had gone wrong, but then I saw that the pupil of the eye was right in the middle.

I cannot emphasize enough what an incredible moment in my life that was. It completely changed things for me. Suddenly I had the wherewithal to look people, literally, straight in the eye, something I had never been able to do with any confidence before. Even better, I was able to look at girls and not be worried that they would laugh in my face. My mum had said that I was about four or five when the problem had first manifested itself, so for the first time in a decade I was able to look at anybody without my glasses knowing my eyes were straight. No longer was my iris retreating to the corner, as if it were hiding!

For months after the operation I took every opportunity to look at myself in the mirror, asking silently, 'Is it going to go back or is it staying right there in the middle for ever?' Once that thought had embedded itself, I stopped looking at my reflection, just in case. Even all these years later, I still dread looking in the mirror. To me, there is nothing worse than when I see somebody with a squint. They look awful, and I feel so sorry for them. I think to myself, 'Why don't you get the operation?' Fortunately it's not something you see so often nowadays. There was a famous old comedian, Mack Sennett, who used to use his squint in his act and was very funny, but it's far from funny in the real world. When mine was corrected, I was ecstatic.

I returned to Huddersfield after a couple of weeks' con-valescence, and it was a great feeling just to go into the ground with the rest of the lads and be normal. Wow! And I could now play football with both eyes open. Anyone who has experienced a bad squint will understand the thrill these simple things gave me. Obviously I still had to be careful, and I was a bit dodgy about heading the ball because I worried that if I sustained a bad knock on the head the eye might flick straight back to where it had been before, but of course that never happened. Three weeks after the operation, though, I did have to go back into hospital because my vision was blurred, and to be honest, it has never been quite right. It was very worrying at the time for a young lad, but the specialist had warned me it might happen.

Still, the freedom the surgery gave me to enjoy things in life outweighed this minor drawback. I was now able to go to clubs, dancehalls and parties and not feel embarrassed. I knew I wasn't the best-looking man on the block, I knew I had too big a nose and all the rest, but it didn't make any difference any more. Suddenly I had confidence. It worked for my brothers and sisters too, but I guess, as a professional sportsman, it really meant the world to me. Can you imagine the stick I would have had in the newspapers and, worse still, on television in the years to follow had I still had my lazy eye? Oh, to be able to go to play against the Sheffield United youth team or whoever and not feel inhibited about joining in without being stared at by a pair of well-centred eyes! I felt like a new man. It wasn't the same feeling as getting a new pair of shoes, football boots, an overcoat or material things like that – and remember, I was just one of many in the area where I lived who were without what would today be considered basics. No, this was different because it made me a different person, the sort of person who could now grasp with both hands all the opportunities the footballing world was offering him.

3   BREAKTHROUGH

MY BROTHERS CAME SOUTH WITH ME AGAIN WHEN I SIGNED ON
with the groundstaff at Huddersfield. I was offered £4 14s. a
week, with more than half that – £2 7s. 6d. – to pay for my board
and lodging. As I was the only one in the family who was earning
enough to send something back home to help, I sent my mother a
pound every week, and I lived on the remainder. It wasn't a lot,
for sure – after bus fares to and from the ground, I was left with
about ten shillings for all my entertainment and clothing needs –
and one way of saving money (and I still can't believe I actually
did it) was to send my laundry home to Aberdeen for my mother
to wash at the cost of another half a crown in postage. Looking
back, it was very silly of me to send my dirty clothes all the way
up to Scotland, spending unnecessary money and giving my mum
even more work. Still, when I made the first team and my wages
went up, so did the money my mother received. I think it got up
to about £5 a week towards her housekeeping – and remember,
that was half my dad's wages from the trawlers.

The lion's share of my club wages, as I said, went straight into the hands of the redoubtable Mrs Clarke at Pond House, my first landlady. I read somewhere once that there were sixteen of us packed into that house, but it was in fact more like seven with periodic intakes of other people. When I arrived, among the group there were Ray Wilson, Jack Connor and Les Massie. With each of us paying over £2 for the privilege, Mrs Clarke was undoubtedly making good money, and as far as we were concerned she was worth it. It was excellent value, and after my frugal home in Aberdeen it was fantastic. In fact, I couldn't believe my luck. There was this big dining-room in the house, and every morning when we came down for breakfast there was toast in the racks. I had never seen a toast rack in my life. There was real orange juice on the table too, a knife and fork, and plates filled with eggs, bacon, tomatoes and sausages. On my first morning there, I took one look and said, 'Wow!' I had never had proper orange juice before, only squash with water. This was a feast, and it was only breakfast.

There were more surprises in store, not least of all hot water round the clock. A hot bath whenever I wanted one! Was this special or was this special? It was just like I'd imagined a posh hotel to be, and to make it even more memorable I was able to meet a lot of other people there, and not just footballers. Mrs Clarke also catered for the local theatre, the Palace, so we used to get Variety stars like Hylda Baker (who later starred in the hit sitcom *Nearest and Dearest*) and Frank Randall (a well-known Northern comedian) staying with us. We met them all; they always seemed to be performing at the Palace. They chatted to us, told us all about their nomadic lives and also gave us tickets to go and watch them. I particularly liked to watch the singers, crooners like David Hilton and others whose names have faded into the past but who were very big at the time. It was a fascinating period for a young lad like me who had never been anywhere to speak of. Pond House was not at all like ordinary footballers' digs, which normally consisted of a room with a couple of beds, a fire and, if you were lucky, a communal lounge. Mrs Clarke had the lot. Hers were the legendary theatrical digs, and the show-business people were happy to share a few drinks with us youngsters.

Maybe those enormous breakfasts were laid on just for me, because the first time Mrs Clarke saw me she shook her head and said, 'Meat pudding wouldn't do you any harm, my lad!' She made it her personal crusade to fatten me up, and I worked up a good appetite to satisfy her ambitions as a groundstaff boy at Huddersfield, what with cleaning the boots, laying out the kit, sweeping the dressing-rooms and terraces, painting the crash barriers, making tea and training in the late afternoon after we'd done a day's work. I was usually ready for one of her big meals. It was always hard work at the ground, in terms of both chores and training; the only thing that wasn't hard was actually playing football. It was so boring running up and down the terraces and around the pitch in order to build up our quads and stamina, and I couldn't wait to have a ball at my feet. That terrace at Huddersfield was huge, mammoth. It was like running to the end of the moon and back, and when you only had a broom in your hand it seemed even bigger. It was genuinely a large stadium, though, and not just through the eyes of an ill-travelled youngster. I remember playing there in cup-ties against West Ham United and Burnley, and there were 58,000 people packed in there. It was like a palace to me in those early years, especially with its full-size snooker table, which was great for us because when the senior players had gone home we were able to play on a real snooker table, though we lived in perpetual fear of damaging the precious green baize.

There was strict control of us groundstaff boys. The head

groundsman looked after us and out for us, but we used to duck and dive with few problems because it was such a big ground and he never really knew where we were. We used to go up to the top of the stairs in the stand in order to pinpoint his whereabouts, and when we spotted him we'd disappear in the opposite direction. It was super fun; we thought it a great adventure at the time.

I wasn't a jack the lad, but after having had my eye done I was certainly a lot more outgoing. But for the groundstaff boys there was still no question of having a drink or going out with girls. We went to the pictures or a dancehall, but pulling birds simply wasn't done at my tender age. The girls would have laughed. I was never a great bird-puller anyway. My major pastime as a youngster was music. The older players like big Jack Connor introduced me to the world of crooners like Frank Sinatra. As one of the younger ones in the digs, though, I was more into rock 'n' roll, avidly following the careers of new stars like Bill Haley and the Comets, Little Richard and, of course, Elvis Presley. Jack and Ray Wilson were regulars at the local dancehall, and after about a year we felt old enough to accompany them. It was Ray who gave me my first ever suit. He was a bit of a teddy boy, was Ray, and the suit he gave me was in a very modern style. The trousers were about four inches wide around the bottom – drainpipes they were called, real teddy boy stuff – and the draped jacket went down past my bum and had velvet on the collar. I'd love to be able now to look at a photograph of me wearing this thing, but no-one had a camera in those days. It was my first real dip into the big, adult world outside, and I thought it was high living indeed.

The only item we missed in the digs was a television, which was still not something everyone had in the mid-1950s, not by a long shot. Fortunately, Mrs Clarke's daughter and her family lived across the road, and she had one. We would go over there to watch special programmes, particularly sport, but she had kids and it was only a small house, so our viewing had to be limited. So it was mainly records we played to kill time at the digs, and as I said, Jack was heavily into Frank Sinatra, and he played his albums over and over again until even I knew by heart all the words to classics such as 'Fly Me to the Moon'. To me at the time it sounded like ancient stuff, but it never lost its quality or appeal, and as I grew older I began to enjoy it more and more. But in my teens I much preferred to listen to the King.

Despite everything, though, I did struggle with homesickness. I had never been away from home before and I soon began to miss the familiarity of my childhood surroundings, my family and my friends. Jack Connor, Les Massie and Ray Wilson were very good to me, but I was fifteen and they were twenty. I used to put myself in their place and imagine that I was the twenty-year-old suddenly having a fifteen-year-old landed in my lap. What do you do? You have to look after the kid, but where do you take him? They were going to dancehalls and to pubs, they were chatting up the girls; at least for my first year there, I was the odd one out. They had spent two years in National Service and had the benefit of that experience of life and all it entails. I think it's a pity that they stopped National Service because it instilled many qualities in young boys that they would go on to appreciate later in life, especially if you played football like Ray and Jack. The great John Charles, of course, played for the army all over Europe while he was still at Leeds United. Ray and Jack also represented their units on the playing field. It was a cushy number, and it didn't affect their club career.

My feeling of being slightly outside the group eased a bit when Gordon Low came to Huddersfield. Gordon had played with me in the Aberdeen Lads side, and I got on well with him. It was interesting the way Gordon's signing happened because Huddersfield manager Andy Beattie, obviously spotting that I was homesick, had actually asked me if I had any pals who were any good. I told him about the lad who played with me for the club and Aberdeen Schoolboys, Gordon Low. They watched him play and decided he was all right both as a prospect and as company for me. It was a good bit of business, too, because Gordon had a good career, playing for Huddersfield and then Bristol City. It was a terrific gesture on the part of Andy Beattie to think of a skinny youngster like me to the extent of bringing in a friend for me.

Gordon used to help me out when I went painting on Monday and Wednesday afternoons. I'd started to do a few jobs in my spare time to supplement my wages. I was a joiner at first, then a painter for seven months, and I also helped in a garage just to earn some pocket money. Huddersfield Football Club sensibly encouraged the youngsters to take up a second trade because they knew that not everyone on the groundstaff would make it in football, and every year a fresh batch of eager young things came in. I quite enjoyed my little odd jobs, but as soon as I got into the team the painting went out of the window.

It was probably a good job too, because Gordon and I weren't very good at it. I remember once we were painting a school in Huddersfield – its toilets, to be exact. We had to lie on the red-tiled floor to get behind the pipes, but Gordon managed to knock over a can of white paint. We had to clean the floor after that, which took a lot longer than painting the pipes. Our jobs seemed usually to be rusted girders, wrought-iron gates and things like that which we had to paint with lead paint. The joinery was another of the trades I fancied right at the beginning. My woodwork teacher at school, who'd also helped to look after the football teams, used me as the class example, showing the rest of the boys how to make a bookshelf or whatever, leaving me with a perfect object which I would take home to my mum as a present. My teacher made all the stuff my mother had, and I believe it was solely because I was in the team. But there was no schoolteacher around in 1955, so I quickly swapped from joinery to painting.

The extra money came in handy, though there wasn't a great deal on which to spend it at that age, just a little Woodbine here and there. Smoking wasn't unusual among players at that time. Several top players indulged. You don't see it now, thank God. Players today know the damage smoking can do, but we didn't then. In those days, our leisure pursuits were all very basic: a cigarette, a pint of beer and fish and chips on a Saturday night – what else could you want? They were happy days. And there never seemed to be any trouble when you went out either. I have never been in a fight in my life, or been hit – off the football field, that is. I suppose for a Scot that must be a record! The last scrape I got into was at school. There was a boy across the road who used to bully me. I was frightened to death of going out, and I used to have a look out of the door before I did; if he wasn't about, then off I'd go to the shops. After a while, I thought to myself, 'This is a load of sherbet!' There was nothing of me, and this guy was a good bit bigger, but one day after some more unprovoked bully-ing I gave him a beating. After that incident he was as good as gold. In fact, we became good pals – strange, isn't it? There was another bully at school, and I gave him a battering as well. Since then, it's always been a philosophy of mine in life, on and off the football field: if you let these people do it to you then they will keep on doing it. You read about kids being bullied today, and you think, 'What an awful life!' Once bullies know you're prepared to stand up for yourself they lose interest and move on. It's the bullies' charter. Sadly, it always seemed to be the retaliator who was suspended at school or sent off from the field of play, never the guy who instigated it.

No sooner had Andy Beattie brought in Gordon Low to keep me company than, it seemed, my status at the club changed totally. In the 1920s under manager Herbert Chapman, Huddersfield Football Club was a big, well-respected side. In five consecutive seasons between 1923 and 1928, they were League champions three times and runners-up twice; they also won the FA Cup in 1922 and were beaten finalists at Wembley on three other occasions. When I first went to the club it was still in the First Division with stars like right-half Bill McGarry, Willie Sinclair, and the captain Len Quested. They finished mid-table in 1954/55, the season I arrived, but it was an ageing team – they were all in their thirties – and there were precious few young players coming through. It was a recipe for disaster, and sure enough they ended the 1955/56 season with just thirty-five points and were relegated to the Second Division. They didn't make it back into the top flight until 1970, and then it was only a brief stay. Since the summer of 1972 they've spent most of their time languishing in the lower divisions. I always felt sad to see such a great club struggling.

Huddersfield's relegation in 1956, however, turned out to be a very good thing for me. Instead of having to wait to force my way into a successful team, I was quickly pushed forward. I was just sixteen years and 303 days old when, on Christmas Eve, I ran out onto the pitch at Meadow Lane for a Second Division match against Notts County. It was a gruelling game on a heavy, muddy pitch – not ideal conditions for a slight young thing – but we won 2–0. Two days later, on Boxing Day, I made my home debut against the same team and we won 3–0. All my Christmases, it seemed, had come at once, especially when I scored my first ever League goal during that return game. To celebrate, my mates at the digs insisted we went out for a drink. It was my first time in a pub as a drinker, and they of course got me drunk. I swallowed a couple of pints far too quickly, then leaned back and landed on the service bell, which kept on ringing until the landlord chucked us out. It was disgraceful behaviour at my age, but it gave everyone a good laugh.

Soon after I had made my debut for Huddersfield, Matt Busby offered the club £10,000 for me. Andy Beattie turned it down, even though it was a record for a kid my age. The facts were confirmed for me quite recently when I met Matt's son Sandy. We were just chatting about this and that, then started to talk about his father. He said, 'You know my dad offered £10,000 for you when you were sixteen, don't you?' I replied that I had heard the story but hadn't been sure whether or not it was just paper talk. He confirmed it for me, saying, 'It's true, that's what he offered for you.' It was an absolute fortune at the time, so it was very courageous of Andy Beattie to turn it down.

I had met Matt for the first time when we played the Manchester United youth team at Beck Lane in Huddersfield. We started really well and were beating them 2–0. I can't remember whether or not I'd got my name on the scoresheet, but I must have done something to impress him, for although we went on to lose 4–2, he introduced himself to me after the game. I'm ashamed to admit that at the time I had never heard of him. I suppose that was unforgivable really as he was already one of Scotland's famous sons; at least I'd heard of the famous Manchester United. It was clear he wanted me at the time to join the developing 'Busby Babes', but, as I said, nothing came of it and I unconcernedly got on with my career at Huddersfield. However, it all came rushing back to me when in February 1958 the club's aircraft crashed in Munich on the way home from a European Cup tie in Belgrade. A chill ran through me when I heard about all the deaths, and I shuddered again when the thought hit me that I could so easily have been on board that aircraft.

My promotion from the reserves over the Christmas period in 1956 was one of Andy Beattie's last acts as manager, for in the new year he was replaced by Bill Shankly. Andy made his way to Nottingham Forest, and his departure came as a bit of a shock to me, but despite this I still felt quite at home; Shankly had been Beattie's number two for quite a while – certainly I had not been there too long before Shankly joined us – and it was, after all, just one Scottish manager for another. (Huddersfield seemed to employ a string of Scots – Beattie, Shankly, Bobby Collins, Peter Jackson, Clem Stephenson, Bobby Collins, Lou Macari – over the years. I wondered if the club had some sort of connection with Scotland, but when I asked no-one could put their finger on a reason why. It just happened that way.) And, despite my age and inexperience, I was being treated really well by my team-mates, too. It seemed I was surrounded by fellow Scots. The two internationals Jimmy Watson and Willie Davis put me on the right road and told me what to do, and when it came to the time to sign professional forms, when I turned seventeen, they told me how to negotiate to get some money for my mum and dad – something I would never have thought of had I been left totally to my own devices. My dad and my sister's husband Billy Bruce (all my brothers were working) came down at the time too; in fact it was 16 February 1957, eight days before my seventeenth birthday, the day of an FA Cup tie with Burnley. We lost 2–1, and they then started discussions with the club about my signing as a professional, talks that went on until eight p.m. the next evening.

I felt very fortunate that there were some good old heads among our Scottish clan who had been through it all before and who were happy to guide me through all the possible pitfalls. Don't forget, there were no agents in those days, and the reality was you were on your own when it came to striking a deal with a club – a young lad, his dad and whoever else, none of whom really had a clue. Bill McGarry, particularly, was a great help to me during those formative years. After a game we used to go to a little pub in Huddersfield which was nice and relaxing for all of us, allowing us to wind down without being bothered. Players couldn't do that today, but it was no problem then. We were footballers, not superstars, and apart from the odd request for an autograph we were pretty much left to get on with our lives. Can you imagine someone like Wayne Rooney being able to do that on Merseyside these days? He'd probably get turned over by the newspapers. I suspect the money these days offers some sort of cushion, but back in the 1950s a few beers in the local was a normal way to relax on a Saturday night after the game. It was during one of those sessions that Bill passed on some great advice to me. 'You are all over the field at the moment,' he said. 'It's no good for you. If you're going to do anything in this game, you have got to be up front scoring goals. That's where you'll do better.'

'But, Bill,' I answered, 'I don't enjoy playing that way. I enjoy lots of work and lots of running.'

But he insisted. 'Trust me. You've got to go up front because you're capable of scoring goals. Come back to the centre of the park now and again and do your stuff there, but your real business is up front.'

A few years later, Matt Busby would say pretty much the same thing to me, but at the time I didn't take much heed of Bill's wise words and kept on doing what I enjoyed most. Now I know Bill was spot on. Goals are gold dust. They were then, they are now, and they always will be.

Through those last months of the 1956/57 season and into 1957/58, Bill Shankly gradually started to ring the changes, bringing in the youngsters in an effort to build up a really good team. Les Massie was up front, scoring plenty of goals; then there was big Jack Connor, who was a good midfield player, Gordon Low, centre-half Ken Taylor, a big, strong man, young winger Kevin McHale and me. Kevin was only five months older than me, and we became the youngest right-wing partnership ever in the history of League football. The team was soon looking like a useful little unit, and it was clear to all that Shankly was making his mark even though he had no money to spend.

The heartening thing for the players was that Shankly immediately took an interest in us and really started looking after us. He made sure, for instance, that we ate properly and drank our milk. He even had the local café, the one we used across the road from Leeds Road, provide us with steaks and wholesome foods for which he used to pay. Steaks and milk – that was Shanks's idea of building up skinny youngsters like me. I'm sure that had I not had Shankly around at that stage of my career, things might have turned out differently.

You heard about youngsters at football clubs all over the country going off the rails because they were away from home with a lot of time on their hands, but Shanks was always there for us, making sure we were healthy in mind and body, even making sure that our parents were all right and that we sent some money home. He was a real, genuine character who insisted that the youngsters in his charge kept tidy, clean and healthy.

Much has been said and written about Bill Shankly and his attitude to football. Certainly the character that became famous later at Liverpool – immortalized in that quip about football being more important than just a matter of life and death – had already developed at Huddersfield, and, no doubt, during his managerial stints at Carlisle, Grimsby and Workington before that. He was exactly the same when I worked under him, maybe even more eccentric. I will never forget one day in October 1958 when we played Liverpool (they were in the Second Division at the time) at Leeds Road because we absolutely battered them 5–0 with what was a very good little team. Shanks came into the dressing-room afterwards and said in his usual grating voice, 'Ah, that team, what a load of rubbish! They're not a team at all, man, shouldn't be in the same division. They cannae play!' A year later, which club did he join? Yes, Liverpool. And what did he say? 'It's the greatest team that ever played!' That was the sort of person Shanks was. Whichever club he took charge of, they were the best, and the players who played for that team were the best in the country. No-one else counted except the team he was managing at that very moment. He was forever looking forward, hammering home the importance of hard work; if you do it, he would say, it will pay off. He was a very effective amateur psychologist and could convince you that every day you woke up was a bonus.

Of course, bound up in that one-track motivational mind of his there were a few quirks, one of which was that he ignored completely any player who had picked up an injury and was therefore unavailable for selection. If you were injured, you didn't exist. Unfortunately, I suffered a few injuries during my four-year stay at Huddersfield because of the way I chased the ball everywhere and wasn't afraid of anyone. I always had the philosophy that if somebody kicks you, you've got to kick them back. Shankly loved the industry, the application and the fearlessness, but not the consequences! I learned a lot from some of the hardened old professionals during this time, especially people like Jimmy Hagan, who was a tough little player. I clattered into him once during a third-round cup replay against Sheffield United, and in full view of everyone at Bramall Lane he stood face to face with me, wagged his finger and told me exactly what he thought of my challenge. Anyway, as I said, several times I would take a knock and miss training in order to have treatment. And at those times, I did not exist.

I remember them well, because at Huddersfield Shankly's office was at one end of the corridor and the treatment room and the gym – well, it was called a gym, but in truth it was a room full of dust and only a few pieces of equipment – were at the other end, and in between you had the secretary's office and the players' dressing-rooms. The first time it happened, physio Roy Goodall gave me a good working over, and as I came out I saw Shankly walking along the corridor in the opposite direction. The corridor was only a matter of six feet wide, so two people crossing could hardly miss each other. He was walking towards me, but he was looking at the ceiling and everywhere else but at me, and we almost bumped as we passed side by side. He didn't even so much as glance at me as he walked by. He never believed anyone was injured and had no time for you if you had tracksuit bottoms on. Maybe it was some sort of a phobia, but it was probably just his brand of psychological motivation again, forcing you into a frame of mind where you wanted to get fit again as soon as possible. He was one of the greatest motivators I ever came across in football.

Shankly's life literally revolved around football. There was a great rivalry between clubs in the north-east of England, especially between Manchester United and Liverpool, though it was not as bitter in those days as it is now. Despite that, whenever Liverpool didn't have a game, Shankly would always be at Old Trafford, and I mean always. He would be in the office or the boardroom with Sir Matt, or upstairs with him in the inner sanctum, talking shop. He used to come to see the players regularly too. He always had on his red shirt and tie, and his greeting was always the same. 'How are you doing, sonny?' he would say to me. 'You shouldn't have come to Old Trafford. You should have joined Liverpool.'

Of course, when Shanks left Huddersfield to go to Liverpool in the winter of 1959, I automatically thought, 'I'll be going with him.' I was quite prepared to follow him anywhere, and when he left Huddersfield he told me it was 99 per cent certain that I would follow him to Anfield. Unfortunately, they did not have the money to buy me at the time. Clearly, Matt Busby had set the benchmark with his huge bid, and as a Second Division club they just couldn't afford that sort of money. I didn't know this at the time, but Shanks admitted as much to me later on. And Busby, by then, didn't have any room for me. Dennis Violett, a survivor of the Munich air crash, was up front scoring goals like nobody's business, Bobby Charlton had also come back successfully, and they had David Herd, formerly of Arsenal, too. He was also hitting the back of the net on a fairly regular basis, so I would have been surplus to requirements.

Shankly and Busby were huge influences on my footballing career. For me, there were three of them in a similar category: all Scots, all different characters, but all with the same aim. The one I had the least to do with was Jock Stein, though we knew him well enough; we were all pals, and he often came down to watch us play. He, too, was a winner for whom everyone wanted to play and do well. Each of these legendary Scots had his own way of going about his business, but the end result was usually the same. The similarity was in their basic philosophy: go out there and play good football. They would say to their players that they knew we could play good football and entertain the people, so go out and try your best. If you get beaten, it doesn't matter as long as you've tried your best. On the other hand, if you get beaten and you haven't tried your best, that's not good enough. To Shanks, before a game, the opposition was rubbish, but that was not how Busby did it. He always showed the greatest respect for the opposing players. But they had the same objectives and the same breed of people around them. Their creed was to look after the people, look after their families, and that did have a bearing on your performance on the field. If you and everybody around you were happy off the field, then it followed that you took no worries with you onto the field. This was the area, I felt, where Busby really scored. He knew the names of everybody's wife, their children and their parents, and he would frequently enquire after them. He'd go up to a player and say, 'How is little Gary doing? How is your good lady? Does she see her mum?' That type of question, sincerely meant, is so simple yet so effective in terms of endearing people to you. Today it's called good man management, and to see it done well is quite a rare thing, then as now. Don Revie was one of the few to compare to Matt Busby in terms of looking after the fine details, sending flowers to your wife when she came out of hospital or sending your mother a box of chocolates when she was ill.

It's a skill that should be applied across the board today, but it isn't, with only a handful of exceptions. There are players a manager can give a hard bawling to, and there are others who need more gentle treatment. In other words, in order to get the best out of them, a good manager will treat different people differently. The manager has to test which one is which because by doing the wrong thing to the wrong player you can destroy him completely. That knowledge comes with experience, but it's still very much the case that some people have it whereas others have to work on it. It's a bit like having children. With the first child you don't know what to do, it's all trial and error; then you have a second, and by the time the third comes along you've got it sussed out. I'm sure it's a similar process for managers, because football players are never easy to handle. And I should think that football players today are even more difficult to deal with because of the amount of money they're earning and their massive public profiles. That must make it more difficult for a manager to get them to listen to him and take notice of what is being said. The attitude, it seems to me, can so easily become negative – 'Ah, so what?' I'm not saying that's generally the case today, but the temptation must be there. There is the danger of a loss of respect between the two parties, and I believe respect is essential for any relationship to succeed.

Shankly and Busby were respected not only by their players but also throughout the game. It was fascinating for me to work under Shanks at Huddersfield, and under Busby for Scotland and at Old Trafford. Shankly went to Liverpool when they were broke and in the lower reaches of the Second Division; four years later they were League champions, and look where they are today. Others followed in his footsteps and achieved tremendous success, people like Bob Paisley, Joe Fagan, Kenny Dalglish and Graeme Souness. They all won trophies, but be fair, Shankly was the one who laid the foundations, as did Busby at Old Trafford – and he did it with three different teams. These guys did their job so well that they earned respect throughout the game, even from the media.

Handling the media was not, of course, as intense then as it is now, but I'm sure Busby would have coped well in the modern game. He had the knack of talking to the press for hours. They would all come away happy, then look at their notebooks and realize that he hadn't given them a single headline story. It was an art in itself, leaving everybody happy without telling them any-thing of note. I'm not so sure Shanks would have done as well, though, because few of today's journalists would have protected him the way they used to. They used to carefully ignore his abrasive little asides, like describing referees as little Hitlers and generally having a go as he wound down after a match. Today he'd be fined every week. But you couldn't help but love the man, and that's why everyone was so protective towards him, even though they sometimes felt the rough edge of his tongue in return.

As I said, and it bears repeating, you couldn't get a more passionate football man than Bill Shankly. When the news came through in 1974 that he had retired from the game, I thought to myself, 'I don't believe this.' It was a real bolt out of the blue, entirely unexpected. He was never the same after that, and I felt so sorry for him. His life was football, and suddenly the carpet was whipped from under his feet. For him to go training at Everton because he was too embarrassed to go either to Anfield or the training ground was heart-wrenching.

One of my great memories of the waves of varying emotion that washed over the great man stems from a game just before Christmas in 1957 between Huddersfield and Charlton Athletic. I wasn't fit at the time and was trying to keep out of his way on the bench, but for once he wasn't worried about injuries or anything else as we cruised into a 5–1 lead. He was, as usual, indicating what a bad side they were and how we were going to rub it in when they suddenly began a remarkable comeback. They levelled at 5–5, and Shanks was going berserk; then they went in front for the first time, although we equalized soon after. But with the final kick of the match, the South African John Summers, a tall midfielder who had already scored four and was sadly to die a few years later from leukaemia, hit the winner in an astonishing 7–6 victory. Shanks was apoplectic and gave Charlton no credit for their fightback. He tore into everyone in the dressing-room, including the reserves, because they hadn't been good enough to get into the team in the first place!

Unfortunately for me, that was far from the only game I missed under Shankly because of injury. I had more than my fair share while I was with Huddersfield. I would not say I was injury-prone, but I did take a few bumps, and in the end Shanks switched me to outside-right to keep me out of the way. I missed seven games at the start of the 1957/58 season, came back and played against Notts County and was injured again, missed ten more, and then returned at the end of November to play against Derby County. It was that winter when I began to earn something of a reputation for being a little cocky, because in one match, with ten minutes remaining, we were awarded a penalty and despite my youth I was given the signal to take it. I did not even think about being nervous, far from it; I tried to unsettle their goalkeeper by making him wait before slotting it.

I twisted my knee badly against Charlton over the Christmas period in 1958, and did it again against Barnsley a few days later. Our physio Roy Goodall had to send me to a specialist surgeon, who discovered that my cartilage was split in three places. I had to have an operation to have the offending body part removed, and it put me out for five weeks. When I came back, I played two games for the reserves to prove my fitness and then played against Sheffield Wednesday. But I trained too hard and this was when Shanks told me he was moving me to the wing. That was a speciality position, particularly in those days. A winger was a winger, and he could rarely be found anywhere else other than getting the chalk on his boots from the touchline. He was just out there to cross the ball to a big centre-forward. You were either tricky and could beat players, or you had pace. It wasn't a position where you were in the game for any length of time, and therefore I never liked it. I just had to be involved in the middle of the pitch. Fortunately, being put on the wing lasted only a few games.

During the last game of the season I got injured yet again, this time a bit more seriously: I damaged a ligament and was put in plaster for ten weeks. It was a choker because everyone else was off on holiday for six or seven weeks and I was stuck in a plaster-cast for two and a half months, missing the entire break, all my pre-season work and the first seven games of the 1958/59 season. The big problem while I was in plaster and on crutches was with my trousers. The only ones I possessed at the time were very fashionable and, consequently, very narrow, and I only had two pairs. I had to have them cut down the sides so that they could accommodate the plastercast. It was a nightmare. All my carefully laid plans were up in smoke, so I just went back up to Scotland and stayed there for the entire period. I couldn't do anything for myself, so my pals used to take me everywhere, which made it even more difficult to chat to the ladies. It was annoying, but when it came to serious injuries I was pretty fortunate and suffered no more than three during my entire career.

My spells out of the Huddersfield side probably had much to do with the fact that I was still growing and asking my body to take on a big workload when perhaps it wasn't quite ready and developed enough. The game was a bit different then compared to today. It was a lot more physical, and I was regularly clattered, but if you took a knock you just kept on playing, which more often than not aggravated the problem.

After Shanks left the club for Anfield at the end of 1959, there were stories in the press about me leaving Huddersfield, and they seemed to get more frequent as the weeks went by and our promotion hopes faded. Eddie Boot had taken over Shankly's job; I thought he was all right, but I never really got on with him, and this no doubt fuelled the stories. There was no serious tapping up going on; initially, I was finding out about other clubs' interest through journalists rather than managers coming to the back door. Boot himself told me that he'd had offers from Manchester City, Arsenal, Chelsea, West Bromwich Albion and Glasgow Rangers. Everton were also keen to land me, and as a youngster – I was still only nineteen – I felt very flattered, even though I was wishing it was Liverpool or Manchester United vying for my services. Arsenal was the team most players would have wanted to go to in those days, with George Swindin as manager. Arsenal's 1930s star Ted Drake was manager at Chelsea, which was another big attraction, and Everton made it clear they were willing to pay a huge £40,000 for me.

It looked for a while as though I was going to Arsenal, who were like the Real Madrid of English football at that time. I had been to London a couple of times with Scotland; it was a big city, and Arsenal were a huge club. I had travelled down with Tommy Docherty, who had played for Arsenal a couple of years earlier. He took me round the ground and pointed out the underfloor heating in the dressing-room and the marble floors and statues in the foyer, and when I saw all that, Arsenal was the club I was going to, no doubt at all! But – and I'm ashamed to admit it, because looking back now it was very childish of me – one of the main reasons I didn't go to Highbury was that they sent their assistant manager to me to talk about the move instead of George Swindin himself. I took it as a slight, and that's why I find my reaction embarrassing now, because one thing I'm certainly not is big-headed. And you know who the assistant manager was? Ron Greenwood, who went on to become the brilliant manager of West Ham United and England.

Alongside the meeting with Greenwood, I had several others, including one with Les McDowall of Manchester City. I was immediately impressed with the guy, and the fact that he was a Scot did their bid – yet another on the table – no harm at all. The fact that Manchester was only across the Pennines made it seem so much closer, and these and a few other factors swayed me completely. It would certainly be much easier to get home to see my folks in Aberdeen. On reflection, I should probably have gone a bit deeper into it than that and had a think about finer details and possible consequences, as well as talking to older players about the situation. Had I had an agent, things would surely have been totally different. I would almost certainly have ended up at Highbury. As it was, in the spring of 1960 I found myself on my way to Maine Road.

4　A BRIEF STAY

MANCHESTER CITY EVENTUALLY PAID A BRITISH RECORD transfer fee of £55,000, of which my share was precisely nothing. The club did offer me £300, but with so much money changing hands for me it wasn't exactly great. If I'd received just 5 per cent of the fees paid for each of my career moves I could have bought myself a very nice detached house. It would also have gone some way towards setting me up with a bit of a nest egg or a pension, but I never got anything. When I moved to Maine Road, all the talk of backhanders was rubbish. Don't forget, I was only twenty, my whole being was focused on playing football, and there was no such thing as a personal agent. We all say, 'I wish I had known then what I know now,' but the maximum wage in 1960 was £20 a week, and that's what I got. I think they gave my dad something extra, but that was the practice in those days; you often heard about parents coming away from negotiations with televisions, washing machines or whatever, according to the quality of their son, though whatever my dad got came in the form of a bit of money. Part of the deal at City was that I also got a public relations job with the local garage, whose owner was a friend of Les McDowall, so that was an extra fiver, which represented a quarter of my City salary. I also earned another fiver for writing a weekly column in the Saturday Pink, the *Manchester Evening News* Saturday-night classified sports paper, so with £30 a week and the prospect of playing Division One football for the first time, I wasn't complaining.

Les McDowall was another Scottish manager struck from the same mould as Matt Busby and Bill Shankly; he even hailed from around the same area, Scottish pit country. He was a good manager, and he'd done really well with Manchester City since joining the club in the summer of 1950, taking them to the FA Cup final in 1955, where they lost to Newcastle United, and then winning it the next year by beating Birmingham City 3–1. George Hannah – who'd actually scored against City for Newcastle in that 1955 final – was in the side then, and Ken Barnes, who taught me a lot during my stint at Maine Road. I was quite happy under Les at Manchester City; it was just that, as had happened at Huddersfield, the FA Cup-winning team was growing old together and losing its effectiveness. They'd finished the previous season, 1958/59, in twentieth place, just one point clear of the relegation zone, and when I started playing at Maine Road in March 1960 I genuinely felt that Huddersfield were a better team than them, and they were in Division Two. Looking back, perhaps I might have picked a team with better prospects. I made my Manchester City debut on 19 March against Leeds United at Elland Road and scored in a 4–3 defeat that left the club fourth from bottom. But that day I couldn't point the finger at anyone else because I didn't play well. Chris Balderstone, who was a useful cricketer as well, had taken my place that Saturday in the Huddersfield side and scored in a 1–1 draw against Shankly's Liverpool.

One young lad who came into the side, a guy called David Shortcross, looked a tremendous prospect, but unfortunately he broke his leg. He was certainly good enough to have made the England under-23 team. David Wagstaff was also an up-and-coming talent, so there were a few of us around, but not enough to disguise the fact that City was an ageing team on the way down. As a result, I soon got itchy feet, but I was determined not to desert a sinking ship immediately; I wanted to help City stay up before thinking about going somewhere else. In April, we beat Charlton 6–1 and 2–1 and I scored in both games, then I netted two against Aston Villa in a 4–1 win that guaranteed First Division football at Maine Road for 1960/61.

It was always a struggle, though. City had been going through a grim time not only in the League, but also in the FA Cup. In fact, they hadn't won a round since beating Birmingham to lift the trophy against the odds in 1956. It was all joy, then, when in January 1961 we beat Cardiff at the third attempt at the neutral venue of Highbury in the third round – and even that one was nip and tuck until I scored two minutes into extra time, Joe Hayes adding another to put us into a fourth-round tie with Luton Town. And what a memory that game provided! We had to travel to the tiny Kenilworth Road ground for the game, and after just eighteen minutes we found ourselves two down as Ashworth scored twice for Luton on a bog of a pitch with the rain pouring down. Then, between the nineteenth and thirty-fourth minutes, I scored my first hat-trick as a professional footballer; just twenty minutes into the second half and I'd scored my second ever hat-trick! It was probably the most extraordinary hour or so of my career, especially when, with seventy minutes gone, the game was called off because the pitch was so waterlogged. Referee Ken Tuck turned to me as he scooped up the ball and said, with a big grin all over his face, 'Denis, I'm afraid your six goals won't count as a record now. Bad luck.' Who knows what might have happened in the remaining twenty minutes! I had scored six only once before, and that was when I was at school. The first game had been drawn, then I'd scored a double hat-trick in the replay. They'd counted, too. In the replay with Luton I scored yet again, so that made my tally seven in one game, and I still finished on the losing side. I recall that after that game I was quoted as saying that but for the goals I would have said I was a bit off form – nice one. Now, I'm not quite sure what I meant by that.

I did enjoy my time with City, and I certainly seemed to earn some respect, even to the point of being appointed captain when Ken Barnes was injured, a role I happily took on. The people were lovely, and in particular I liked George Hannah and Ken Barnes. It was just such a shame that City wasn't a really good team. It was said that I didn't like Manchester City, but nothing could have been further from the truth. I loved Maine Road. Of course there were things I didn't like – the rubbish kit, for example. I'd always thought that when I joined a First Division club the facilities would be so much better, especially at a big club like Manchester City, but I have to say the kit arrangements were awful. Pictures from inside modern-day dressing-rooms show the kit hanging on individual pegs, freshly laundered and smart, with clean boots underneath; at Maine Road in the early 1960s there was just a pile of shirts on the floor and you grabbed whatever you could. It was hardly something to fill you with pride, especially for me: I'd just come from a Second Division club where every-thing had been laid out for you. Now, whenever I pulled a shirt from the pile, I would find there were big holes in the sleeves. It was really poor, and the lads who were there at the time will con-firm that I'm not having a whinge. We really did have some tatty kit. Maybe it was a Manchester thing. Certainly when I first went to Old Trafford a couple of years later things were much the same, just a lot of old gear scattered about inviting you to help yourself. Now, of course, it's all ironed and laid out; with kit sponsorship, it's probably brand-new for every session.

The playing staff at Maine Road weren't in much better shape than the kit, with only a handful of top players such as Barnes, Hannah, a young Alan Oakes who was then very inexperienced, and goalkeeper Bert Trautmann. We all knew how good and brave a goalkeeper Bert was – it was he who had soldiered on between the sticks during the FA Cup final against Birmingham having broken his neck – and we also knew that Ken and George had been terrific players in their time, but they were no longer the players they had been. Alan went on to enjoy a marvellous career with City, but he wasn't quite ready in 1960/61. It was the ideal time for some rebuilding work, but the attitude to it was poor. They went about it in the wrong way, with one big signing in and another one out instead of building up the squad. It was Bobby Johnson who left before I came in, and when I left Peter Dobing arrived. That was no way to improve the quality of the side and rediscover the form of the mid-1950s, and I felt it was not the right time for me to be playing there. Clearly the financial side of the club was not as healthy at the time as it became a few years later, and they just weren't able to buy enough players.

What always made it worse for me was the fact that I knew I'd left behind a good team on solid foundations which Bill Shankly had built. I knew that the likes of Ray Wilson, Jack Connor, Gordon Low, Kevin McHale and Les Massie were the nucleus of a very good team if they were nurtured properly. There was a youth policy at Maine Road which was to pay dividends eventually, but you can have too many youngsters in a struggling side. I have seen what happens to bright prospects when the team around them is mediocre or poor; it does not help their cause or that of the team. Nonetheless, it is important they come through, not only in terms of team development but also from the point of view of future financial rewards, but when it comes to kick-starting a team you need a delicate balance of youth and experience. Things didn't really change for City until the late 1960s and early 1970s when Joe Mercer, and then Malcolm Allison, arrived to breathe new life into the club. With the likes of Mike Summerbee, Colin Bell and Francis Lee in the side, they really took off and established themselves as the best side in England for a while, reassuring those wonderful fans who stand by the club through thick and thin like nowhere else. And I mean that. I once told a journalist in confidence that if City went down I didn't want to go down with them because I felt I was heading in the opposite direction. Unfortunately it became public knowledge, but the fans understood what I was trying to say and didn't turn against me. Perhaps it was because they could see I was giving my all and scoring goals, which eventually helped to keep us up.

Another aspect that made Les McDowall and George Poyser's regime seem that it was getting a bit too long in the tooth was the dramatic changes in wages going on at this time. The PFA, under the chairmanship of Jimmy Hill, managed to get the £20 maximum wage abolished from 1961 onwards, and because of the stance of George Eastham, who was seeking a declaration from the FA that the retain-and-transfer system was an unreasonable restraint of trade, players had a little bit more say. All of a sudden they were renegotiating terms, and different clubs started to pay different wages. We'd known it was coming, but I don't think any of us realized quite how the figures would rocket: overnight, it seemed, it went from £20 to £100. Well, certainly Johnny Haynes was given £100 a week, but others were now pulling in £60 or £70, which was three times the wages we had earned before. The changes were immediately evident. Players began to exchange their bicycles for cars; maybe only one or two footballers owned a car before then. Some of the older managers found these unfamiliar circumstances hard to come to terms with, as was the case more recently when wages went through the roof because of television money; they just couldn't accept that the players were becoming a bit more powerful, that they couldn't control them as much as they had before.

I must say, when you think back to how big the crowds were after the war, it was all very slow in the coming. The grounds were packed with thousands at every game. The money must have been pouring in, but where did it all go? They certainly didn't spend it on improving the grounds, none of which were improved until the 1966 World Cup; neither did they spend it on players: most good teams kept the same line-up for years with just the occasional buy to spice things up. And these standards applied to big as well as small clubs. When I first went to United, Old Trafford was as awful as the training kit. On the far side it was just fencing with pointed tops. It was like a shed, painted red and white. Between 1945 and 1964, nobody spent a penny. When you add into the mix that until 1961 the maximum wage was in operation, I ask you again, where did all the money go? Certainly a few chairmen were quite happy and drove about in rather nice cars.

Another factor that helped push me towards making a quick move was the training itself, which, under Jimmy Meadows, was poor. It was just running and more running. There was nothing to inspire the younger players and no work on developing skills or tactics. That was dispiriting for everybody. When I went to Italy, it was a different world: the training was excellent, completely different from anything I had experienced in England, and everything was done with a ball at your feet, even the running. We hardly ever saw a ball during training at Manchester City – and it wasn't just City: many other English clubs, Manchester United among them, prepared their players in this way. The weak theory at the time was that if the ball was kept away from players during the week, on a Saturday they'd be that much more eager for it. Speaking personally, I needed the ball to work with in order to improve. My career wasn't in athletics; when I trained for football, I wanted to do it with a ball.

As I said, the standard of the training, allied to the fact that we were losing more than we were winning, led to a decline in the spirit among the players, and that's always a recipe for failure. We had gone out to Portsmouth from Division Two in the new League Cup and lost to Luton from the First Division in the FA Cup in the match I described earlier. On our way home we heard that local rivals Manchester United had lost 7–2 to Sheffield Wednesday, which comforted us a little. At least the entire city would be in mourning, not just half of it. It was only natural when you lost a match to hope that your city neighbours lost too; if they did well while you struggled, it made your efforts look even worse. I remember that night that the *Manchester Evening News* carried the headline UNITED IN NINE-GOAL THRILLER. Well, it all depends on how you look at it, doesn't it!

When I moved to Manchester in the spring of 1960, the rivalry between the players and fans of the two clubs was immediately obvious. Things took a nosedive – from our point of view at least – when we lost 3–1 and 5–1 in our two derby games in 1960/61. I'd never experienced anything like it. Neither Aberdeen nor Huddersfield had had any real local opposition, so I'd never been involved in a derby game before. The only one I had really taken any notice of was the big Glasgow derby between Celtic and Rangers, and that was certainly explosive with all its religious overtones. Initially, I could never understand why some of my team-mates in the national side did not get on with one another just because they played for opposing clubs. Surely, I thought, this was Scotland and we should all be together? As I got older, I began to understand the situation much more clearly, and it must have been uncomfortable for the players from the two Glasgow clubs suddenly to be playing with one another in the same side when there was such animosity between them during League matches, fuelled by the supporters on the terraces. When I was playing in Aberdeen I can honestly say I never thought of who might be a Protestant and who might be a Catholic; to me, it had nothing to do with football. It still seems strange to me that it is allowed to seep through into sport. Rangers would not sign a Catholic until Graeme Souness bought players like Mo Johnston. Certainly the players don't concern themselves with such trivialities these days, particularly now that there are so many overseas players in both sides, although the supporters still hold a religious bias.

There was not quite the same sort of intensity in Manchester, but there was certainly a lot of passion during a derby. That was new to me as a player. You know you've got your fans on one side and the other fans on the other, and that it's a huge game that's going to affect the city, people at work and in the pubs. The pressure is on for days before the match, and nerves come into it to a much greater extent. And as I said, in the 1960/61 season we were battered by United in both games. The fans had to live with those results for a year – in fact, longer than that, because City didn't beat United until September 1962, at Old Trafford. When the two teams are not in the same division, as was the case between 1963 and 1966 for example, there's not the same feeling, the same intensity in the city. But, boy, those Manchester derbies were big games.

I only stayed at City for just over a year. I scored nineteen goals in thirty-seven League appearances, not too bad for a side down the bottom. And it was a relegation battle all the way through that spring of 1961. In mid-April I wanted to play for Scotland, but City needed me to play for them against West Ham. I went to join the national side, but I should have stayed: City drew 1–1 and Scotland lost 9–3 to England. But then, how could I have not wanted to play for my country at Wembley? Manchester City rallied to finish the season in thirteenth place on thirty-seven points, just five points ahead of the relegated teams Newcastle and Preston. Although I scored a few important goals, it was a team effort. One player never makes a team. He can make a difference, but he certainly can't make a team.

And after that I was free to concentrate on a new career opportunity abroad. There had been a break from the slog of the League battle in November 1960 when I was selected for the Football League side to play the Italian League in Milan. We had a good side that day – Cliff Jones (Spurs and Wales), Jimmy McIlroy (Burnley and Northern Ireland), Johnny Haynes (Fulham and England) and Peter McParland (Aston Villa and Northern Ireland) were playing – but we lost the match 4–2. I was impressed with the standard of the Italians' play against a side as strong, if not stronger, than the England team. (Ironically, twelve months later I would play in the same fixture, but this time for the Italian League. We won 2–0, but that was the day I told Matt Busby how desperate I was to come back home.) With that experience in the forefront of my mind, and what with the maximum wage disappearing and players jockeying to see how much they could earn by playing football, Italy became the lure. The Italians had big money. I don't know where they got it from, but all of a sudden they were buying top players from Europe and South America, though they very rarely bought British players. Big John Charles had gone over there and was the exception to the rule, and a lad from Charlton, Eddie Firmani, who had Italian blood. City were keen to keep me and were prepared to up my wages to £80 per week if I would stay, but by that stage my mind was fixed on trying my luck abroad. I needed to spread my wings and see how good I was. I felt Italy was going to be a land of sunshine, wine and roses.

I was reading in a Manchester hotel about how Johnny Haynes had turned down a big move to Italy when I was approached by a director of Inter Milan. He offered me a signing-on fee of £20,000 to agree to a three-year contract for £20 a week basic plus bonuses of £1,000 a season which, he explained, came to £200 a week all together. A fortune! The Inter Milan representative returned to Italy without clinching any sort of deal with City, but, foolishly in retrospect, I did sign a note saying that I would be prepared to join the club if a deal was sorted out. I thought no more about it at the time, but it was to come back to haunt me later.

Then the famous agent Gigi Peronace, who had signed John Charles for Juventus from Leeds United, approached me on behalf of Torino. It was not as much money, but it was still good and I wanted to go, despite the warnings I was receiving from all quarters about how difficult it would be to settle. The strongest of them came from Manchester City chairman Alan Douglas, who told me, 'Don't do it, Denis. Don't be led astray by the big money and the glamour Torino is offering. Think of the other side of it. You will be in a foreign land and you will soon discover there are other things in life besides money.' But I wasn't really listening to what he had to say; my mind was made up. I felt that playing in Italy was my destiny. Like a good Aberdeen lad, by playing in Italy I felt I could secure my future and give myself a pension – a valuable thing given the nature of the game and a player's uncertain role in it.

Looking back, I was probably being a bit big-headed, saying the sort of things you say in the flush of youth. But when I left

Huddersfield it was to go from a Second Division outfit to a First Division club. It was a logical progression. I was ambitious, and I wanted to keep moving forward. Towards the end of the 1960/61 season, when the Torino transfer deal was being put together, it really was beginning to look increasingly likely that City was going down, and I did not want to retrace my steps. I'd been down there, I didn't want to go back. I had tasted the top division, and I wanted more of that standard of football. Once you've been at the top level, it's where you want to stay. I should probably have kept quiet and waited to see what happened; had the worst happened, I could then have gone to Mr Douglas to say I didn't particularly want to play in the Second Division. I suppose to come and say it before it had happened must have seemed a bit arrogant, as though I couldn't wait to get away from Manchester, but the truth is that I enjoyed my stay in Manchester. That's why it has been my home ever since I returned from Italy. When I came back to England to play for Manchester United, I went back to the same digs I had used when I played for Manchester City. Mrs Atkins, the landlady, had looked after me brilliantly; she'd even pressed my shirts and my suit for a Saturday night out.

Although I was very keen to seal the deal with Torino, I insisted that instead of my signing-on fee of 10 per cent of the transfer fee paid to Manchester City being spread over the two years of the contract, I wanted it to be paid straight away, not in instalments. I really dug my heels in over the issue, telling Torino that I would not sign unless it happened. It was all legal and above board because once the fee had been decided it was up to the player to negotiate his own signing-on fee and how it was paid in direct and private negotiations with the president of the club. They tried every trick in the book to deter me, but in the end they gave me a third of the fee when I signed and the remainder after I had played a couple of games. In terms of negotiating wages, I went on instinct because I didn't know what anyone else was getting in the team, including Joe Baker who had also signed for Torino from Hibs, and I didn't have the unbiased advice of any sort of agent. (By a strange coincidence, Joe Baker's brother Gerry was at Manchester City while I was there. He was something of a jack-the-lad at the time, but he was a good lad.)

I played my final game for Manchester City on 7 June 1961 in a friendly in Turin, which was part of the transfer deal. I started off playing for City and scored a goal after eighteen minutes, then the sky opened, torrential rain soaking the players and water-logging the ground in spectacular style. And there was me thinking I had escaped from the Manchester rain to a sunny climate! Despite the conditions, we came out for the second half – this time with me in the Torino strip – played for a couple of minutes, and then the referee called it off to everyone's relief except the paying customers. I couldn't for the life of me under-stand the timing until it was explained to me that had the referee called the game off before half-time the fans would have been entitled to claim their money back.

Welcome to Italy!

5 CIAO, ITALY, AND ARRIVEDERCI

THE STORM THAT BROKE OVER OUR HEADS DURING THAT JUNE 1961 friendly wasn't the only one I ran into on my arrival in Italy. Inter Milan, it seemed, were intent on challenging the Torino transfer deal because, they claimed, I had signed a pre-contract with them. They made all sorts of threats, including having me banned from the game for ever. As far as I was concerned, though, I had signed that troublesome scrap of paper simply to signify that I would accept the terms they offered if the transfer was agreed between Inter and City. Gigi Peronace told me to go home and play some golf or lie on a beach while the problem was sorted out, and to return to Italy in July. Inter soon dropped their claim on me, but for a while my future seemed in jeopardy, and on top of this I had a niggling worry about an impending seven-day suspension by the FA as a result of a little problem that had arisen during a game against Leicester City in April. Luckily, the FA ruled that the ban should start on 14 August, before Serie A kicked off, so that particular problem was easily swept under the carpet too.

When I returned to Turin, it was to a film star's welcome. I was greeted at the airport by a crowd of directors, press, television cameramen and players waiting to meet their new signing. Gigi told me I needed to make sure I spoke to all the directors in order to get them on my side – easier said than done, because there were fourteen of them all told, every one with different opinions. Neither Joe Baker nor I spoke any Italian so we were very reliant on the personable Gigi, a lovely man, but it was annoying having to pass all our responses through him and having to ask him for all the snippets of information we needed. Sometimes he could be a bit sparing with his answers – let us say diplomatic. A prime example of this was when he told us to report at the club one afternoon soon after we joined without telling us what for. Joe and I strolled up only to discover we were being taken straight off to a training camp three thousand feet up in the Alps for a fortnight. We were bundled onto the coach and into the foothills without even being able to pack so much as a travel bag, and there we stayed for the full two weeks. It was like being back at school, except that we had the very best of everything in the fabulous luxury hotel where we stayed. I thought this was the real life, the big time, and we ordered off room service, telephoned home and all the rest to our hearts' content. What they hadn't told us, however, was that they were keeping a running total of expenses. When we moved out, we had to settle our own accounts. Mine came to a staggering £400!

There were lots of incidents like that during my brief stay in Italy. Despite the tremendous wages and the creature comforts, they could be exceptionally mean in other areas, particularly when the team lost. I discovered how quickly the atmosphere could change after my very first Serie A game, in Genoa against Sampdoria, when we went down 2–0. All sorts of officials and directors piled into the dressing-room afterwards, and although neither Joe nor I could understand a word that was said, it was fairly obvious from the sharpness of their tongues and the looks on their faces that not too many compliments were being handed around. That I could understand, but not what happened later when we returned to our hotel for dinner. I ordered a salad because I wasn't hungry after the match, which was played in hot weather. I waited, but nothing came. When I enquired as to the whereabouts of my meal I was told that the club secretary, Mr Giusti, had cancelled my order. I tackled him about it, and was angrily told I could either choose only from what was on the menu or go without. Win, and I could eat and drink whatever I wanted; lose, and there was nothing.

Everything depended on results, and the bigger the win and the better the opponents, the bigger was the little bag full of lira – though if we got beaten there was a fair chance we would be fined instead. I wasn't happy with this system, it was too erratic, and I began thinking, 'What kind of club is this?' My first experience of being given an envelope stuffed with money came right after our first victory of that 1961/62 season. It took me totally by surprise, but I was very, very appreciative. But the other side of the coin was daunting. Our first game, away to Genoa, was a real eye-opener. It was boiling hot, and Joe and I were absolutely roasting. We were completely knackered after the first half. Torino lost, and I immediately realized what Italian football's all about: no-one talked, no-one dared smile, and no envelopes stuffed full of cash materialized. When there were no cash bonuses, it was tough. Club secretary Mr Giusti was a regular visitor to our hotel over stoppages in my wages and official bonuses, which always came in the form of a cheque which then had to go to the bank; I'm sure that if they could have had their way I wouldn't have been paid at all. Mr Giusti was the archetypal secretary of any football club from any country who treated the money he was giving you as his own. It was in stark contrast to the situation at our neighbours in the city of Turin, Juventus, who seemed to look after their players so much better (probably because at the time they were winning more often). What house do you want? You want 500,000 or 600,000? Do you want this car or do you want that one? But at Torino, we had to battle for everything. It was a sad state of affairs, because I know I could have settled in Italy. I loved everything Italian – except for one other crucial thing: the style of football.

The 1960s was the wrong age, the wrong period in Italian football for an industrious forward like me. It really wasn't until Enzo Bearzot, who was my captain at Torino, became the manager of the national side that things began to change. Suddenly he was using an attacking full-back in Antonio Cabrini. There had never been an attacking full-back in the history of Italian football, as far as I know, but it worked for Bearzot: after getting away to a bad start in Spain in the 1982 World Cup and being jeered by their own fans, the Italians went on to win the competition, playing some nice football. Enzo liked to play what I'd call proper football because he was a good footballer himself, unlike many of his fellow Italian managers at the time. Sadly for me, when I joined Torino he was coming to the end of his career. You could see he had been a fine player, maybe two or three years earlier, but at least he still tried to play football, and he was one of the few people in the Torino side who wanted to do that. He didn't want to rely on the *catenaccio* or 'chain-link' system – at its most ruthless at Inter Milan under the management of Helenio Herrera – with everybody back behind the ball.

Football people are usually the biggest copy cats in the world. Alf Ramsey and England were the classic example: almost every club in the country switched to 4–4–2 after he had been successful with it. But the rule of thumb did not apply in Italy. Look at

Juventus. They played wonderful attacking football throughout the 1950s and won the Scudetto several times, but no-one copied them. The rest remained defensive. The result was always all-important, no matter how you played. For the supporters it must have been really dull to watch, just absolutely boring, apart from Juventus and the occasional team that tried to break away from the yoke. I found myself wondering why they came to watch this garbage. It has improved, of course – it had to – and though the national team is experiencing something of a mediocre patch at the moment, at least most of them are going out and playing football. When we were there we didn't play football at all, not at all. It was awful. And not only was it boring, it was difficult to play against as well. At home you had to get past nine people just for a sight of goal.

Another of my problems came in the form of Luigi Cillario, the Argentine-born millionaire builder and chairman of the Torino Financial Organization and the Torino Supporters Club, who had put up a large slice of the transfer fees for both Joe Baker and me. Unfortunately, as a result he thought he owned us. His position went completely to his head, and often he was known to overrule the club president on important decisions. He told us on more than one occasion that he had the power and the money to put us out of the game for good if he so wished. Once, at the airport after returning from Palermo and a 1–0 defeat, he ordered Joe and me not to accept a lift with a friend because he happened to be a Juventus supporter. He ordered us out of the car and back onto the team bus to go to the ground.

The press weren't too keen on me either. The sports paper *Tutto Sport* gave me the symbolic award of a lemon as the most uncooperative player in the country because I wouldn't fall in line with their constant demands for interviews when my Italian was in its infancy and their English wasn't much better. The lemon was another thing in Italy we didn't really have back in Britain. There, we'd probably only talk to the media pack on a Friday, and it would be a short session. Don't forget, there was very little football on television in England at that time. There was radio coverage, but even that was very limited in football terms, and it was basically just before a game and immediately afterwards when you gave a couple of quotes and everyone went away happy. But in Italy, the requests came by the bucketful every day. Television, radio, newspapers – every single day without a break. And when you don't speak the language, that can turn into a nightmare. They asked a question, someone interpreted, then I answered it, and he relayed it back to the journalist. And this wasn't just for one or two journalists, this was easily twenty people every day. It would take an hour just to get a few quotes over to them all, but you had to do it. Well, I'm not saying you *had* to do it, but it was certainly expected of you because it was the norm. The problem with translation is that things get changed in the telling; it's like the old joke of 'Send reinforcements, we're going to advance' being transformed into 'Send three and fourpence, we're going to a dance'. I never had any major problems with what was reported, but the words were rarely representative of what I'd said. So after a bit of that I got fed up, shrugged and said 'No more'. That's when the press gave me my own special lemon. It was a proper trophy, a real lemon embedded in a plaque! I loved it, and put it on the wall. I kept it for ages. I'm sure I've still got it at home somewhere, maybe in the attic.

The alternative award for the most cooperative player was an orange, which I never received. But the press and I weren't always at odds. I remember one of the headlines proclaiming me as Valentino Law, after the local favourite Valentino Mazzola. This was quite an honour, as Mazzola was the Torino captain who died in the team plane crash in 1949. The memory of that air crash still dominated proceedings at the club over a decade later, and there were constant reminders of the seventeen players who perished that day and the destruction of a side that was dominating domestic soccer in Italy. High above the city of Turin on the hills above the River Po, the huge Superga basilica was built in their memory, a permanent tribute to the team that won the Scudetto three seasons in a row.

Amid the various difficulties of life with Torino, it was helpful that there were a few British players around, for it meant Joe and I didn't feel quite as isolated as we might have done. In fact, something of a British community was developing, with me, Joe, John Charles (at Juventus), Gerry Hitchens (Inter Milan), Jimmy Greaves (AC Milan) and Eddie Firmani (Sampdoria) all playing in Italy. But even here a spanner was thrown into the works. Such was the rivalry between the two local clubs in Turin that meeting up with players from Juventus was frowned upon, which to us seemed a nonsense. We would meet King John Charles for dinner, but we would have to go out of town if we wanted a meal. That seemed even more ridiculous because John had his own restaurant – called, appropriately, King's – but because of the problems associated with 'fraternizing with the enemy' I doubt whether we ate there on more than two or three occasions. I was told in no uncertain terms that it wasn't good to be seen in John's restaurant. Football was the Torino fans' lives; I didn't realize how intense the football scene was until I was over there. They were so jealous of Juventus because they had taken over from Torino after the air crash. Before the disaster Juventus weren't in the equation; Torino supplied something like nine of the national team. The nearest English equivalent I can think of would be if the current Manchester United squad was virtually wiped out after suffering, God forbid, another disaster.

John Charles was a great comfort to both Joe and me in times of anguish in Turin. He was always available, always friendly, and no-one dared say a word against him. He was loved not only by his own supporters but by the Torino fans as well. He was Gentleman John to our fans from the day he put the ball out of play instead of into the net after accidentally injuring one of our players. He was also the first to come and see us in hospital when we were recovering from a car crash, bringing us all the newspapers with pictures of Joe's smashed-up Alfa Romeo.

That accident happened in February 1962 – the seventh, to be precise. It's a date that's inscribed in my memory, and could have been inscribed on my tombstone, for I was extremely lucky to survive. My brother Joseph had come out for a visit, and I was enjoying my first evening out for six weeks. The three of us went to dinner and then on to a dance, having a laugh as we sat in Joe Baker's new Alfa Romeo going for a spin through the streets of Turin. We cruised up to this huge roundabout, but instead of going round the right way, Joe started to go towards the left, as he would do in England. I quickly alerted Joe to the fact that he was going round the wrong way, but as he reacted and turned the steering wheel, the car clipped the kerb, which was about a foot high. That's the last I remember. Apparently, the car did about six somersaults on the tarmac. Joe was thrown completely out of the car and hit the road face first; I was tossed into his seat like a rag doll. That saved my life, without question. Ironically, had I been wearing a seat belt I would have been a goner, for where I had been sitting the car roof was flush with the dashboard, completely flattened. I shuddered when I saw the photograph.

Poor Joe, he was so unused to his new car. It had only thirty miles on the clock, and prior to that I'd done all the driving in a little Fiat 600. When I came to in the hospital, the first thing I saw was photographers taking pictures of us in our hospital beds (fortunately, my brother had escaped without injury). I looked over at Joe, and he was in a bad way. He reminded me of the Invisible Man, with his bandaged head and his body covered with a blanket from feet to neck. His face was a total mess; he'd broken his jaw, his nose, virtually everything. They had to perform an emergency operation, and he was in hospital for seven weeks being fed through a drip attached to his neck. Joe was very fortunate to survive the accident, but he was a strong man and made an incredible recovery. Had our roles been reversed, I'm sure I wouldn't have pulled through. He was also lucky, as was I, that no damage had been done to his legs. His face had taken the full impact. The operation to patch him up cost around £3,000, but fortunately for Joe the club's insurance paid for it.

Needless to say, the reports in the newspapers the next day had us attending a drunken orgy and crashing a high-powered car at speed in a haze of alcohol, but all we'd had all night was a couple of lagers each, and we were travelling at about thirty miles per hour when we hit the kerb.

Maybe the reaction had something to do with the fact that by that stage of the season things weren't looking too good for Torino. In the early 1960s it was a middling sort of club in terms of cash (three years before I arrived the club almost went broke) and talent, generally depressed at having to play second fiddle to Juventus, and it was unfair to believe that Joe Baker and I could change it around on our own – with, of course, the help of Torino's better players: left-back Ezio Cella, left-sided midfield player Roberto Rosato, his right-sided partner Enzo Bearzot, a good young goalkeeper in Lido Vierri, and the rugged Giorgio Ferrini, later that year to be sent off during a violent World Cup tie with Chile. Our biggest day had come earlier in the season when we beat Juventus by a single goal scored by Joe in front of a sell-out 70,000 crowd at the shared Stadio Comunale. After the game we passed a funeral procession complete with hearse and Torino mourners pretending that they were burying the body of Juventus. It was a rare victory, and they were determined to make the most of it. That night we had healthy envelopes, and we were allowed to order whatever meal we desired with no intervention from the secretary.

But even that early in the season Joe and I had had plenty of evidence of the sort of defending we would be facing. In fact, during our first home game, against Lanerossi, it became clear that we were going to have to cope with some rough, underhand tactics. There is no doubt that a year playing in Italy made me a better player. It was tough, and those Italian defenders took no prisoners, but there were also some cowards around. We were 3–1 up and coasting in that match with Lanerossi, Joe Baker having scored twice and made the other, when the Lanerossi defenders started to target him. He took the treatment until one of their players tried to poke two fingers in his eyes, at which he lashed out with his boot. The visiting player rolled around on the ground until Joe was sent off. After that, we were lucky to hang on for a 3–3 draw. Joe was noted for being a clean, fair player at home, but he was sent off a couple of times in Italy because he stood up for himself against dirty players. It was the first time he had ever been sent off anywhere. Subsequently, Joe was fined by the club and the Italian Federation, and suspended. In total, the incident cost him a stunning £500. No-one had warned us about that level of punishment when we signed. When we played Lanerossi at their ground, it was my turn to find myself in trouble with the referee when, after being hacked to the ground, I sought a touch of vengeance. The Federation fined me just £10 and banned me from the next game against Inter Milan, but then my own club fined me £200 for missing the game!

It was an awful lot of money to be docked for silly things.

Whenever we were presented with our little cash bonuses in envelopes we could see a little bit of corruption going on there but we readily accepted a few quid; in a way, they were giving us back with one hand what they were taking with the other. The Italians run hot and cold anyway. Sometimes you think people are angry when the volume rises and the hands start going, but then they surprise you because it turns out they're happy. If you cut off their hands, I doubt they'd be able to talk. I was only in Italy for a short while, but I was fined a total of over £500 for various offences. Having said that, the rewards for success were huge. Every club did it, and when the Federation caught up with Torino they were fined £1,100 for the payment of illegal bonuses.

The most I was given in a single go was £150 for that victory against Juventus after which the Torino fans staged a mock funeral. In the very next game we hammered Vicenza 4–1 away. Our skipper Bearzot was handed a large package for distribution and he gave each of us £80 above the allowed amount. We earned every penny of it though, as we had to crouch on the floor of our coach after the game, the home supporters throwing stones and bottles at us.

For a while after that things went surprisingly well. We went eight matches without defeat, taking thirteen points out of sixteen, but then we went on an unsuccessful trip to Britain to play friendlies against Manchester City and Hibernian, Joe's former club, as part of the transfer deals. Joe scored a hat-trick for us at Maine Road and we were drawing 3–3 when his brother Gerry scored the winner for City. A week or so later we lost 2–0 to Hibs, and in between we flew home to play Atalanta, who at the time were joint second with us in Serie A. We lost 2–0.

This was the beginning of a drop in our form and results, and that was when it became hard and expensive to play for Torino. It was hard not just because of some teams' *catenaccio* tactics, but also because of the continuing violence on and off the pitch. Violence in the Italian game was a problem long before the finger was pointed at English clubs and their fans. No-one fancied playing Palermo in Sicily at the time, for instance, because their players kicked lumps out of you and their fans were the nastiest I have come across. They threw at you anything they could get their hands on – bottles, coins, oranges, you name it. I was even spat upon once when I went to take a throw-in. As a result, I have to admit to being quietly pleased when Palermo snatched a late winner, but it was a case of out of the frying pan and into the fire as our fans displayed their anger when we returned home. It was mayhem. As I said, we definitely earned our extra money and bonuses when they came.

Similar things happened in Venice, too. The city is renowned as a beautiful place to visit as a tourist, and you'll be made welcome there, but as visiting footballers we were spat at and pelted with rubbish from every bridge when we took a gondola down the canals. That trip to play Venezia was the occasion for one of the more serious incidents when Joe and I posed for a local photographer outside the hotel. Not satisfied with the snaps we gave him, he began to follow us. We told him to go away and leave us alone, but he kept popping up and taking pictures. He was becoming increasingly bold, and suddenly he crept up behind Joe. I shouted a warning to my team-mate, and the next thing I knew Joe, who'd been severely provoked for a while by this stage, was fighting with him and rolling around on the floor. There was hell to pay for that, and it was us who suffered, not the paparazzo. Joe had to pay compensation for his broken camera, and he earned further notoriety because the photographer had been injured during the fight. The press loved that one.

There always seemed to be some sort of aggravation going on. Against Spal, towards the end of my brief stay in Italy, I laid out a player on the pitch and was attacked in the tunnel while coming off at the end of the game. It was in some ways the release of months of pent-up frustration, and come the spring of 1962 I was determined to look after myself. When we played this little club on their little ground I had not one but two of their defenders marking me, and I mean marking. I could only take so much, so, waiting until the referee was out of view, I punched one of them right in the jaw and he was stretchered off with blood running dramatically from the corner of his mouth. The home crowd went potty, and I feared the worst when the referee, the international official Lo Bello, came striding over towards me. He spoke good English and told me he hadn't seen what had happened but had a good idea. I should behave myself for the remainder of the match or I would be off. He was a good official, and he knew what I'd had to put up with; still, if he'd offered me a bit more protection earlier I'm sure the incident would not have occurred.

When we came off the pitch after the final whistle, I saw a group of Spal players and officials waiting for me in the tunnel. They literally piled into me, punching, kicking and behaving just like their defenders had during the match. I needed the help of some of my Torino team-mates to reach the safety of the away dressing-room. It may sound dramatic, but this sort of thing was going off all the time. It was only a narrow tunnel at Spal, too. Attacking a player in the tunnel, however wide, is not to be recommended!

If I had decided I was going to give a knock for a knock and stand up for myself as best as I could, then Joe went one stage further when he threatened to go on hunger strike – a tough call given the quality of Italian food. He was, like the rest of us, fed up with the three-day-a-week *ritero*, or 'players' rest', in the mountains in a small twenty-bedroom hotel, which was such a dull and regular experience. The club went mad when Joe refused to come to the dining-room, and he hadn't eaten for almost two days when they gave in and took the team back to Turin. We never went back, much to the delight of every player, who thanked Joe profusely for his one-man stand.

Under such circumstances as these, Joe and I were never more than a few yards away from each other on and off the pitch. We shared a luxury hotel room together for five months and took breakfast there every day to avoid being hassled. We might have been paid well to be there, but it felt like a prison. After breakfast we would take a taxi to the ground for the ten a.m. roll-call, which made sure that no-one had skipped town or was sleeping in, and then it was straight back to the hotel. The highlight of our day was the afternoon training session.

What can healthy young men do when they have so much spare time on their hands and they can't go out for fear of being photographed and reported on? We sometimes broke the monotony by having a drink in the hotel bar, away from prying eyes. Ours was a hotel stuck up a side street so it wasn't that busy; the clientele was mainly business guys from out of town. We knew Giuseppe, the barman, and he knew what we wanted. We sometimes had a few beers, just to pass the time, but we weren't big drinkers. We certainly didn't drink in our room. Because of the drink culture back home there was always the temptation when we were bored, but it wasn't booze we were craving, it was conversation. We went downstairs to the bar not necessarily in order to have a beer, but to find some company, quite often over a cup of tea or coffee. We also played cards and draughts in the hotel room because there was nothing else to do other than go to bed early. The only break from this tedious routine was when we went away three days before a game. It was just another hotel with the same restrictions, but at least it offered a change of scenery. Unsurprisingly, I became a good card player and a lethal draughts player. I killed my opponents, even when I gave them a two-draught head start.

Yes, of all our problems out there, boredom was the biggest. The club kept promising that an apartment would soon be ready for us, but we waited and waited. When Joe and I finally moved in, the place turned out to belong to Luigi Cillario, the Argentinian who had put up the money for us. It was almost as though he wanted to keep an eye on us all the time. The apartment was brand new, which was the reason why we'd had to stay in the hotel for so long. Originally we were going to live in another apartment in town, but that wasn't convenient for them and it was cancelled. The new apartment was perched on top of a hill, had five bedrooms, and was absolutely luxurious, but it was bare, totally without furnishings and any other homely touches. It was a relief to move in initially, but it soon got very boring there too with no visitors, and as neither of us could even so much as boil an egg at the time we just used it to sleep in and store our clothes. It was a bit better than the hotel because we had more privacy, but it was so cold and lonely. The most remarkable aspect of this entire period was that my relationship with Joe stayed amazingly good. With two guys stuck together for that length of time under such circumstances, it's a wonder how we didn't get on each other's nerves. I suppose adversity and traumatic events bind people together. Joe and I are still friends, we're still in touch.

I had been so determined to see out my two-year contract with Torino. To demonstrate my commitment to them I'd even started to learn Italian from a friend, Marco Garadi, so that I could hold my own in conversation and get a better understanding of what was being said about me. But the boredom, the style of football, the violent man-marking, the struggle to get my wages – everything just wore me down in the end, and I wanted to leave. My transfer requests were ignored that April, though, and the club wouldn't give me a decision on whether I would be released to play for Scotland against Uruguay, even though it was written into my contract that I could play in such games. I eventually missed the match, which made me very bitter and hardened me further against Torino. The club president, Angelo Fillipone, wanted me to play in the Italian Cup, but that was just a non-event. I think there were about two thousand spectators at the game. For them, the Italian Cup was nothing, totally unlike the FA Cup, which was huge and known throughout the world. It was just another nail in the coffin as far as I was concerned. Why didn't they let me go and play for Scotland? To be fair, the Uruguay game was only a friendly, but it still meant earning a cap for my country, and it was important to me as I'd been left out of the side, and out of sight is out of mind. I was desperate to win my place back after the 9–3 defeat at the hands of England the previous April.

It was a horrible period for me. I felt trapped, especially because I'd just spent seven weeks on my own in the apartment with Joe in hospital after the car crash. The final straw came in that Italian Cup game on 25 April against Napoli, in which Joe was making his comeback. It was a poor game played in stifling heat, and after an hour or so of running about I innocently went to fetch the ball for a throw-in only to be confronted by our coach Beniamino Santos shouting and screaming at me. Torino skipper Bearzot and the perplexed referee joined in the fun, and the next thing I knew I was being sent off for the first and only time in Italy. Gigi Peronace was on the spot to guide me to the dressing-room, and he told me that Santos had asked the referee to expel me from the game because I'd been told not to take throw-ins! I had never heard an excuse like it. If it had not had such serious consequences, I would have laughed. I had made it known I was looking to leave the club, and they'd all turned instantly against me. We went on to lose the game, and any respect I had left for the coach and the club totally disappeared in that one crazy, unique moment. After a few well-chosen words with our president, I walked out. I was promptly banned from the ground for two weeks and was a virtual prisoner in the flat, with just Joe and occasionally Gigi to keep me company and tell me what was going on.

Santos, an Argentinian, was a reasonably good coach, but he was totally dictated to in terms of the way the game was played in Italy at that time. He wasn't a fluent Italian speaker either, which didn't help his cause. His training routines were excellent, but when it came to the game at the weekend I'm sure he was manipulated from above. He certainly didn't appear to have the sort of control a manager would have in England. He was a nice enough guy, but that row and the sending-off finished any relationship we might have had, regardless of whose orders he might have been following. I wasn't going to be treated in that fashion, and I had no doubt at all then that I was off.

I was eventually instructed to travel to Switzerland, where Torino were due to play Lausanne in what was called a Friendship Cup tie. It turned out not to be a sudden apology and recall to the team, but something much better as far as I was concerned: it was an invitation to meet Matt Busby. Well, actually he met with Fillipone privately in a hotel room and I wasn't allowed to attend, but when Matt came out he was wearing a big grin and it seemed that everything was fixed. In October 1961, during the Italian League versus Football League match at Old Trafford, Matt had approached me and asked if I was happy in Italy. Even then I'd replied, 'No, not really. Everything is nice enough, but the football isn't great.' He'd added that he would be in touch, and that was all he'd said. He'd known for months how desperate I was to get back home, and now, at last, he'd come to my rescue.

Dennis Violett had left Old Trafford and gone to Stoke, and Matt was trying to rebuild his team, a team that was breaking up. I knew Matt from my Scotland games, and for me it was inevitable I was going to sign for him one day.

But then, a few days later, came a very strange twist – even for Italy, where nothing, it seemed, was ever straightforward. I was ordered to a meeting with the president of Juventus, Umberto Agnelli, and Fillipone, and they told me how glad they were that I was going to Juventus. Yes, the president of Torino had sold me to Torino's rival club for £160,000! I was informed that it was all perfectly legal and backed up by the small print in the papers I had signed on my arrival. I was theirs to sell off to whom they wanted. They also asked me how I fancied playing alongside my friend John Charles and the wild South American Omar Sivori. I sat there stunned. I thought I'd been sold to Matt Busby just a few days earlier! When I recovered my breath and the power of speech, I said to these two men, who virtually owned the city of Turin between them, 'No thanks.' I was a footballer, not a side of beef. I told them I was going home and that I wouldn't ever kick a ball for Juventus, and with that I pushed the registration forms away and walked out. I reckon that cost me around £50,000, but I'd had more than enough of Italy and I vowed that I would never work abroad again.

I went back to the flat to pack a few things, left a note for Joe, and rang a taxi driver I knew. Then I flew home to Aberdeen via London. When I got home there was a telegram from Fillipone demanding my return. I still haven't replied. To be honest, I'd planned to stay just for four or five days before going back, but when it was confirmed that I'd been sold to Juventus without any consultation I accepted that there was no point going back at all. I was backed up in this by the much-respected secretary of the Professional Footballers' Association Cliff Lloyd, who agreed with me that if Torino had their way it would be pure slavery.

I improved my golf handicap and tried to persuade Mum and Dad not to worry, which wasn't all that easy. By coming back home when I did and turning my back on Torino I had left myself open to all sorts of possible reprisals. Had Torino wanted to take it all the way, I could have been banned from the game. The only place I would have been able to play football would have been South Africa, which wasn't under FIFA jurisdiction. But I gambled on the fact that there was only one way the argument could be resolved because Torino, unlike their neighbours Juventus, were not sound financially, so the £100,000 or so they would get from my transfer was a lot of money to them. If they banned me worldwide they would get nothing. They needed the cash transfusion as much as I needed to play football, therefore I was sure my move to United would go through. As the weeks passed I admit I became less and less certain of my position – I presumed that Juventus's £160,000 was still on the table, muddying the waters – but I was determined to hold my ground. There was even a time when I seriously contemplated going to South Africa. I mean, what else could I have done? I was a football player, that was how I earned a wage. If things had gone against me I would have had to move there. Then, at last, I received a call from Gigi asking me to meet him at Edinburgh airport to sign for Manchester United, the team for whom I'd always wanted to play. I would have walked from Aberdeen to sign that contract. It was like signing a peace treaty. I was overwhelmed, and even little Gigi wept. I'd been bought by Torino for £125,000 from Manchester City on hire purchase and sold to Manchester United for £115,000. Not only did Torino lose out on this deal, they also lost an option on the talented Spanish inside-right Luis Del Sol Miramontes, known simply as Del Sol, who joined Real Madrid instead, and all because of their prevarication over my transfer to

United. In fact, Matt Busby had become so annoyed with their delaying tactics that at one stage he'd walked out and slammed the door on the deal altogether. Thank goodness he changed his mind!

I suppose it sounds all bad, but it wasn't. There were the odd moments of sunlight. Being a good Scot, I was delighted that I'd won a fiver off Joe Baker on a wager that I would find a club back home before he did. I signed on 10 July 1962 for Manchester United while Joe had to play seven more games for Torino to prove his fitness before signing for Arsenal. And it was very flattering when the Italian journalists voted me the number one foreign player, especially after the lemon award and everything else, and even more so when you looked at the quality of the opposition I had faced. At that time there were excellent players from all over the world enjoying the high wages offered by clubs in Serie A. Alongside my British compatriots were the likes of Sivori, the Swede Kurt Hamrin, and the Spaniards Luis Suarez and Del Sol. They were all top players, so to receive that accolade was a big honour. To cap that, the Torino supporters had protested when they'd heard the news that I was being sold to Juventus. The weirdest postscript of all came eight weeks after my move to Manchester United when Fillipone tried to buy me back. It was suggested it was because of the anger of his fans, who would soon be voting on his position, but I had no wish to talk to the man, and going back to Turin was the furthest thing from my mind.

Without Gigi Peronace we would never even have survived in Turin, because when we were unhappy with something it was very difficult to communicate with the Torino officials. Very few of them spoke English, and whenever we had a problem none of them spoke any at all. Everything had to go through Gigi, and he was always under a lot of pressure. As an agent, Gigi wasn't even

ABOVE LEFT: Denis Law was born here! The house at 6 Printfield Terrace.

ABOVE RIGHT: Me, aged five, with my mum.

RIGHT: Winning the Subbuteo Trophy in Aberdeen.

BELOW: Hiding my squint, aged ten, in the Kittybruster school team (*front row, far left*). The schoolteacher, Mr Wright, switched me from left-back.

THE SIX SORROWS
OF DENIS LAW

Ditherer then
dazzler
that's Briggs

Brian
keeps
score
down

This match
had final
touch

Rain stops City

OPPOSITE TOP: Playing for
Huddersfield against Sheffield
United in September 1958. This
one didn't go in! *Action Images*

OPPOSITE BOTTOM: The Huddersfield
club line-up with me on the far
right, third row. Spot Bill Shankly!

ABOVE: Can you believe it!
I score seven goals in a cup tie
for Manchester at Luton and still
finish on the losing side. *Action Images*

RIGHT: Signing for Manchester City
the first time around with manager
and fellow Scot, Les McDowall.

LEFT AND MIDDLE: Postcard home to Ma and Da from Turin in 1966. The front of the postcard shows the eighteen Torino players killed in the plane crash of May 1949.

BOTTOM LEFT: Posting my letters home from Turin. Does that boy look homesick?

OPPOSITE TOP: Me, Garry Hitchins and Joe Baker preparing to play for the league of Italy against the football league at Old Trafford.

OPPOSITE MIDDLE, LEFT: Discussing my life with Torino captain Enzo Bearzot, eventual to become the manage of Italy.

OPPOSITE MIDDLE, RIGHT: Don't worry, you haven't lost your good looks! Checking out Joe Baker for scars after our car crash. *Empic*

OPPOSITE BOTTOM: Another inter-league match, but this time in Milan and this time I am playing and scoring for the English league in November 1960. The goalkeeper is Lorenzo Buffon and in the background is Villa's Peter McParland.

Topham/AP

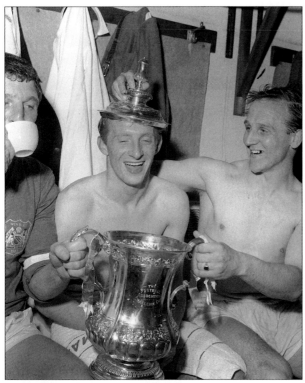

ABOVE: Looking smooth in my white socks as I sign for Manchester United, watched by (*left to right*) Gigi Peronace, Matt Busby, Jimmy Murphy and Howard Staff.

LEFT: So this is what it feels like to win the cup! Two-goal David Herd prefers a cup of tea while Maurice Setters crowns me Kir

Action Images

OPPOSITE TOP: See how much it means as I score against Manchester City for United in May 1964.

OPPOSITE BOTTOM: They don't make shirts like they used to, as Jack Charlton proves in March 1965 when Billy Bremne and Bobby Collins join the fray.

Action Images

Our wedding day, December 1962

attached to the club, yet he was there all the time, trying to make sure his assets were happy. We gave him many a rollicking, usually telling him to do the same to the club, and he had to do that on our behalf. I doubt whether he used exactly the same words, of course, because Gigi was quite the little diplomat. In the early days he was a bit of a jack-the-lad and we thought we'd made a mistake, but as it turned out he was a good lad, a very shrewd cookie, and he was excellent for us. I liked him, and I was very sad in the early 1980s when I heard that he'd died in Rome. He was due to fly off to South America that morning with the Italian team. Gigi was fifty-two then and looking forward to the World Cup in Spain because he was very friendly with Enzo Bearzot. He was also still friendly with me. I was working for the BBC at the time and Bearzot was big news because of the threat of the sack hanging over him; Gigi would pass valuable snippets of information on to me.

In fact, both Joe and I became good friends with Gigi. He was something of a father figure to us, and he looked after us well. Occasionally we were invited back to his home for a meal with his wife. That sort of thing is very much appreciated when you're stuck in a hotel in a foreign country. I'd do exactly the same if a friend came to Manchester United and I was married and with a family; I would have him in my house for a meal, because I know what it feels like to be on your own. It's homely things you miss most. If you can overcome that problem with good foreign players, then you're on to a winner. That's why so many clubs buy two overseas players from the same country, so they have some company.

Soon after I'd managed to extricate myself from Turin, at the start of the 1962/63 season, that likeable English striker Gerry Hitchens was sold by Inter Milan to Torino without any consultation. That was just the way it was, it seemed. There was little or

no choice for the player himself. Gerry learned very early on that
he had to battle it out if he wanted to survive, and he coped well
and earned everyone's respect. He was an honest, strong guy, he
could handle himself and he was good in the air. He didn't mind
being marked because he could take it and dish it out. John
Charles, of course, was another success in Italy, but he was past his
best when he moved to Roma. His form went very quickly after
leaving Juventus. He'd probably have performed better for Roma
at centre-half, but they wanted his goals.

I'm happy to admit that I went to Italy for the money. It did not
work out, but I would do it again – though perhaps a little differently with the benefit of hindsight; I was too young and immature
at the time, a twenty-one-year-old with little sophistication –
because I reckon I had the best of the bargain. I earned three times
what I would have earned over a similar period in England, even
though Torino had the final word where money was concerned
by doing me out of two £500 bonuses they owed me. In addition,
I did a lot of growing up while I was there which stood me in
good stead for my stay at United. Previously, as with any English
club, I'd been looked after and taken everywhere. If you were
travelling, the club had your passport, ticket and everything you
needed there for you, but in Italy you had to look after yourself.
Nowadays, youngsters travel all over the world during their gap
years, but that wasn't the norm in the early 1960s. To travel
around Europe on your own in those days was a bit of an ordeal.

The nature of the football over there, which I've already
described, made me grow up quickly too. It was the dirtiest football I had ever been involved in, and it was a shock to someone
who thought he could handle himself. I became more aware of
where people were on the field than ever before, and consequently
I had better insight into the game. When I was at Maine Road I
hadn't really thought about that aspect of the game before. I just

did my job. But when I returned to Old Trafford I was very aware of football's nuances, a game's shape, its possibilities. When you're aware of where people are and what they might do, it gives you a huge advantage. I also became more self-sufficient. I had to be able to look after myself. Sometimes you lash out without thinking, but that's just instinct. It's not premeditated, but invariably that's what got me into trouble. It was always retaliation; I was never the instigator. You know when a game is going to be hard, so you have to set yourself up for it. Leeds, for example, were always a hard team to play against, as were Liverpool with Tommy Smith, Chelsea with Ron 'Chopper' Harris, and Arsenal with Peter Storey. They were all hard, top players. We had some too at Old Trafford: little Nobby Stiles, Bill Foulkes and Pat Crerand could certainly dig in when necessary. It was a man's game, and my Italian experiences taught me a lot more about how to handle myself.

I'm convinced that those of us who had played in Italy could look after ourselves much better, not only in terms of how to ride a tackle, but also how to ride a punch. You need to know where your marker is and what he's likely to do at all times, and you also need to watch out for all the play-acting. That was certainly something I hadn't experienced before going to Italy, because in England you felt you had to show your opponent that he hadn't hurt you. You might have been in pain, but you didn't want to show it. But the Serie A guys were like Laurence Olivier at his best, rolling around the deck in agony. Well, if they were going to do that, you made sure you hit them properly so that they could give full rein to their acting talents; after all, it was no use being done by the referee for a mild challenge or none at all.

It's just not in the British nature to be rolling about or pretending, nor is it in our nature to spit at people, unlike, in my playing and spectating experience, those of a more Latin temperament. Of all the nationalities I played against, the South Americans really were the kings. We must be on our guard in Britain. Because of the recent influx of overseas stars there is now more acting and shirt-tugging than ever before. Referees need to get a grip. If I were an official today there would be a record number of bookings. I'm sorry if that sounds like poacher-turned-gamekeeper stuff, but what goes on now is awful. Take an average corner-kick in the Premier League; there'll be six players holding onto other players' shirts and others standing there with their arms raised. If I were a referee, I simply wouldn't be retained because of too many bookings and penalties. I detest shirt-pulling, and how players get away with it is beyond me. The authorities have successfully cut out things like tackling from behind and going over the top, and that can only be good for the game, so why not clean up other aspects of the game too? If referees were strong and booked players and awarded penalties, all foul play would soon stop because the coaches would insist on it. No-one wants to play a match with nine or ten men.

The sickness of the Italian game in the 1960s didn't seem to end with dirty play on the field either. There were constant stories of drug taking – though I have to say I saw none – and bribery, with rich clubs accused of paying smaller clubs to throw matches. This sort of corruption was eventually exposed by the British journalist Brian Glanville of the *Sunday Times*, among others. I was often suspicious about the quality of some of the decisions made by certain referees. While I was in Italy, Roma's Francisco Lojacono was sent off four times, suspended for a month and fined a fortune. Success in Europe was not only financially rewarding, it carried much prestige in Italy, and consequently we saw some really dodgy results – but who's to know how deep the problem really went? The players certainly talked about it among themselves, debating whether or not strange decisions had been made by accident or by design, and it was hard to take. As a player, you expect to be treated fairly by the match officials, you expect the referee to be doing his job as best he can. Obviously he'll make mistakes like anybody else, but when you harbour doubts about his honesty, that's a different matter altogether.

But, as I said, despite everything, I wouldn't have missed the experience. It was so completely different from anything I'd experienced in Aberdeen, Huddersfield and Manchester, and now I felt able to bring to United, a club hungry for European success, a good amount of valuable international experience gained not only with Torino, but with Scotland too.

6 SCOTLAND THE BRAVE

MATT BUSBY VERY NEARLY DIED AS A RESULT OF INJURIES sustained during Manchester United's plane crash in Munich in February 1958, but he made a remarkable recovery and was appointed manager of Scotland that October (in the days when you could be a club and international manager at one and the same time). He had obviously been keeping an eye on my progress, and presumably he'd seen enough potential in me to pick me for the senior squad. It was very flattering. When I was selected for the game against Wales in Cardiff on 18 October, my mind went back to that week in February when I'd seen pictures of him in hospital with an oxygen mask to help him breathe and tubes everywhere to keep him alive. It had been touch and go for a while, but now here he was preparing for an international match, and his assistant at United, Jimmy Murphy, who had missed the fatal Belgrade trip because of international commitments, was in charge of Wales.

It's often funny listening to how other players learned of their call-up to their national side – via the manager, a phone call, a telegram, a television or radio announcement, from the wife who'd taken a message, even, nowadays, text messages. Me? I learned I was to become the youngest Scot to be capped so far that century from a newspaper seller. In those days, Scotland used to inform the club, saying, 'We would like to select such and such a player.' But me, I was walking through the middle of Huddersfield when I heard the good news. There used to be a guy called Eric who sold the local papers in the city square, and he was the one who told me.

'Hey, Denis,' Eric said as usual by way of a greeting.

'Hi, Eric.'

'I see you've been selected to play for your country,' he continued.

'What? Are you sure?'

'It's right here in the paper.'

And, sure enough, there it was. I had no idea at all I was even being considered, none whatsoever. It was the greatest feeling, a real honour. It still is today, really, but it felt particularly good in those days when, of course, only eleven players were selected (there were no substitutes). To know, at the age of eighteen, that someone of Matt Busby's standing thought you were one of the best eleven Scottish players on the mainland was something special.

The build-up to the game, even the matchday itself, passed in a complete blur. I must have been doing something right to be called up, though I think the fact that Matt had taken such a close interest in my career weighed hugely in my favour. Had someone else been appointed to take charge of the national team, I might not have been selected. It was definitely to my benefit that he was plying his trade down in England, in Manchester, and he used his local knowledge to pick an all Anglo-Scottish forward line, which was most unusual: he named Tommy Docherty (Arsenal),

Graham Leggat (Fulham), Bobby Collins (Everton), Jackie Henderson (a left-winger with Arsenal), me (Huddersfield) and David Herd (also with the Gunners). The Scottish media weren't too happy about it and there was a great deal of controversy north of the border, especially because one of the Anglos was only a young Second Division player with a team in England called Huddersfield. 'Who?' they asked. I had only played a couple of under-23 games, so I can't blame them for hardly knowing me.

We were under a great deal of scrutiny that day, especially as Wales, with the likes of Jack Kelsey, Mel Charles and Ivor Allchurch, had that summer reached the quarter-final stage of the World Cup in Sweden. Phil Woosnam, then playing for Leyton Orient, won his first cap for Wales that day, and Terry Medwin was picked to play centre-forward having just left Swansea for Spurs because he wanted to play on the wing. Both were good performers, particularly Woosnam who was a beautiful player, and a lovely man.

Dave Mackay, then with Hearts, was the Scotland captain, and he missed a penalty in the first minute, though it scarcely registered with me. I had no recollection of the incident until Dave reminded me many years later. He made a big impression on me that day and was a great inspiration. His words before the kick-off had me all fired up and running all over the pitch. I soon found myself gasping for breath as this was a cut above anything I had faced so far in the Second Division. Even so, I managed to make an impact of sorts. Our first goal came when I found the speedy Jackie Henderson, who tore down the wing and crossed for Leggat to head us into the lead. I scored – if I can use that term – my first international goal in the second half when David Herd crossed the ball and I jumped for it with Dave Bowen, whose firmly struck headed clearance hit me on the head and flew in past the surprised Kelsey. To cap what was a satisfying debut, I laid on the third when I headed down John Grant's long ball to Dave Mackay – a good way of thanking him for the way he had helped me settle before the game – and he played in Bobby Collins to score. Still, I had to read the papers to see what I had done and how the goals had come about. For me, it was all a blank.

At the beginning of November, I played my first home international against Northern Ireland. We were unchanged after our healthy win in Cardiff, but the Irish team was a strong one with the likes of Uprichard (Portsmouth), Keith and McMichael (Newcastle), Blanchflower (Spurs), Bingham (Luton), Simpson (Rangers), McIlroy (Burnley) and McParland (Aston Villa). It was a side that had also just reached the quarter-finals of the World Cup, while both England and Scotland had come home early. Their key player was undoubtedly Danny Blanchflower. He was an icon to all of us, a majestic and influential player who could take complete control of a game. Matt Busby naturally wanted us to keep a close eye on him, but sometimes, particularly when you are young, you can take things too literally. Matt said to me before the game, 'Make sure you stop him because this guy starts everything for them. You are the inside-forward, make sure you watch him.' To be honest, I am embarrassed to this day about what I did to that great player. I chased him all over the field and gave him a good kicking. It was effective, but it was totally wrong, and I apologized to him many times over the years as I got to know and respect the man. I was only eighteen, a young boy, and I kicked him off the park. I didn't play any football, I just swiped at him every time he got the ball. It was an absolutely disgraceful performance. Danny, quite rightly, was disgusted by the time the final whistle went. I can't remember whether or not he spoke to me after the game, but I was well aware he wasn't happy. But

Danny was a good man, and he accepted that I was very young, charged up in my first ever international in Glasgow.

I was always a fiery player who gave it my all in every game, giving as good as I got, but I overdid it on this occasion. But, for the first time, this was Hampden Park, and I was playing for my country! I had heard so much about this famous Scottish battle-ground. What's more, this was a big game in those days, a home international. It was no friendly. Northern Ireland were a good team, too. The others told me that if I could stop Danny Blanchflower we would stop a lot of their moves, so I got carried away and went completely over the top. The strange thing was that Matt said nothing to me at half-time; he didn't tell me to calm down or anything like that, so I thought I was doing well. We were actually leading 2–0 at one stage, but the Irish eventually earned a draw, so it was a disappointing result for us at the end of the day. I'd expended such a lot of nervous energy charging about the pitch, and when I tired Danny started to take control and led the Irish back into the game with his perceptive passing.

And to think my mother and father were watching me as well for the first time. They must have seen a different player to what they expected. Neither Mum nor Dad had ever seen me play as a professional footballer before that day, and all they witnessed was me trying to pummel the life out of the great Danny Blanchflower. To cap that, on their journey home my parents were injured in a car crash. That Northern Ireland match was the first and last time they watched me play for club or country.

As I grew older, the game often came back to haunt me, particularly when some youngster out to make a name for himself marked me out for a kicking to help his reputation, which tended to happen when I was playing the occasional reserve game on the way back to fitness. Danny accepted my apology because he was a gentleman, and we became good friends. I was also very friendly with Dave Mackay, John White and Bill Brown, who were all team-mates of Danny's at Spurs. Occasionally, over the years, we'd meet and have a drink. Mackay would laugh and remind Danny that I was from Aberdeen and no-one could expect any better. 'These guys from Aberdeen have no breeding whatsoever,' he'd quip. The next time we played Northern Ireland, twelve months later in Belfast, I'd grown up a bit. Matt had moved me to centre-forward, and we won 4–0. By then Danny was acting manager as well as skipper of the team and had more than enough to occupy him without having me snapping at the backs of his legs. In the late 1950s I counted myself very fortunate to be play-ing with great players such as Danny at my tender age, especially as Huddersfield at the time were not doing at all well and I could never be sure of my place in the national side.

My first trip abroad with Scotland, to Holland, came in May 1959 along with John White (then of Falkirk, before he went to Spurs) and Bertie Auld (Celtic, before he went to Birmingham). Bertie was a strange character, a bit like Desperate Dan: he always seemed to have a five o'clock shadow, rounded off with a pro-nounced dimple. He was a good, tough player though, and he could dig as well as any defender. The first game was a warm-up against Jutland in Aarhus, and I scored the first goal in a 3–3 draw. It wasn't a good result, but then we beat Holland 2–1 in Amsterdam in a very rough match during which Bertie was sent off on his debut in injury time. Bertie had been given a torrid time by his marker so we were all baffled as to why he was the one to be ordered from the pitch. It was a real home decision! Then the squad moved on to Lisbon, where we lost to the Portuguese by the only goal of another rough encounter.

The following summer we went on tour again. On 29 May 1960 we were thumped 4–1 by Austria in Vienna, then in early June we drew 3–3 with the Hungarians and went down 4–2 to the

Turks in Ankara on a rough pitch on a very hot day. My contribution to the tour was minimal as I'd damaged my ankle in the twelfth minute of the very first game, so it wasn't a happy trip personally, or for the team. There was unrest among the players before the game in Budapest. When they turned up for a practice match two days before the Hungary fixture they found some two thousand paying customers in the stadium. The last time this had happened a special fee had been paid to the squad, so after a meeting we sent captain Bobby Evans to enquire after its whereabouts. Andy Beattie, who'd by then taken over from Busby as manager, gave a very blunt reply in the negative, and that was the end of the matter.

Newspaper reports of a wild party in Ankara didn't help matters. Sure we had a few parties and a few drinks on those end-of-season tours, and after playing on a baking summer afternoon and becoming dehydrated the wine at the banquets tended to go straight to the head. In those days we always had a banquet after international matches, and matters could sometimes get a bit out of hand. Dave Mackay was the leader of the pack, and I know there were a few shenanigans going on at the top table. The problem in Ankara actually started in my room, which I was sharing with Dave. We spent a rather boisterous night there with a few other players, and at some point Dave dropped a marble-topped table on the floor and cracked it. There were no complaints from the hotel or from its manager, but when the story appeared we read that we had wrecked six hotel bedrooms. God knows, then, what went on in the other rooms; I only saw ours. It was the last game of the season and everyone was letting their hair down, but in those days the media stayed in the same hotel as the players and they were probably getting their own back because we hadn't invited them to join in the celebrations.

The Scotland team was like a family. We were a highly bonded unit, and we battled for one another. From what I heard, that wasn't always the case with England. It was said it was because their players came from all over the country, and with the different regional accents and what have you it tended to get very cliquey. But we were widely spread too, with players from both England and Scotland, and we didn't experience anything like that. I believe our closeness was more to do with coming from a small nation, and the consequent need to be in it together, as a team, if we were to taste success. We played hard together, and then we played hard together off the pitch.

End-of-season tours were often a bit like a holiday. After a tough season we needed to relax. Obviously we gave our all in international matches, friendly or not, but at other times during those summer tours we were unwinding after a long season. It wasn't as if these games were World Cup qualifiers or anything like that. We only played a handful of international matches during the course of a full season, and three of those would be home internationals. It was not until later that Scotland started to play something like fifteen games a year. Nowadays, before you know where you are you've got yourself fifty caps, but in the 1950s and 1960s you'd have to be picked for your country for ten years to reach that sort of number. A good example of that is John Charles, who in a long and well-respected career played only thirty-eight times for Wales. Unbelievable. Even when the World Cup qualifiers came round there were only four teams in a group, and it was tough, with only one team progressing. Often teams would fail to reach the finals simply through bad luck, poor refereeing or badly timed injuries.

The home internationals were once used as a qualifying group, for the 1968 European Championship in Italy. The ties were played over two seasons between 1966 and 1968, and for the first time the British teams were thrown together in a home and away group. England, of course, went into the competition as world champions, having just won the World Cup at Wembley in July 1966. Our own little World Cup final against England at Wembley was scheduled for 15 April 1967 – and more of that in the next chapter – but before that we had to go through a nightmare in Cardiff.

On the morning before the game, at exactly 9.15 a.m. on 21 October 1966, tragedy struck. It wasn't a player breaking his leg, someone being dropped or even a player breaking curfew; no, this was a real, gut-wrenching disaster. A waste tip slid down a mountainside straight onto a small Welsh village called Aberfan. Who can ever forget seeing those harrowing scenes on television or listening to the news unfold on the radio as the slurry engulfed a farm and then Pantglas Junior School minutes after the children had sung 'All Things Bright and Beautiful' at their morning assembly? The mudslide, soaked by heavy rain, was unstoppable, and after the school it ate up another twenty houses. One hundred and forty-four people died in Aberfan that day, and 116 of them where schoolchildren. People from all over Wales rushed to the scene with shovels they'd thrown into the backs of their cars, while journalists in Wales for our game were despatched to Aberfan to report the unfolding horror. We were long gone by the time they recovered the last body almost a week later. Can you imagine, under those circumstances, having to play a game of football in Wales the next day? I suspect that had it not been a European match it would have been abandoned immediately. Unsurprisingly, the match was played in a sombre atmosphere. All the while the death toll rose; it was just horrendous. To be honest, the game meant nothing, other than the fact that we managed a score-draw against a side England had thrashed 5–1. In the end, we just missed out on qualification for Italy.

That was very much Scotland's story in the 1960s in terms of qualifying success. We were certainly very unfortunate in 1961 during our attempt to book a place in the 1962 World Cup finals in Chile. I was dropped that May for the games against the Republic of Ireland and Czechoslovakia. I was stuck in Italy with Torino at the time, away from the eyes of the selectors, and I began to feel I'd had it as far as Scotland were concerned. But I was recalled for the return game against Czechoslovakia at Hampden Park on 26 September into a forward line that boasted Alex Scott, John White, Ian St John and Davie Wilson – good enough to give any defence in the world a hard time, I thought – and I celebrated by having one of my best ever matches for Scotland. We were twice behind in the match, but I scored twice – the winner coming seven minutes from the end when I lost two markers and beat goalkeeper Schroif at the far post – and I reckon I covered every blade of grass on the pitch – twice. It was a satisfying win for two reasons. Firstly, we'd been thumped 4–0 by the same side in Bratislava a few months earlier. Secondly, Czechoslovakia were a big, powerful, athletic team with some outstanding players. Josef Masopust (voted European Player of the Year) certainly stood out, but they also had the likes of Popluhar, Bomba, Novak and Kvasnak, all of them very talented players. I played with two or three of them for a Rest of the World side a couple of years later, so I speak from good experience. At that time they were, to my mind, not far away from being a great team in the mould of the Hungarians of the 1950s. That Czechoslovakian team jetted off to Chile the following summer and reached the World Cup final, so to beat them 3–2 at Hampden Park was huge by any standards. The only person who wasn't dancing with joy was manager Ian McCall. After the game he went on at us about the chances we'd missed and the goals we'd given away!

After that superb victory our hopes were high of going to Chile, but then, at the end of November, we had to play the Czechs again in a play-off in Brussels, a game that turned out to be a great disappointment. I was having big problems in Italy when Torino didn't agree to release me until the last minute; as it was, they sent three officials along to keep an eye on me. One was my friend, the agent Gigi Peronace who had seen through my transfer from Manchester City, and the other two were very large gentlemen who could easily have deterred any football hooligan from interfering. We used to have trouble getting time off from our clubs to play international matches in those days because there was no FIFA law yet forcing clubs to release players, even for European and World Cup matches. There was always trouble in Turin whenever I wanted to play for Scotland. It made me so mad; we weren't even guaranteed to be released for the World Cup finals themselves! John Charles, for instance, was only given permission by Juventus to attend the 1958 finals in Sweden at the eleventh hour. Torino were so worried about their investment that they made the Scots take out a £200,000 insurance policy every time I played for Scotland.

Anyway, any hopes we had of competing in the 1962 finals disappeared in Brussels on an absolute mud heap of a pitch. Our main problem that evening was one that no longer applies. Nowadays, on the Saturday prior to international qualifying games, domestic fixtures are cancelled, but in those days you played on, and just before that vital tie with the Czechs we lost four of our players through injury: Bill Brown, the goalkeeper, Alex Scott, Davie Wilson and Billy McNeill, who was crucial in the middle of our defence. In effect, the heart of our team was ripped out. All the same, we put up a mighty performance against this very good side and only succumbed in extra time. We were actually leading 2–1 with around ten minutes remaining; all we had to do was hold on and we would have been through. But they grabbed an equalizer to take the game into extra time, and that's when they took command and scored another two goals. That was a hugely disappointing game for us, but I can't help but wonder how we might have done had we been given the Saturday before the game off. We would certainly have been a lot fresher to face that period of extra time. Mine was a very depressing and lonely journey back to Turin after that. A few of the guys in the Torino side played for Italy. They knew they were going to Chile, so they too were disappointed for me because they'd thought we would all be going together.

Scotland was a good side in 1962, certainly the best team in the home international tournament that year with three wins out of three. Just look at the sort of players we could call on: Bill Brown, Pat Crerand, Billy McNeill, Jim Baxter, John White, Ian St John. But it was so difficult to qualify for the World Cup in those days. The game was still in its infancy worldwide, and in a way it was a non-event outside Europe and South America; certainly no-one was going to win the World Cup from outside those two major zones. In Europe, the top teams were all knocking one another out. Nowadays you're not as likely to get two top sides in the same group, and if you don't qualify in top place you can have a little play-off. In contrast to the European nations, the South Americans had it easy in terms of qualifying, with Uruguay, Argentina and Brazil dominating. I always said it was probably more difficult to qualify than to actually win the cup once you were in the finals, because in the preliminaries you had to play teams on their home ground, top teams like West Germany, Italy, Czechoslovakia and Poland. Everyone knew they faced a major battle to qualify for World Cups and European Championships.

My other most disappointing World Cup failure came in the

run-up to the very next tournament. Had we qualified for the 1966 finals, it would have been like playing at home, and who knows what might have happened? We were in a tough group, with Italy, Poland and Finland, and only one to go through. We beat Finland at Hampden in October 1964, then in May 1965 we drew with the Poles in Chorzow and beat the Finns again in Helsinki. We also beat Italy in Glasgow. The crucial match for us turned out to be the Poles in Glasgow in October 1965. We went close, leading the Poles 1–0 courtesy of Billy McNeill with just five minutes to go, but then they equalized. And then they scored a winning goal. If you look at all the games that team played in – alongside me, the likes of Bill Brown, Jimmy Johnstone, Willie Henderson, Billy McNeill, Dave Mackay, Paddy Crerand, Ian St John, Bill Steel and Danny McGrain – that would easily be in our top three when it came to gut-wrenching results. Looking back now, when we went one up against the Poles the older pro-fessionals should have said, 'Right, let's keep it quiet and close it down.' I hate the expression, but in such a crucial game we shouldn't have been looking for more glory and goals. With the players we had we would have been more than capable of closing it down. We were not the professionals we should have been. Fortunately, we did become more professional as the years passed and the home internationals were dropped, and we took our place in the World Cup finals as England failed a couple of times. Swings and roundabouts.

That match against Poland was such a blow. Up until then we'd been flying; we'd taken five points out of six. The 2–1 win against the Finns in Helsinki in May had set us up for what we all believed would be a celebration night at Hampden Park – until those last five minutes or so. Amazingly, history was to repeat itself eight years later at Wembley when England, also needing to beat Poland to qualify for the 1974 World Cup, drew 1–1 after holding the lead and assaulting the Polish goal. The knives were out for me and the other Anglos after we had been knocked out, and once again I was dropped. The Scottish media needed someone to take the blame, and obviously felt it had to be some of the Anglos.

We still weren't officially knocked out, though: we could still beat the Italians in Naples on 7 December and go through. I was back for that one, but on the Saturday before the game I was kicked during a game at West Ham. I was clearly going to have to withdraw, and fortunately Scotland's manager Jock Stein was at the game and I was able to show both him and the suspicious national press how my ankle had ballooned up. I didn't want to be accused of ducking out of a tough encounter, and as it turned out I would rather have played than be forced to sit and watch my country crash out 3–0.

Playing for Scotland is, without doubt, the greatest honour anybody could ever have bestowed on me. It really doesn't matter if it's rugby, football, athletics or whatever; it's a massive honour to represent your country, though particularly in football as it's the national game. It was always a thrill to be informed that you were playing, no matter whether it was against Jutland, Norway or Brazil. As the old saying goes, you'd play for your country for nothing; the money side of things doesn't even come into the equation. That certainly holds true for me at any rate, and that's why I get so disappointed at times when players are unavailable to play for their country and all of a sudden fit and raring to go in the very next game for their club. I have never been able to understand why anybody with talent does not want to play for his country. There have been those who have actually come out and said they don't want to play for their country. The mind absolutely boggles. Some very good players have done it, but I just can't understand it at all.

That's why the biggest disappointments of my footballing career are based around international rather than club football, and I collected another clutch of them during the qualification tournament for the 1970 World Cup in Mexico, even though my involvement was limited to just two matches because of injuries. I played and scored in our first game at Hampden on 6 November 1968 against Austria, which we won 2–1, and I also played in the home draw six months later with West Germany, who went on to win the group by four points and reach the semi-finals before losing to Italy 4–3 in extra time. It was a thin time for me in international football: I'd had just the two games in 1966, against England and Wales; three in 1967, against England, Russia and Northern Ireland; just Austria in 1968; only two in 1969, against West Germany and Northern Ireland; and then nothing until April 1972, when I scored in the 2–0 win over Peru at Hampden Park. As a result, it's our failure to qualify for the World Cups in 1962 and 1966, when we really could have put out a very good side, that rankles. We underachieved, there is no doubt at all about that, me included. I'm not saying we could have gone on to win the World Cup in those years, but we felt we were as good as any team. We were afraid of nobody, and I'm sure we could have made a big impression in Chile and England. We had some fine players, most of whom I've already mentioned, and there were other very good players who couldn't get into the team. Don Gibson, who was a good little player for Leicester City, was in the frame, and then there was John White, of course, the brilliant Spurs midfield player whose talents were so tragically denied to Scotland when he was killed by lightning in 1964 while playing golf.

One of the problems, as Matt Busby had found out back in

1958, was the Anglo-Scot rift, the players who were plying their trade south of the border to the irritation of some journalists and fans. I often felt I had to play twice as well as the home-based Scots to remain in the national side. It was a real honour to be selected for my country because the competition was so fierce, but you felt that not everyone was pulling in the same direction. There was nothing between the players; whether they played for Celtic, Rangers, Aberdeen, Manchester United or Arsenal, it didn't make any difference as far as we were concerned. We were just glad to be there and be part of the team. The media was the biggest problem, because apart from the Anglo-Scot stuff there was also a bit of Edinburgh/Glasgow rivalry in there as well. I felt it, and so did other players, but we were careful to keep it to ourselves rather than ignite a proper war.

Things have changed since then, mainly because the Scotland manager is now dedicated to international duties. In those days, of course, it wasn't a full-time position. Matt Busby was the first, Andy Beattie, Ian McCall and Jock Stein did stints in the 1960s, along with the Rangers goalkeeper Bobby Brown, and there were a few others after that, including Tommy Docherty and Willie Ormond. Who did I rate most highly? Sir Matt, of course. Andy Beattie, too, was a good manager and someone I knew well, as I did Bobby Brown – a very nice guy. Willie Ormond was excellent during the 1974 World Cup. He had been one of the famous five of Hibs, and he was a delightful guy. Crucially, he seemed to know what the players wanted, and was very flexible when it came to matters such as scheduling training sessions. Being the manager of an international squad is extremely difficult. You have twenty-two guys from different clubs with differing person-alities vying for eleven places; some need one thing, some need something else, which makes things difficult, particularly when the team is away from home. Everyone wants to follow the routine they are used to with their club, and get away with what they usually get away with when they are with their club. That is the hardest thing for a player, and it's an even more difficult balancing act for the international manager. To be able to make them all feel at home, to leave them feeling content, is a real art form. There can also be problems when it comes to pairing players up in bedrooms. Some guys like to read, some don't; some like the light on, some don't; some snore, some don't. Many times I asked the manager if I could have a room on my own, and more often than not he would let me. It was the same when I was with Manchester United. I needed a proper night's uninterrupted sleep in order to play at my best. I think players and managers are a bit more aware now of issues such as these than they were thirty, forty years ago.

The international scene is undoubtedly more professional and luxurious these days, but the players pay for this with an intrusive media spotlight. With us, it was just football; rarely did it become personal. We used to go out with some of the journalists for a drink and a night out, but now there is little or no such fraternizing. Ironically, we had much more of a private life by mixing with 'the enemy', because we got to know whom to trust and whom not to go out with. That applied not only to Scotland but to club sides as well. After a game abroad, we would all go out and have a few beers. It was part and parcel of your life. One group would go out for dinner, another would go out for a drink, another might fancy a nightclub.

That must be the most difficult thing for a manager of any side: to know when to allow leeway and when to crack the whip. It is essential that he has a good staff he can trust, because he can't be everywhere all the time. There's usually a bad-apple player who will overstep the mark, maybe have a drink before the game, things like that. Dealing with situations like that is down to the manager; it's not up to the players to sort it out. Some think that one of the players should go up and say, 'Hey, watch what you're doing,' but you can't really do that. It's never easy for one player to lay down the law to another; it must be left to the manager and his staff to nip problems in the bud by saying something like, 'Listen, this is your last chance,' or 'If you behave like that you need not come with the team.' Having said that, sometimes a blind eye needs to be turned, particularly at the end of the season – as was the case on that summer tour to eastern Europe and Turkey in 1960.

It was small consolation for me that, for the first time since 1958, we qualified for the World Cup in 1974 in West Germany. Our qualifying group for 1974 featured the developing Danes and the always strong Czechs. We beat the Danes home and away in the autumn of 1972, which was to prove crucial because the Czechs surprisingly drew in Denmark, leaving the door open for us. We beat them 2–1 in Glasgow in September 1973, and although we lost in Bratislava the following month, it didn't matter. We were through.

I equalled George Young's record of fifty-three caps in the friendly against West Germany in Frankfurt on 27 March 1974, and number fifty-four came against Northern Ireland at Hampden on 11 May. We lost that match 1–0, and I had a poor game. I was left out of the next home internationals against Wales and England, and then the squad for West Germany was due to be picked the following Monday. I and many others thought my last chance of a World Cup finals had gone. I hadn't been selected to play that often for Scotland in the early 1970s; it was only when Willie Ormond took over as Scotland manager in 1973 that I began to be picked more regularly. Mind you, I had been playing fairly well for Manchester City, to whom I'd returned by this time, and I'd scored a few goals. Despite that, I was still surprised when I heard that I'd been named in the squad. 'Whoops!' I thought. 'That'll do for me!' It certainly came as a bit of a shock at the age of thirty-four, but Willie had ignored the press and gone with the fact that I was doing reasonably well up front and had the experience. I was the older man of the team, of course; all the others were youngsters like Kenny Dalglish, Joe Jordan and Jim Holton, and it was nice to think that I could give them the benefit of my experience. I think Willie picked me as a gesture, really, on the strength of what had been achieved against the Czechs several months before, which was very nice of him because he could easily have left me out. To my mind, it was one of those selections where the player might be able to contribute something valuable in part of the game, maybe not the whole game but somewhere along the line.

In many ways we were unfortunate to be playing unknown Zaïre in our first game on 14 June, and we were quite satisfied with a 2–0 win in Dortmund with goals from Peter Lorimer and Joe Jordan. I played the full ninety minutes, but was left on the bench for the second game against Brazil in Frankfurt where we matched Yugoslavia with a goalless draw against the reigning World Cup holders – no mean feat. I was also left out of the final group game against Yugoslavia on 22 June, and again we drew, this time 1–1, Joe Jordan notching up his second goal of the tournament. That meant that, although all three of us finished on four points, Yugoslavia topped the group by virtue of their 9–0 thrashing of Zaïre and Brazil took the second qualifying place because they beat the Africans 3–0. We had been eliminated by a single goal despite not having lost a single game.

Soon the lads came to appreciate their achievement: we were the only team to leave that World Cup unbeaten. We were knocked out because we had played Zaïre first. Nobody knew about the qualities or weaknesses of Zaïre then, so once we went two up we were satisfied to safeguard the win rather than press on for goals. By the time Brazil played them, of course, they knew they only had to beat them by a margin of more than two goals to be certain to qualify. It was a pleasant enough experience as far as I was concerned, and it's nice now that I can say I was there, but unfortunately for me by the time I got to represent my country on the world's biggest stage I was past my best. That game against Zaïre in June 1974 turned out to be my last appearance not just for Scotland but also in professional football.

I was extremely disappointed, though, not to get a fifty-sixth cap against Brazil. I didn't think my exclusion was merited as I felt I'd played well enough against the Africans to keep my place, or at least to play a part in the Brazil game. But I accepted it, even though I would have loved to play against the world champions, and I have some good memories from that time. Yugoslavia, as always, were a talented side. They always played good football and were tough physically, as all those eastern Europeans seemed to be then. Their only fault was that they were never the greatest away from home. They were hard, but then they lived hard lives, didn't they? Whenever you played them you knew you were in for a battle because these guys had so much to play for. When you came back from some of those Eastern Bloc countries you'd be thinking you were glad you didn't live there. They got the best out of life as footballers, but even that was pretty awful. Now, of course, those countries have broken away from the Soviet yoke and are not so depressing to visit. Czechoslovakia, Hungary and Poland are beautiful countries.

I felt my place in the squad was justified because, apart from a couple of injuries, I had played well during the 1973/74 season. It was a good idea to have a sprinkling of older players in the squad, especially with so many youngsters. I'm not saying that they looked up to me, but I was the oldest on the team and I hope they felt some respect and had no problems with it. I certainly didn't complain when I was left out of the side, and as far as I was concerned we had a lovely World Cup within the team – at last.

7 THE AULD ENEMY

A VERY SPECIAL ATMOSPHERE ALWAYS SURROUNDED MATCHES between England and Scotland, and out of my fifty-five appearances for Scotland nine of them were against the Auld Enemy. Four of them we won, two were drawn, and I scored in just three of them. It's a great shame we don't play each other regularly any more. There was talk about the fixtures coming back, but nothing developed. I always thought it a far better tie than, say, playing Chile or teams like that in friendlies, which Scotland started to do in the 1970s, games which were of no consequence whatsoever. The home international was a platform for younger players to come through, and it was very important particularly for Wales and Northern Ireland, huge games that brought in much-needed income.

Those games against England were the be all and end all for many Scots. Some would save up for two years in order to attend the Wembley game. It was a massive emotional occasion to play England at either Wembley or Hampden Park. When I was a kid, the fixture was the highlight of the season. We were brought up on tales of the Wee Blue Devils; those stories were embedded in your brain. The thirty-first of March 1928, when Scotland beat England 5–1 at Wembley, is a day etched in the mind of every true Scot. There were 145,000 at Hampden Park for my first game against England on 9 April 1960, a 1–1 draw, and in 1962 135,000 turned up, before it was eventually restricted to 100,000 because of crowd safety. The Hampden Roar was famous worldwide; it raised the hairs on the back of not just our necks, but our opponents' as well. You stood in the line-up before the game, glancing left and right at your heroes, you heard the swirl of the bagpipes and the national anthem, and you thought, 'Aye, this is what it's all about!' Suddenly, you were standing a foot taller. The singing of that national anthem before the game was something you couldn't buy. All you could hear, standing there in front of this enormous crowd, was 'Scotland, Scotland, Scotland!' echoing around the stadium. It was appreciated, I can tell you; it made the players puff out their chests and think, 'Yes, we cannot be beaten here!' You can imagine walking out into such an atmosphere, when virtually everyone in the ground was a Scot; hardly a single English voice could be heard outside the press box. There never seemed to be too many English voices for the games at Wembley either!

If there was one thing any young Scot dreamed about, it was to watch Scotland beat England at Wembley; when you became a player, you dreamed of playing in one of those games and scoring the winning goal. It might not have meant as much to the English, but to us it was everything. For me, as a player, it lived up to everything I had dreamed of.

But, can we forget the 9–3 game, please! What a strange game that was – it really was. My blackest day, 15 April 1961, should never have happened. England started well enough. Bobby Robson opened the scoring, and they were leading 3–0 at one stage, but we never felt out of it and we came back to make it 3–1 through Dave Mackay, and then Davie Wilson scored. At 3–2, England were rocking and we were back in the driving seat; we were still trailing, but we had our tails up. Honestly, England looked down and out. Then we conceded a stupid fourth from a free-kick, and suddenly they were back in command. We were, to say the least, dodgy at the back with Celtic goalkeeper Frank Haffey having a nightmare game (to this day, if a goalkeeper has a bad game it is known as 'having a Haffey'), and don't forget, this England side was on a roll having scored twenty-three goals in four matches (the run ended at an astonishing forty goals in six games). Sure enough, once that fourth goal went in they ran away with it.

Can you imagine being in a Scotland team that's beaten 9–3 by the English? It might be just about acceptable in a schoolboy match, maybe even in a club match, but certainly not in an international match, and most definitely not at Wembley. For the rest of our careers that result made the Scottish players all the more determined on the pitch, because we continually had to try to live it down. In fact, I think we're still trying.

That day, Jimmy Greaves was, as ever, lethal. You might not know he was there for eighty-eight minutes, and he still might finish up on the scoresheet with a couple of goals to his name. Greaves was a different player compared to me and other forwards. He was the best pure striker, the best goalscorer, I have ever seen. When he had the ball in front of goal there was always absolute panic among the opposing defence. They knew it was probably either going to end up in the net or miss by inches; there weren't that many chances he fluffed. I was a different type of player. I was an old-fashioned inside-forward, doing work all over the pitch, which included scoring goals. Greaves, though, was an out-and-out poacher. He just waited up front, prowling around the penalty area. I have always tried to judge a player's qualities by asking myself if I would like him in the opposition when I'm playing. I didn't want Greaves playing for the opposing team at any time. That's how good he was.

There were also plenty of gifted Scottish players I would never have relished facing. Dave Mackay, for one. I wouldn't have wanted to play against him once a season, never mind once a week, and the same goes for Billy Bremner. Kenny Dalglish was another player whose name you never wanted to see on the opposition teamsheet because he could hurt you. Graeme Souness, for different reasons, was another I wouldn't like to have played against. That was how I judged players: if they could hurt me in any way, physically or by scoring goals, I wouldn't want them around to oppose me.

Gordon Banks was another England player who fell into that category for me. Whenever I saw him between the sticks I knew it was going to be bloody difficult to get the ball into the back of the net from any range. I rate him as the best goalkeeper I have ever seen, even though the Russian Lev Yashin was reputed to be the best around. I once played with the man they called the Black Flash for a Rest of the World side, but I didn't see him play much and he wasn't on television often enough for me to be able to assess him properly. (It was the advent of the European Cup in the late 1950s and early 1960s that changed that situation; suddenly we were all able to see the great players in action, particularly the outstanding Real Madrid side. I, for one, drooled over players like Ferenc Puskas, Alfredo Di Stefano and Francisco Gento. Instead of just reading about them, at last we could see them on screen in full flow.) There were a few very good goalkeepers around in those days, and one of my favourites was the big Irishman Pat Jennings – a quiet man with hands like dinner plates who performed miracles for both Spurs and Arsenal – but if I had to pick the best, as I said, I would definitely go for Gordon Banks.

I managed to score a couple of goals against him, as it happens, and when I did I always felt it a better goal than when I scored against any other goalkeeper. I got much more satisfaction out of sticking one past Banksie, and I told him so when I scored against him in the 1963 FA Cup final, and, of course, at Wembley against England. It was Banks who made the best save I, and probably most other people, have ever seen when he somehow tipped a goal-bound header from Pele up over the crossbar during the 1970 World Cup in Mexico. That will go down as one of the best ever.

But that stuffing we took in April 1961 was before Banks's day; it was Ron Springett who let in our three goals. Looking at that horrendous scoreline now, it looks as though we were absolutely demolished, but as I said, it just wasn't like that, as daft as that may sound. Still, it was bad enough in 1955, when I was in my last year at school, when England beat Scotland 7–2 at Wembley with Dennis Wilshaw scoring four, Nat Lofthouse two and Don Revie one. I felt that one, too, because the Aberdeen keeper Fred Martin was in goal. Those who played in that one were lucky because it now pales in comparison with our 9–3 result. There will always be an Englishman around to remind us of that one.

It was only my tenth match for Scotland, and I had only been on the losing side twice, both times by the odd goal, so it was a shattering defeat for me personally. I couldn't even return to Scotland with my tail between my legs like some of the others; not only did I have to go back to Maine Road, I also had to play against English players every week. The English media also had their fun, of course, and not only with the scoreline. The television cameras had caught me being a naughty boy right underneath the royal box, with Her Majesty the Queen in attendance. Bobby Robson kicked me, and I kicked him back.

Fortunately we shook hands, apologized to each other and are still good friends. I think it's written into your contract that when you play at Wembley you're not allowed to do things like that in front of the Queen, and one of the English papers made a big play on it, announcing that 'Law had the audacity to kick Bobby Robson right on the centre circle in front of the Queen.' Maybe our minor act of hooliganism put Her Majesty off, because we haven't seen much of her at football matches since. Bobby still maintains it was me who started it! Moi? Bobby, you know it was you who started it!

Bobby Robson wasn't a dirty player at all, but he could put his foot in. He played at right-half and I was at inside-left, so we came into contact when we played against each other; I would be trying to stop him going through and he would be trying to stop me. He was a fine player. In fact, West Bromwich Albion were one of my favourite teams at the time. I liked the broad, bold stripes they wore and the quality of their players, such as Ronnie Allen, the elegant Ray Barlow and the giant England inter-national Derek Kevan up front – not to mention the elegant Robson. They gave good value for money, and they caught the eye because in 1954 they won the FA Cup, beating Preston North End 3–2.

Bobby had the last laugh that day, and clearly we were going to suffer for the defeat. I was immediately dropped after the game, along with poor Frank Haffey, who understandably bore the brunt of much of the criticism, as did Motherwell's central defender Bert McCann, and I don't think either played again for Scotland. But the biggest surprise as far as I was concerned was that Dave Mackay was also left out for the next game. The next sequence of games were the World Cup qualifiers against the Republic of Ireland and Czechoslovakia, and I must admit I was annoyed at being singled out among the forwards, especially as we had scored enough goals to win a normal game. It has to be said that I always felt as an Anglo I had to do something special to keep my place in the national side. Not a lot was said publicly by those who played south of the border, but it's true to say that we all felt we had to do something special to get noticed. If somebody was going to carry the can, I thought it would be an Anglo. Having said that, if you're in a team beaten 9–3 by your biggest rivals, somebody has to go. But it's a bit tough blaming the forwards. Now, looking back, I suppose I must have had a mediocre game, or I'm sure I wouldn't have been dropped – even for kicking Bobby in front of the Queen.

It was an unhappy end to an unhappy week for me as in those days they retained a full League programme on the day of the international. All the clubs played that Saturday afternoon, and Manchester City were going through a bad patch. The club was desperate for me to play, but I insisted I played for my country. They were unhappy about it – we were struggling near the bottom of the table and City needed all their players to be available – and I remember having a right barney with Les McDowall. I had never played against England at Wembley before, and you never know when your last chance is going to come. Football is too unpredictable to take chances. As it turned out, I wish I'd stayed to play for Manchester City on the day!

The profound shock of the 9–3 defeat, coupled with our disappointment at not qualifying for the 1962 World Cup, was eased somewhat in April 1962 when we at last beat England for the first time in Glasgow since 1937. That was an enormous amount of time in football terms, and the nation heaved a great sigh of relief. I made the first for Davie Wilson, and the second was a penalty scored by Eric Caldow. It went some way towards demonstrating that had we qualified for the World Cup we – Bill Brown, Alex Hamilton, Eric Caldow, Pat Crerand, Billy McNeill, Jimmy

Baxter, Alex Scott, John White, Ian St John, Davie Wilson and me – would surely have made our mark. Certainly it was one of the best Scottish sides I played with, and they were all young lads with more to come. The win was even more satisfying because England had fielded a very good team that featured the likes of Ray Wilson, Jimmy Greaves, Johnny Haynes and Bobby Charlton – in fact, almost the same side that had thrashed us a year earlier.

The national side lost much of its impetus in the summer of 1964 when John White was killed by a freak accident, struck by lightning on Crews Hill golf course near his north London home in Enfield. The lightning apparently missed the trolley but struck a ring on his finger as he was sheltering under a tree. And he was just beginning to fulfil his fabulous potential at the tender age of twenty-four. It has been said that had John been around I might not have won as many caps as I did because he was an inside-forward too, but I don't necessarily agree with that. Certainly we were both inside-forwards, but we were so different in the way we played the game that I'm sure we would have continued to complement each other.

His was a great loss. I don't think I've ever seen a more skilful guy with a ball at his feet than John. He was just phenomenal in terms of his control and his distribution. Playing keepy-uppy and all that was never my forte. I could juggle it maybe half a dozen times, but you never do that in a game, so what's the point? But John, well, he really could put the ball anywhere he wanted. If you stuck half a crown in the ground twenty yards away he was capable of chipping the ball and knocking it flat. I couldn't have done that. I could probably have passed the ball and knocked the coin over, but I couldn't chip it the way John could. He could even, quite deliberately, knock a dead ball against the crossbar time after time. His death was a real tragedy, because all his best years were yet to come and there was nothing to stop him becoming a truly great player. He was part of the double-winning Spurs side of 1960/61 – still the best English club side I have ever seen. They weren't far behind Real Madrid at the time, which is a huge compliment, because Madrid were (still are) the best club team in the world. I say 'have ever seen' because I never got to watch the 1955–58 Manchester United team which was reputed to be the best, and quite possibly so. I can, of course, only talk about the teams I saw. The comparisons between those two sides are worth considering. I have often pondered what Spurs and Scotland might have done had John White lived to play a full career, just as I've wondered what Manchester United might have achieved but for the Munich air crash and, in particular, the loss of the fabulous Duncan Edwards. Edwards was an English John Charles, and you can't give any praise higher than that. Here we are, going back over forty years, and we're still talking about these brilliant young players whose careers finished so early. Obviously, the younger generation would have no idea.

The best international team I've ever seen was the 1970 Brazil side. For me, and for many others, they were the very best – legendary players like Pele, Rivelino, Jairzinho, Gerson and Carlos Alberto. They effortlessly combined the skills of South American midfielders and forwards with the solid defence of the Europeans. Because of the kicking they'd taken in England during the 1966 World Cup, they'd toughened up a bit. It's an age-old debate, people asking you if you'd be able to compete in today's game. Well, there's one thing that never changes, whatever era you played in, and that's skill. It is the one facet that remains unaltered, and those Brazilians had it in bucketloads. The shape of the ball is constant, and if you were able to control it forty or fifty years ago you would be able to do the same today. In fact, you would be even better today because the ball is lighter and is much less affected by climatic conditions. Passing, control, heading and shooting remain the essential areas of the game, and one thing you can never take away from any player is his skill. It is said – and I would agree with this – that the game is much faster today, the combatants fitter, but I also contend that the runner who was great half a century ago would be just as great today because he would adapt to the training. Don't tell me Madrid players like Alfredo Di Stefano and Ferenc Puskas could not have lived with the Zidanes, Figos and Ronaldos of today. I played with them for the Rest of the World, and I know how good they were. I was twenty when I watched them destroy Eintracht Frankfurt at Hampden in the European Cup final.

But the best players were not necessarily foreign, not when you look at the likes of George Best, Dave Mackay, John Charles and Bobby Charlton; they stand shoulder to shoulder with the likes of Ernst Ocwirk, Josef Masopust, Franz Beckenbauer and Johann Cruyff. The list goes on, too, because over the years Britain has produced many outstanding players. Of those I played with, I would have to include Best, Charlton and Nobby Stiles among the best, while for Scotland I would pick out Dave Mackay, Billy Bremner, Jim Baxter, Billy McNeill, Pat Crerand, Ian St John, Davie Wilson, John White, Jimmy Johnstone, Alan Gilzean – there weren't many better in the air than Alan, and he had a lovely touch – Danny McGrain and Bill Brown. Prior to breaking his leg, Eric Caldow was a fine player as well. Bremner and Mackay, particularly, should have played many more times for Scotland than they did. I think, though, that John White would have been the best of them all had he lived – maybe not quite a Pele, but close. You would want John in your team along with Bremner, Mackay, Baxter and wee Jimmy Johnstone – five foot nothing with a touch as soft as a butterfly. They would be the first names in, and you'd quite happily build your team around them.

With all that quality in our ranks, it has to be repeated that we underachieved throughout the 1960s, and into the 1970s, even though we of course had our bright moments – like when we became 'world champions' by beating England 3–2 in a European Championship qualifier in 1967 when they'd not been defeated for ages. Indeed, they'd beaten us 4–3 at Hampden the year before, World Cup year, and, I have to admit, they were by far the superior team that day despite the one-goal margin. By April 1967 we knew we had to win at Wembley to keep alive our hopes of going to Italy for the 1968 finals. It was a fixture all Scots will remember, especially the sight of Slim Jim Baxter standing on the ball, doing his tricks and taking the mickey out of the World Cup winners on the very ground where they had beaten the Germans. Everyone had expected us to be slaughtered, but we weren't because we had no fear of England whatsoever. We knew we had a good team, and we knew that if we played the way we knew we could play we would cause an upset. I have played in games when I have not been in the best team but won, but this time we were the best team, and nobody could argue about it.

Englishmen will, however, argue that they were down to ten men. Big Jack Charlton went for a ball with Bobby Lennox less than fifteen minutes into the game and limped off with a damaged foot, though he came back after half an hour and played up front. So what? England were stronger than for the World Cup final, with Jimmy Greaves back in the side for Roger Hunt, and this made us even more determined to beat them. I opened the scoring off a rebound. I scored a lot of goals for United that way because of Davie Herd and Bobby Charlton, both of whom had tremendous shots. I always felt when they had a go there was a fair chance that if the keeper saved, the ball would rebound because of the power. They were, after all, belting it goalwards at around eighty miles per hour. Whenever I saw them lining up for a shot I was into the keeper, probably distracting him at the same time, and if he dropped it I was always there with a chance of knocking it into the net. This time I think it was Willie Wallace shooting, and his strong shot came back off Gordon Banks. He didn't get hold of it and it fell for me. In you go, 1–0.

The atmosphere, yet again, was fantastic; I swear there were more Scots than English in Wembley that day judging by the noise when that goal went in. Bobby Lennox added a second, but England would not lie down and the injured Jack Charlton pulled one back. Jim McCalliog restored our two-goal gap, but still England came at us, and Geoff Hurst's loopy header off a Bobby Charlton cross pulled it back to 3–2. But we held on for a glorious victory. Once again we weren't as professional as we might have been. When we were 3–1 ahead, instead of hammering home our advantage we let them off the hook, Jim Baxter and others playing to the crowd. That almost let England back into the game when we still had something to spare. But it was a good victory, even if Big Jack continues to insist it was because England were down to ten. My answer? 'Jackie, you're a bad loser, man.' Jack, however, had the last laugh, for although the win gave us the 1967 home international title, there was still another round of matches to play for the European Championship place, and England, needing only a point, secured it in Glasgow the next season thanks to a Martin Peters equalizer.

I think – and it has been said before – we paid too much attention to those England games. Treating that April 1967 game as an unofficial World Cup final was unprofessional, really. I know how important it is for Scotland to beat the English, but I often think that if our approach had been a bit more disciplined we could have done a lot better than we did in competition football. Still, the high points of my sixteen-year career for Scotland, apart from my one game in the World Cup, were more often than not those games against England. I mean, I know our attitude in 1967 was probably a bit childish, but England were the reigning world champions and to think that we'd gone and beaten them on their own ground felt very good indeed. I loved playing at Wembley. It was quite rightly a famous stadium, a beautiful pitch to play on. If you couldn't do your stuff on the Wembley turf, you couldn't play on anything. I was sad when the old place was demolished. Outside the England games, I suppose the highlight was the win against Czechoslovakia at Hampden Park in September 1973 that guaranteed our passage to the 1974 World Cup finals, even more so than Zaïre in the finals itself. They had reduced the crowd to 100,000 that night, but I have never heard noise like it in my life. When I played in the Maracana in Rio against Brazil during a summer tour in 1972, there were 156,000 people there and they made some noise, but I tell you what, Hampden that night probably doubled those decibels, because apart from anything they realized what had been achieved. We hadn't qualified for the World Cup since 1958, after all.

I can't help but feel when I recall those England games what a shame it is that the fixture no longer takes place. I know there was trouble later on when the fans invaded the pitch, and that was bad news; one of my brothers claimed to have seven penalty spots from Wembley, and he sold them all! Still, I think generally that Scottish fans were pretty well-behaved, as they prove every year when they travel abroad, and I think London enjoyed having them. They certainly enjoyed going down to London; I don't think half of them saw the game, but it was certainly an occasion. We felt we were playing at Hampden Park at times. There was always a wall of noise and a sea of Scottish flags, tammys, kilts and all the rest. Those fans were sensational. In 1978 I was in Argentina with the BBC, and some of those guys had travelled the world to get there; it's reckoned that some of them still haven't got back! Whenever I've been doing some commentary work around the world at Scotland matches, the fans have really been good, and I'm not saying that simply because I am Scottish. I cannot remember any real trouble. We seem to take with us the best of our supporters, while England seem to attract the worst of theirs. It's a strange thing, and hard to explain. One of the key factors, I think, is that the Scots take defeat with good grace.

They've been really good fans for us, and they deserve something to cheer about, but, sadly, I don't think anything's going to happen for a wee while unless things change dramatically. It's clear to me that the West German World Cup winner Bertie Vogts has got an extremely difficult job on his hands; there just don't seem to be top-quality Scottish players about any more. That really is tragic, and it's not Bertie's fault. The way things have gone, whoever had taken charge of the national side would have had the same desperate problems. That's why I think Craig Brown did a marvellous job with what he had. He really blended that small group of players into a team, and it's amazing the results they achieved when you look at the state of the Scottish game.

In the past, you could guarantee that half the squad would come from Celtic and Rangers, with the odd player from Aberdeen, Hearts and Hibs and the rest from south of the border. But look at the teams now in the top divisions in Scotland and England and they're filled with overseas players. There always used to be talented Scots playing at Manchester United, Liverpool, Leeds, Arsenal and Spurs, but now there are none at all. Where are the players going to come from? What chances do young Scottish players get nowadays? They must be there somewhere along the line, but the clubs are no longer waiting for anybody to come through and don't seem to be developing local youngsters because they just go and buy established players from around the world instead. It's a great pity, because I maintain that it is easier to qualify today for the major competitions than it was in the 1960s and 1970s. The bigger the tournament, the more teams there are in it, with an ever-increasing number of minnows to embarrass the unwary. But whoever you are, you're going to struggle if you can't put a decent team together.

As for Scotland having a foreign manager for the first time, well, look at England. You would never have dreamed the Football Association would have gone abroad for a national manager, but they went headlong for Sven Goran Eriksson. I feel it is a bit of a slight on your country if you can't find a native to manage your team, especially if you're a world power like England. Can you imagine Brazil, Argentina or Germany appointing a foreigner? I must say I feel the same way with Scotland, but that's just the way the game has gone and you've got to roll with the changes. Who would have thought French managers would be at Arsenal and Liverpool? Maybe it's not so bad in cosmopolitan London, but somehow it seems surprising in a place like Liverpool with their history; somehow, a French manager on Merseyside doesn't seem right. But they and Arsenal have done well, and I suppose you must judge solely on achievements.

I think the main problem with a foreigner being the national manager is that, while he might know the international scene and the likely opponents, he can't know the domestic football scene in any depth. It took Bertie Vogts a long time to find out what he had available around the country at clubs like Dundee, Aberdeen and Hibs, even in the lower divisions in England – and by 'find out' I mean getting to know their character as well as their play-ing ability. Of course he knew about the senior established players, just as a Scottish manager in Germany would know the stars of Bayern Munich or Borussia Dortmund, but loads of smaller clubs can contribute to the national team as well. A smaller club might have one player who is really top class, or is a bright prospect, and it would be very difficult to know about it without local help. If you're Scottish to start with, it seems to me you'd have a head start, and I think that's crucial.

It is important now that the SFA starts a search for the next Scottish manager. Among the leading contenders as I write is David Moyes, who having done well at Preston is now doing an outstanding job at Goodison Park. Everyone speaks highly of him. Then there is Alex McLeish, who after a fine career with Aberdeen, Hibs and Scotland has resurrected Rangers. I have spoken to him and he strikes me as an extremely intelligent guy who has done remarkably well. I would say that those two at the moment seem to be the ones, although I don't suppose anyone would object if Irishman Martin O'Neill were to be persuaded away from his job at Celtic.

I suppose in many ways it is a good thing to see overseas players in different teams not just in England and Scotland but also in other countries around the world, a world that has shrunk considerably since I stopped playing. Who would have thought that Brazilians, Frenchmen and Italians would be playing in English football? But a word of warning: if the trend carries on, England could have a similar problem to Scotland in the years to come. If one goes back just twenty-five years there were only a handful of non-English players in England, mainly Scots, Irish and Welsh. In those days an England manager was able to pick perhaps fifty contenders for his squad before whittling it down to twenty-two. I don't think Eriksson could now pick fifty English players of international quality because they just aren't out there. I honestly don't think there are even thirty of them. As the years pass, that number will dwindle. As a national manager, you want to pick your players from your top clubs, but when you look at Premier

League sides today there aren't that many Englishmen, although Sir Bobby Robson seems to be trying to stem the tide at Newcastle. Newcastle and Manchester United seem to be an exception, but Liverpool, Chelsea and Arsenal are packed with overseas stars, although under their new Russian chairman Chelsea seem to be altering their format somewhat. I recently read an article in *The Times* that put the number of foreign players in the English game at something like 374, and that was players outside the United Kingdom. That's over thirty teams' worth. Add to that the fact that the British don't tend to export players. Brazil probably has hundreds playing around the world, but England and Scotland have no more than a handful.

If you're a manager of a club side, your national team is probably not at the forefront of your mind, because that's not what you're paid to worry about, especially if you're French or Scottish and in charge of an English Premier League club. Therefore, if there aren't any Englishmen in your team you're not particularly bothered, as Bolton's Sam Allardyce showed when he kept Bolton Wanderers up in 2003. If you feel that the Frenchman is better than any of the Englishmen you have, or there is a Brazilian waiting to be snapped up and you can afford him, then the Englishmen will be ignored. This has to have a detrimental effect on the national team in the long run. A similar scenario confronted the Italian game in the 1960s, when Big John Charles went over there to be followed by strikers from all over South America and Europe. All of a sudden the Italians could not find any strikers because the top teams had foreigners in those positions. Italy played defensive football as well as any team in the world, but they couldn't score goals and therefore they weren't winning games. So, sensibly, they put a bit of a block on it for a short period and started to bring through some young players.

The warning is there for us all.

8 UNITED AT LAST!

THE FIRST TIME I EVER ATTENDED A GAME AT OLD TRAFFORD, after the Munich air crash in 1958, it was more of a pilgrimage than just going to watch a football match. I made the journey from my digs in Huddersfield and paid eight times the value of the ticket – the first and only time in my life I paid black-market prices. The face value was half a crown (two shillings and six-pence in old money), but I handed over one pound, a huge slice of my meagre wages. Everywhere I have been since, football fans have claimed they were at that particular game. Had all of them been telling the truth, there would have been a world record 400,000 attendance. But I was genuinely there. It was my first ever visit to Old Trafford, and what an emotional occasion it was! The programme listed the teams, as usual, but almost every name for Manchester United was A.N. Other. It was a First Division game against West Bromwich Albion, and Shay Brennan scored two goals on a day when the Midlands side was rolled over in a display of incredible emotion.

Between then and signing for United in the summer of 1962, I had been back of course: once with the Italian League side and once with Manchester City. But this was different. I was now a Manchester United player, and a very expensive one, too! That didn't go to my head though, as I went straight back to my old digs, now with Mrs Atkins, where I was made most welcome, though I had to be driven to Old Trafford on my first day because I didn't know how to get there! I'd never been to the ground, other than in a coach. My digs were on the other side of Manchester, in Withington, where I stayed until I got married. Still, I was back home, and I didn't have long to wait for my first game as we kicked off the new 1962/63 season in August. It was still a strange feeling turning right to Old Trafford instead of left to Maine Road in my borrowed car, but it felt good to be back in English football, and to add to my sense of anticipation Mrs Atkins promised me my favourite chicken curry for dinner after the game.

Quite often you feel like a complete stranger that first day you walk into a new club, but Old Trafford was not like that at all for me. I knew Matt Busby from his days coaching the Scotland team; there was Maurice Setters, with whom I'd exchanged a little banter after swapping bruises during a practice match earlier that week; and Bobby Charlton I also knew. He was there, although he wasn't playing because of an injury. There was also a familiar Aberdonian accent from the teenaged Ian Moir, who was standing in for Bobby.

Despite this, and all the important games I had already played in England, Italy and for Scotland, it was still a nerve-racking time, my first game at Old Trafford. My first game with a new team.

Thankfully I got off to a good start against West Brom on 18 August, and the team did even better as Davie Herd put us one up within a few minutes of the start and I added a second when I glanced Johnny Giles's perfect cross past the goalkeeper after just seven minutes. Two up at half-time and we felt like world-beaters, but the first game I played typified our season: brilliant in patches and ordinary in others. The classic example of this was when, in late October, we were thrashed 6–2 at White Hart Lane, then ten days later we played Alf Ramsey's reigning champions Ipswich Town at Portman Road and I scored four as we beat them 5–3 to send them into the relegation zone. That was a day it all went right for me, with superb service from Albert Quixall, Bobby Charlton and Davie Herd, who scored the other goal. Four days after that, I scored another four for Scotland against Northern Ireland. But we were totally inconsistent in the second half in that match against West Brom and allowed them to pull back to 2–2. It wasn't a good start, but we'd shown our capabilities in pre-season friendlies, drawing 2–2 with reigning European champions Benfica at Old Trafford and beating Real Madrid 2–0 in the Bernabeu, the first British team to do so.

We were a good one-off side, at least, which was encouraging given United's struggles in the aftermath of Munich. They hadn't been doing particularly well, but this was a new dawn with Sir Matt building a new team, which obviously takes a bit of time. Alongside me, he'd brought in Noel Cantwell from West Ham, Maurice Setters from West Bromwich Albion and David Herd, of course, from Arsenal. Bobby Charlton was still there, a corner-stone on which the side was to be built. It was all done in the space of a very short time really, and we were aware of our terrific potential in that 1962/63 season because we had some outstanding players. These were the new 'Busby Babes', players like Johnny Giles, Nobby Stiles, Phil Chisnal, Jim Nicholson and Nobby Lawton. Little did we know how good it was going to get over the next five years or so. Still, in our first year together we were nearly relegated. It's strange when you look back at the ironies.

People are quick to remember the goal I scored with the last kick of my League career for Manchester City which helped put Manchester United down, but how many remember me sending my old club City down in my first year? It was mid-May 1963 at Maine Road, and City needed to win to stay up. We were trailing 1–0 when a ball was put through to me. I was going nowhere, in fact I was headed towards the corner flag, but I was still within the penalty area when goalkeeper Harry Dowd charged at me and pulled me down. It was baffling because I was no threat at all; I can only assume he panicked, given the circumstances. Albert Quixall wasn't going to refuse such a gift, and he popped in the spot-kick for a 1–1 draw that sent City tumbling into the Second Division. It was a good game considering it was between two teams struggling at the wrong end of the table, and perhaps that showed the quality and depth of the teams in the First Division that season.

We'd been doing all right until the freeze set in in January, and by the time we came back we were embroiled in the FA Cup and trying to play out the backlog of fixtures. We just seemed to keep on losing in the League, and with just four games remaining we were still in trouble. Orient were already down and it was between ourselves, City and Birmingham for the other relegation spot. We lost at Birmingham on 10 May, drew with City on 15 May, then came back from one down on 18 May to beat relegated Orient 3–1 while City lost 6–1 to West Ham on the same day. That rather vindicated my decision a couple of years earlier to quit Manchester City because they were going nowhere.

It was mainly because of the FA Cup that we managed to save our season, reprising the emotional time in 1958 when United reached Wembley with a side cobbled together by Jimmy Murphy only to be beaten 2–0 by Bolton Wanderers when Nat Lofthouse shoulder-charged Harry Gregg and dislocated his shoulder. This was just five years later, and it was everybody's dream to win it for Matt Busby, as well as, of course, to play in the final of the most famous knockout tournament in world football. Leicester City, our opponents, were a very good side at the time with the likes of Gordon Banks, Frank McLintock, Colin Appleton and Ken Keyworth, seven of them survivors from the 1961 Cup final when Spurs won their memorable double, and they'd been chasing the double themselves only to slip up and finish fourth in the League – but that was fifteen places higher than us, so they were strong favourites to win on 25 May 1963.

For some reason, we'd always come good in our cup ties that year, beating my old team Huddersfield 5–0 (I scored a hat-trick), Aston Villa 1–0, Chelsea 2–1 and Coventry City 3–1. They say you have to have luck to win the FA Cup, and we had our share when we avoided Leicester and Liverpool in the semi-final and drew underdogs Southampton, who we beat by a single goal, one of my luckiest. The ball just came across, bobbled up, I took a swing, missed, and finished up on the floor where I found myself with a second chance; the ball hit me on my calf and bounced beyond unlucky goalkeeper Ron Reynolds. (They all count, especially in a semi-final!) All these matches were played within six or seven weeks because 1963 was the year of the big freeze that paralysed everyday life throughout Britain for a few months, and fixtures were thrown into chaos. During the enforced seven-week lay-off we mostly had to train indoors. We had very little room for manoeuvre at Old Trafford, and our training ground, The Cliff, was still in the planning stages. Basically, whenever we were outside we trained by the Ship Canal, which was just down the road, occasionally even in the corridors at Old Trafford, or up and down the terracing. We went to Ireland once to play because that was the only place free of ice. It was a bad time to try to stay match fit. Everything was cancelled, not only football but racing and every other sporting event. The FA Cup third round was played in March, and as a result the final was three weeks late.

It was a big year, 1963. President John F. Kennedy was assassinated in Dallas, Texas; sex and politics had proved to be a combustible mixture in the Profumo scandal; almost three million pounds had been stolen in the infamous Great Train Robbery; and Lord Home succeeded Harold Macmillan as Prime Minister. But for me, despite my fascination with history, the FA Cup remains the big event of that year. The thick sheets of ice had given way to typical Cup final spring sunshine which provided for us the perfect backdrop to give everyone a glimpse of what was to come in the near future from Manchester United, represented that day by David Gaskell, Tony Dunne, Noel Cantwell (captain), Pat Crerand, Bill Foulkes, Maurice Setters, Johnny Giles, Albert Quixall, David Herd, me and Bobby Charlton. We went into the game without Shay Brennan, who had been a rock all season, Nobby Stiles and Harry Gregg, who had been unable to win his place back after injury. When we gathered for the team talk we also thought that we'd lost Paddy Crerand, only for him to be found standing in the tunnel wearing only his jockstrap, listening to the emotive singing of 'Abide With Me'.

Leicester had the better of the early exchanges, but we were passing the ball about well and took the lead just before the half-hour when Crerand intercepted a throw from Banks and fed the ball to my feet; I was able to spin and shoot low past Banks's left hand.

I was loving every minute of it, and almost had another goal a short while later, but McLintock cleared the ball off the line. We stayed on top, and when Banks failed to hold a Bobby Charlton screamer, Davie Herd was on the spot to tap in the rebound to make it 2–0. But Leicester would not lie down, and they came back at us with a goal towards the end when Keyworth launched himself at the ball and saw his horizontal header deflected past Gaskell off the toe end of Dunne's boot. We were determined not to lose, though, and after I had headed against a post, the beaten Banks gratefully clutching the rebound, the outstanding England goalkeeper failed to hold a cross from Giles and Herd tapped in his second of the day. Winning the cup on that May afternoon at last proved to us that we were championship material.

Playing in that final was undoubtedly special. I know it's a bit clichéd, but it was a dream actually to be at Wembley for the showpiece of the season. The FA Cup final was a game I had always listened to on the radio or watched on television. It was a huge day, and this one was made even more special by the fact that the Queen was in attendance to present the medals afterwards. And our bonus for that historic win? Twenty pounds! A year earlier Burnley had reached the final against the double-holders Spurs and were paid a bonus of £1,000 for losing. Still, bonuses had to be set out at the start of the season, so the club was quite within its rights to dig their heels in. Anyway, although it's a terrible thing for a Scot to admit, I would have paid to play in my first ever Cup final. It was simply the biggest game of the season, and not just in England. My memories of it are sketchy, but I do remember how intense the week was leading up to the final, the media following you everywhere. It was a different experience entirely. After the game, someone asked me what I'd thought of it. 'Well,' I replied, 'I'm delighted to have been in the final and I'm delighted to have won as well. I really don't care now whether or not we come back again.' It wasn't perhaps the best choice of words, but I was just feeling so satisfied that I'd been there and done it. Still, God must have thought I was being serious because I never did go back. United didn't return to Wembley in May until 1976, when they lost to Southampton. It was a bitter disappointment because I would have loved the opportunity of a second attempt, if only to savour the moment a little more on that heady day.

But the Cup final success couldn't erase our poor performances in the League that first season. We were erratic, and spent far too much time flirting with relegation, mainly because we couldn't sort out our best midfield, and the defence was poor. Personally, I would have preferred to see Bobby Charlton out there wide on the left because he could have done a fine job for us there, even though both Matt Busby and Alf Ramsey preferred him in a midfield role. For me, on the wing Bobby was the best in the world. Certainly as an opponent of Bobby's, when he played for England, I was always happier to see him in midfield rather than on the flank with that magic left foot of his that could tear a defence apart. Probably our most consistent player that season was Johnny Giles, who did play on the wing when he should have been playing in midfield. He wasn't, however, a great player then, and I wasn't surprised when he moved on to Leeds where Don Revie turned him into one of the finest midfield players in the country.

The most significant date of the season was 6 February – not only the anniversary of the Munich crash, but also the day United signed Pat Crerand from Celtic. I have to admit I was instrumental in the deal. Matt confided in me that he was going to sign either Paddy or Jim Baxter, and he asked me what I thought. He preferred Jim, but I said, 'Well, to be fair, Jim Baxter is a better player than Pat Crerand, but if you want a long-term investment I think you'd be better off buying Pat Crerand.' Jim Baxter was the more skilful player, of that there was no doubt, but he was too much of an individual at times. I just felt that if Matt was building for the future, Crerand was a stronger, more dedicated player who would give the club more value. Matt bought Paddy, and Jim went to Sunderland, which wasn't a particularly good move for him. Ian McCall had become the manager of Sunderland and they were pals, but Jim should really have gone to London or Manchester. Sadly, we never saw the best of Jim Baxter, just like, in my opinion, we never saw the best of George Best, and in both instances the cause was alcohol-related.

I don't think Matt Busby would have coped too well with Jim Baxter off the pitch, because he liked his players to get married and settle down. So it was with Matt's full blessing that I married Diana Rosemary Leith Thomson in the middle of the football season, shortly before the onset of the infamous deep freeze which shut down football and virtually the entire country. I had only met Di in the summer, at a dancehall in Aberdeen when I was back home during the close season. In those days, that was where everybody met their future wife. She was not from a well-to-do family, but she'd certainly enjoyed a much higher standard of living than my family, a few steps up the ladder with an inside toilet and hot water all the time. I was smitten straight away; I knew I had found someone special. A few weeks after meeting Di I went down to sign for United. I was reluctant to leave her for any length of time after that, so I decided I would return to Aberdeen after our games on a Saturday. Doesn't sound too difficult today, does it? Manchester to Aberdeen, an easy little journey. Not so then: it was three flights to get there and three flights to get back with British European Airways. It was almost as bad as coming home from Turin! It was just too much, so I thought the best thing would be if we were to get married. I asked her, she accepted, and I took her to Manchester.

The reason 11 December was picked as our wedding day was because her mother had got married on the eleventh. We were just following family tradition. It was a Tuesday, and the middle of the season, but as I said, Matt was one of those managers who liked his players to be married. He felt that if you were married you would calm down, leave the nightclubs and the pubs alone and live a cleaner life. I suppose he must have worried I was going to run wild after being closeted in Turin, especially as I had already been in Manchester before and knew a few good places for a late night out. In fact, Matt was so keen on having his players married I'm sure he would have given me a Saturday off to tie the knot.

Matt's 'family' management philosophy was great, and I have tried to apply it myself in certain family situations. If you had a bad game, he wouldn't give you a volley. His attitude was that if he still felt the same way twenty-four hours later, then you would get it in the neck, but invariably it never happened because he had calmed down. He believed that if you say things in the heat of the moment you might say things you'll regret; but if you feel the same way twenty-four hours later, then you know you're right in what you're doing. That philosophy has stayed with me through my life, especially when it came to dealing with my kids. I would keep quiet at the time, but if I felt the same way the next day, then they would get it. I would know it was right then, because you do say things in the heat of the moment you wish you hadn't.

Di wasn't a football fan; her first Cup final was that 1963 match against Leicester. It must have been really boring for her down in Manchester at the start. When I met her she was working as a secretary in a solicitor's office and led a full life. She didn't work when we came to Manchester, and that could have been bad news, but it wasn't too long before our first-born arrived. A baby is a full-time occupation in itself, so after that I didn't worry about her so much when I was away playing and training. We'd set up home in a club house in Chorlton-cum-Hardy with no central heating and no carpets, just a bed, a television, two armchairs and a cooker. The club houses were a good perk, a throwback to the days of the maximum wage when no-one could afford to buy a house of their own. Everybody was in a club house with a cheap rent. They were also good assets for the club.

Sir Matt and his wife Jean looked after Di in those early days; Lady Jean, in particular, took care of her when Matt and I were away. She would make sure everything was right for Di because she had no car at the time. Jean also took me around Manchester house hunting, because I hadn't a clue with regard to looking for a house prior to getting married. We would see a house and I would say, 'Oh, that's fine, it's near the club,' and Jean would point out that there weren't easily accessible shops or many good schools around, sensible things like that, things I would never have considered. When we finally chose a house it was handy for the shops and the school was just down the road, and all that was down to Jean Busby. That was the type of thing Matt and his wife were good at, making sure the family was settled, because he believed that was as important as your performance on the field. He was right, too; it does make a big difference if you are content and happy off the field.

Then, of course, early in 1963, the big freeze struck. It was a nightmare; the ice was five or six inches deep in the streets. It took everyone by surprise. We went up to Scotland for a couple of days for the New Year, then rushed back. We could have saved our breath, because we didn't play a single match until the end of February. It was incredibly frustrating as game after game was called off due to brick-hard pitches, and of course when we finally returned to action we had to catch up on the lost weeks.

In one way, it was a pity the bad weather had not set in earlier. Had it done so, I might have saved myself a huge amount of hassle following an incident which was to plague me for at least three years. Four days after my wedding I was playing against West Bromwich Albion and had a dreadful run-in with referee Gilbert Pullin. He had made a remark during the game which was completely out of order, to the effect of 'What a waste of money!' And he kept on having a go at me throughout the first half. It was so bad that I had a word with Matt at half-time. Pullin was totally out of order, and we agreed he should not be refereeing with an attitude like that. Whenever I shot and missed, he would pop up and say something along the lines of 'Oh, you're a clever bastard, you can't play.' Matt told me to put it out of my mind, but it was almost impossible with him chirping away in my ear. It put me off my game – the first time ever that had happened.

The only incident I can recall even remotely close to Pullin's treatment of me was with the very amusing Roger Kirkpatrick, a bald-headed, wealthy extrovert who could run backwards faster than most could run forwards. It happened during a game at Old Trafford several years later when Brian Kidd headed a super goal but Kirkpatrick disallowed it. As he was running past me back-wards, he said, 'If it had been you who had scored it, Denis, I would have given it.' Many years after that, when I was doing some summarizing for the BBC at Maine Road, there was a bomb scare in the stadium just prior to the game. These things were taken very seriously at the time, and the crowd fell as silent as a church congregation, but Roger walked out to the centre of the field, picked up the ball gingerly, shook it and held it to his ear. Everyone just cracked up, and we got on with the game. He was a good referee, Roger Kirkpatrick, and I liked him a lot. The other referee who used to talk to the players was Jack Taylor. He would come up to you and say, 'Listen, I'll let you get away with that, but don't do it again. Just play your game and don't get involved.' He was very good at defusing situations, and players responded to him; he was just as likely to swear at us as we were at him, and he was, without doubt, the best referee around at the time. But as the years passed by referees seemed to become very aloof. Instead of having a quiet word with somebody, all of a sudden there were yellow cards all over the place. I think if referees understand the game, they appreciate that things can happen on the field in the heat of the moment, but they know it's not intentional, or that you're not that type of player; they can simply have a quiet word and tell you to settle down and get on with it. But you still get referees who pose about the place saying 'Watch it!' or 'Come here, you!', pointing all the time to show they're in charge. There were some good referees in those days, but there were also some poor ones.

The 3–0 defeat at the hands of West Brom that December day had nothing to do with the fact that we decided to report Gilbert Pullin to the Football Association. It was a grave error. We were called to a disciplinary meeting at Lancaster Gate, and after hearing what everyone had to say, the Football Association severely censured Pullin. He didn't like the decision, and promptly quit. I had mixed feelings. While believing and knowing that he'd been completely wrong to say the things he'd said, I still felt sorry for him – at least I did for a while. I believe that as a direct result of my protest and Pullin's resignation, I was victimized by certain referees over the next three seasons.

9 THE PATH TO THE TITLE

THE 1963/64 SEASON BEGAN WITH GREAT EXPECTATIONS AT OLD Trafford. Despite having finished near the foot of the table the previous season, our victory over Leicester in the FA Cup had not only put us into Europe but also fired the imagination to such an extent that we fancied ourselves for the League title. And as it turned out we were coming into a terrific period for the north-west of England, the start of the great rivalry between Matt Busby's Manchester United and Bill Shankly's Liverpool, now back in the First Division. For the next four years, the League title alternated between these two clubs in what was a remarkable sequence. For me, it was almost like keeping it in the family: if United couldn't do it, there was no-one else I'd rather have seen win it than my old boss Shanks.

I felt sharp and ready for the new challenge. That close season I scored three in a 3–4 defeat in Bergen, Norway, and was feeling really good by August. I always enjoyed playing against the Norwegians; indeed, I went one better for Scotland at Hampden Park later that year by hitting the back of the net four times. That

June I'd also been given the honour of skippering Scotland in the absence of the injured Dave Mackay, against the Republic of Ireland in Dublin, but ours was a dismal performance and we lost 1–0 before making up for it in some style a week later in Madrid, putting six goals past Spain. I was on the score sheet in that game, too. The entire five-man forward line scored, with Frank McLintock, playing in midfield, scoring the other. It was a tremendous result because Spain were a good side, and to beat them in the Bernabeu was a special treat, especially as I was captain.

The domestic season, however, got off to a bad start: as Cup holders, we were hammered 4–0 by the League champions Everton in the Charity Shield. It did its job, though, and gave us a jolt. We responded brilliantly by thumping Everton 5–1 at Old Trafford in only our third game of the season, and followed this up on 3 September with a 7–2 win at Ipswich. The previous season I had scored four against them, now I slotted three. I began to wish we could play them every month. It seemed I could not stop scoring, and after seven matches United were top of the table with just two points dropped.

I have no doubt at all that it was those early-season goals, plus my international goals in the summer, that pushed my name forward for the Rest of the World side to play against England at Wembley on 23 October to celebrate the Football Association's centenary. It was a fantastic experience playing alongside the likes of Alfredo Di Stefano, who had by then won five successive European Cup winners' medals, Ferenc Puskas from that great Hungarian side that had twice annihilated England, and a host of other world-class stars. We were together from the Sunday, when we met up, until the Thursday after the game, and what a few days they were. It was such a big squad, with so many world stars. I wasn't at all sure I'd be playing, but not only was I picked, I scored a goal and played for the full ninety minutes as our Mexican coach used sixteen players. The forward line in that first half was me, Kopa (France), Di Stefano (Spain), Eusebio (Portugal) and Gento (Spain); in the second half, Puskas came on for Eusebio. Conversation was tricky, but as I said, to be part of that super side was very, very special. Just take a look at the other members of that Rest of the World team: Yashin (USSR), Djalma Santos (Brazil) and Schnellinger (West Germany), and the three Czechs Pluskal, Popluhar and Masopust; other than Puskas, the substitutes used were Soskis (Yugoslavia), Eyzaguirre (Chile), Baxter (Scotland) and Seeler (West Germany). Despite the lack of training and the inability to communicate, the football flowed as the Rest showed their full range of skills while England worked hard to get a result, which they managed, 2–1. It was Puskas who opened the way for me to score my goal; his pass was a dream, and I found myself beating Gordon Banks at Wembley for the second time in a few months.

Playing with such outstanding players is an experience I will always cherish. To be picked to represent the Rest of the World was a singular honour, as it was for my mate Jim Baxter, who came on for the brilliant Masopust in the second half. And it wasn't just on the pitch that it was special; we mixed with those greats in our London hotel, too, and watched the likes of Puskas and Di Stefano knocking back the whisky with Jim Baxter and lighting up their cigarettes. I wouldn't have been surprised if it was Jim who'd introduced the two superstars to his favourite alcohol. It was also the first time I had met Eusebio, and I was impressed with this lovely gentleman. In fact they were all really nice guys who provided me with memories to last a lifetime. We certainly let our hair down and had a bit of a wild night after the game before the troops departed on Thursday morning. I doubt whether anything like it could ever happen now. What a pity for the players, not to mention the fans, to miss out on experiences like that. It was all done very properly, and we were kitted out with blazers, slacks and all sorts of stuff including a beautiful gold watch, which I have kept to this day, engraved with REST OF THE WORLD V. ENGLAND. It is one of the few things I have kept and treasured. Sadly, I don't know where my shirt is. I also played once for the Rest of Europe, and that was a privilege as well, though not as big a game as that truly memorable tie at Wembley in October 1963.

I was having a wonderful time. Everything was going right for me. Then, on 16 November, the rug was pulled from under my feet and I was sent crashing back down to earth. In an away game against Aston Villa, a match we lost 4–0, I was sent off for the first time in my career (discounting that ludicrous Santos affair when I was with Torino). To rub salt into the wound, the Football Association then promptly banned me for twenty-eight days. A month-long suspension then was not like it is now. I was not only denied the right to participate in six matches, I also missed training and I was on no pay. I wasn't even allowed to go to the ground. It was a nightmare.

Was this a post-Pullin December backlash? I wondered. In all, I was sent off and banned three times, though in fifty-five matches for Scotland I wasn't even so much as cautioned. Suspiciously, all three came at roughly the same time of year – Christmas and New Year. I seemed to always find myself up in Aberdeen enjoying myself while England was beset with the most horrible weather for playing football. I used to call it my mid-term break. It's easy to joke about it now, but imagine having all your money stopped over the Christmas period when you're buying presents and all the other bits and pieces that come up at that time of the year with a growing family.

What really hurt was that I felt I was being harshly treated, punished for things for which others regularly escaped scot-free. Take that first incident at Villa Park in 1963. I was sent off for kicking a defender named Alan Deakin, who throughout that match played me more often than he played the ball. I was black and blue. I was especially furious when in the second half he launched himself on a sliding two-footed tackle and ended up between my legs. As he lay on the ground I made a gesture towards him with my thigh as if to warn him. I didn't make any contact, but referee Jim Carr of Sheffield immediately pointed to the dressing-room. Matt Busby always pleaded with me to count up to ten whenever I was kicked, but I'm afraid counting was never one of my great assets and I rarely reached beyond five before taking the law into my own hands. But this was no more than shadow boxing. It would have been easier to take had Deakin been ordered off with me.

My second sending-off happened in Blackpool nearly a year later, the result of a clash with fiery redhead Alan Ball, one of many over the years for club and country. Pat Crerand joined in the verbals, and in the heat of the moment I swore and was sent off by referee Peter Rhodes because he insisted I'd sworn at him. That was another twenty-eight days, plus a £50 fine. For the second year in succession I was home for Christmas. What really hurt about that incident was that Rhodes admitted to making £7,000 from selling his story to the newspapers after sending me off, while I had lost about a grand. There was some consolation, however, when seven days after the start of my suspension I was named 1964 European Footballer of the Year. I have to confess I enjoyed the break, but I was getting fed up when it happened a third time. My third red card was shown after a clash with my fellow Scot Ian Ure. I confess that I did throw a punch at him, but I missed, so again I was punished severely for something I hadn't done. But then, as I threw the punch the referee turned round to see what the fuss was about, and he couldn't do anything else. It was suggested by 'Sneaky Meeky', properly known as David Meek of our excellent local paper the *Manchester Evening News*, that I had it all planned. I told him that of course I'd planned it, adding, 'I mean, what is the point of being sent off if you're not going to be sent off at the right time? Who wants to be in Manchester on a cold, dank night in December when you can spend Christmas and the New Year at home?' It was naturally tongue in cheek, but he still printed it in the local paper and said he'd done it with his tongue firmly in his cheek as well!

I was indebted to my fellow players, who had a whip-round to help pay for Christmas. Even then the FA tried to stop it. What a cheek! Not only had they forced me to pay a fine and prevented me from being paid, they also wanted to deny my team-mates chipping in to help me out! It was positively feudal, the system in those days, and my long suspensions broke new ground. It looked as though there was a separate page in the rule-books under the heading 'Law, Denis'. The FA's attitude was totally wrong, and illegal I may say, as it defied the Treaty of Rome and restraint of trade. It also forced clubs to break FA laws by slipping suspended players a few quid. I wasn't officially paid, but I did get a few quid slipped to me through unofficial channels, apart from Christmas 1963, that is, when I didn't get a bean. It was a while before the Professional Footballers' Association managed a minor victory, forcing a change in policy so players could be paid part of their salary while under suspension.

It wasn't just a question of money anyway. In that 1963/64 season I was flying, and I finished with thirty goals in as many League matches, with fifteen more in cup ties. Because of suspensions and injuries I missed another twenty games, which set me wondering: how many goals might I have scored had I been available for all those games?

That first time was particularly annoying; in my final game before suspension, on 7 December against Stoke City, I'd scored four in a 5–2 win. I was in cracking form, and among the games I missed was the two-legged European Cup Winners' Cup tie against the holders of the cup, Spurs.

United had got off to a dreadful start in that competition on 25 September by drawing 1–1 with the Dutch part-timers Willem II Tilburg. I missed that one through injury, but I made my comeback in the return leg and scored a hat-trick in a runaway 6–1 victory. It was much the same story in the second round when we crashed 2–0 at White Hart Lane in the first leg, then beat them 4–1 in the second leg with a couple apiece from Bobby Charlton and David Herd. That was the day when Noel Cantwell broke Dave Mackay's leg. I was horrified as I watched my Scottish team-mate and great friend sustain a double fracture of the left leg, and I was in the dressing-room when they carried him in, looking absolutely awful. His face was a ghostly white as they cleaned him up and took him off to hospital. I don't think I would have survived had it been me, but he was so strong. It was just a mis-timed tackle between two of the strongest men in football. They went for the same ball, and although it was clear he was going to lose it, Mackay was not the sort of person to pull out of a tackle. I was up in the stand watching when it happened, and if memory serves, the ball had run away from him and he went lunging in for it. I don't think Dave should have gone for it. I'm not saying it was his fault, though, and it certainly wasn't Noel's either; it was just one of those freak incidents that can happen in sport. Dave was in plaster for sixteen weeks, and when it was removed his left leg was four inches thinner than his right. He came back quicker than anyone expected, though, in less than a year, only to break the same leg again in a reserve match against Shrewsbury. Even that couldn't stop him. He returned to the game and saw out his career without ever avoiding a tackle or a challenge for Spurs, Derby County and finally Swindon.

That 4–1 win was a fine one because Spurs were, without doubt, one of the very best sides in Europe at the time. They played some of the best football I have ever seen, and Mackay and Danny Blanchflower were huge influences on their style and class. I had massive respect by then for Danny, who I hoped had forgiven me for my youthful indiscretions in a Scotland shirt. And it didn't end with just Danny and Dave. From Bill Brown, Scotland's goalkeeper, right the way forward, Spurs had quality players. In front of Brown they had the powerful Maurice Norman at centre-half; John White was their ace schemer, while Cliff Jones was an outstanding winger and a great header of the ball who would help provide the service for two England inter-national strikers, Bobby Smith and Jimmy Greaves, the finest striker I ever played with or against. I'm not so sure we would have got past them that season but for the loss of the majestic Mackay.

I was back for the first leg of the quarter-final against Sporting Lisbon in February. In front of a home crowd, I scored a couple of penalties and added a third in a surprisingly unconvincing 4–1 victory. We were annihilated 5–0 in the return leg in Lisbon, though, a result that prompted even the mild-mannered, even-tempered Matt Busby to blow his top, such was the paucity of our performance.

At the time of the first leg against Sporting Lisbon, we'd still been chasing trophies on three fronts, but because of an incredible congestion of fixtures we won neither the Cup Winners' Cup, the FA Cup nor the League title. We played seven major games in just twenty-one days at the sharp end of the season, and it proved too much for us. I was still suspended at the beginning of our cup run when we beat Southampton, but I was back for the fourth

My first call-up for Scotland. Matt Busby casts a fatherly eye over me. Note the shirt!

TOP: The great John Charles and I tussle for possession at Hampden Park in 1959. *Empics*

MIDDLE: Same match, but this time foiled by the man Gordon Banks. *Empics*

BOTTOM: We became the first team to beat the World Champions at Wembley in April 1967 – and I scored! *Empics*

The Zaire goalkeeper Kazadi stops
Buhanga stamping on my head in my
one and only World Cup Finals match.

The Rest of the World team: (*back row, left to right*) Puskas, Santos, Popluhar, Yashin, Pluskal, Schnellinger, Soskic, Mosopust, Eyzaguirre, Baxter (*hidden*), Seeler; (*front*) Kopa, Law, Di Stefano, Fusabio, Gento.

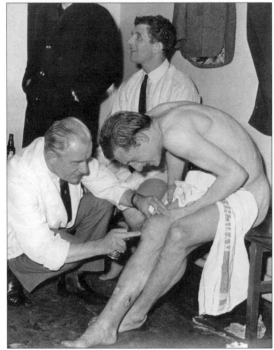

ABOVE: Watching the European Cup Final from my hospital bed.

LEFT: Counting the latest scars! Ted Dalton tends the battered legs while David Herd can't watch.

BELOW: Look at those old dressing rooms! But it doesn't seem to bother David Herd or me.

OPPOSITE BELOW: I remember you! Last time we met we were both sent off (see ABOVE). Ian Ure and I shake hands as he joins United in August 1969.

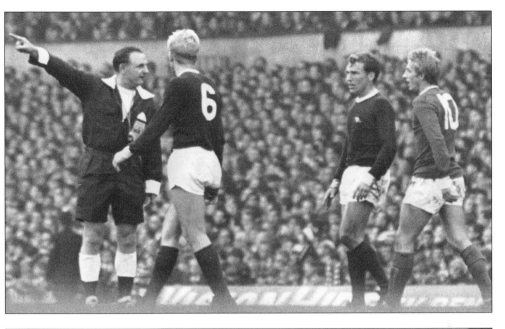

Scoring a typical header against Arsenal in 1966.

One of my tricks, this one against Spurs in September 1967. *Action Images*

round with a hat-trick against Bristol Rovers. We then put four more past Barnsley in mid-February, and the draw for the sixth round gave us a home tie against Sunderland. We were naturally confident, but with six minutes remaining we found ourselves 3–1 down. Somehow, Bobby Charlton and George Best managed to force a replay. We were behind again twice in the replay before forcing another draw after extra time thanks to their excellent goalkeeper Jim Montgomery, who never did have the best eyesight, who cleared the ball straight to my feet when he could have kicked it anywhere. Our third meeting took place at my old ground Leeds Road in Huddersfield. Again we went behind early on, but this time we came back majestically to win 5–1, and I helped myself to another hat-trick. It was a fine win, but the long slog of a tie had not only taken it out of us, it had also forced a logjam of fixtures. We faced a semi-final against West Ham just five days later, and not helped by a heavy, rain-sodden Hillsborough pitch we lost 3–1 to the underdogs.

Our season disintegrated in those three weeks. In that time we'd been asked to play two legs of a European tie, four FA Cup ties including extra time, and two League matches. Crashing out of two major cup competitions within five days in mid-March was devastating, and we were shattered both mentally and physically. We could not believe we were going to win nothing after such a tremendous season. Injuries to key players played a big part, though, and it must not be forgotten that we didn't have big squads at the time; the game has changed dramatically in that respect. You had to have an awful lot of luck to go through a season without major injuries and, in my case and a few others', long suspensions. Liverpool won one of their titles using just fourteen or fifteen players. That's why doubles were so infrequent, until top clubs realized that with all the fixtures they were required to play they needed greater depth in their squad and some rotation of players to help keep the side fresh and eager.

Liverpool were our main rivals in the League that season. They were bristling with quality. The all-important game between the two clubs came at Anfield in April, by which time a win was essential for us. They beat us comprehensively by three goals to nil, and the title was lost. We hadn't quite taken off as we had hoped, but we still felt we were on our way.

I was buoyed almost immediately the season had finished by the arrival of Gary. I was a proud father. It was lovely to have a son, and it was also good for Di because she needed something to fill her time, particularly when I was away. Now she is a working mother, and has been for the last four decades. It was tough for Di, though, in the early days because the world revolved around me. On the day of an evening game at Old Trafford, for instance, Di would have to take Gary out for the day because I had to rest during the afternoon before the game. So it wasn't easy for her, but at least things were positive on a personal and professional front.

John Connelly was a great buy by Sir Matt for the 1964/65 season. He turned out to be a very good asset, a good crosser of the ball. It was especially good news for me because I knew how good a supplier he was; he had given a first-hand demonstration of his skills the previous season when he helped Burnley to a 5–2 victory at Old Trafford. If I was going to score more goals, I needed people to give me the ball in the right areas. And Connelly wasn't just a winger, he scored goals as well, as he showed immediately on our pre-season tour when he hit the target twice against Hamburg in West Germany. He was a fine striker of the ball, and his arrival gave us balance. With him on one flank and George Best on the other, me and Davie Herd down the middle, and Bobby Charlton making runs from midfield, we were a powerful attacking force. We were also a lot stronger and more resilient in midfield with Nobby Stiles and Pat Crerand, and at the back Shay Brennan, Tony Dunne and Bill Foulkes looked solid, as did Dave Gaskell in goal before Pat Dunne took over. We felt in good shape to challenge not only for the League, but everything else too.

We were looking forward to the new campaign with eager anticipation but were quickly brought back down to earth when we scraped together just five points from our first six matches of the season. Strangely, a pattern was beginning to emerge, for this was not the first time we were to recover from a poor late summer to win the title the following spring. Another curious fact was that John Connelly made his League debut against the same team both George Best and I had faced for ours – West Bromwich Albion. But after this we embarked on a run of fourteen League matches dropping only a single point. We were scoring goals for fun, and by the end of November we had taken thirty-two points from a possible forty and led the First Division by three points from Tommy Docherty's young Chelsea side. At last I was playing for a winning side, and I can't tell you how good it felt after all the complications of previous years. It was good football as well, good to watch and good to play in. We felt it was all coming together.

Much of this was due to Sir Matt's philosophy, which ran along these lines: 'Go out and play your football. It doesn't matter if you win, lose or draw as long as you try your best and play your football. You know that's what you do best.' We were more than aware we were performing in the Theatre of Dreams, where the fans had once appreciated the skills of the 1948 side and the artistry of the 1958 side. This was the side of 1964, and there was a great air of expectancy at Old Trafford. We played it simply and we looked for goals. Many people claimed we played it totally off the cuff, with no plans for anything including free-kicks, but that does Matt Busby and the players a disservice. We had our own structure and worked as diligently as most clubs on set plays. We were well aware when we conceded a free kick who should be in the defensive line-up, where we all were in relation to the play and who to pick up when we were not in possession. We all had our jobs to do. It must have looked as though it was played off the cuff, that it came naturally to such gifted players, but it didn't. We worked hard at it, even when we were in possession in open play. Had we not mastered the basics, it would have fallen apart and we would have been chasing our tails. If Bobby Charlton made runs through the middle someone would know to drop off, and if I was not getting any joy up front, I would just go to the right side and let somebody else come in. Bestie could always play through the middle, and I never minded going out wide for a while. It was often like a game of chess at times. If things are not going right for you you have to be disciplined enough to make adjustments, just as you would in a game of chess or on the battlefield.

We might ask the question, 'When we're defending, what do we want the opposition to do?' And the answer would be, 'Well, we want them to knock the ball up the middle and then we'll win it back.' Then someone might say, 'If that's what you want them to do, why are we doing the same thing at the other end? If we're knocking a ball down the middle and there's a big centre-half waiting up there, then life's a doddle for the defending side.' So I might say, 'Let's stick it down the wing, then, and get in behind them.' There's nothing worse for a defender than being turned. He wants to be facing the game all the time; he doesn't want people to be going round the back. It's a simple example I've given here, but that was how we tackled the games, that was our philosophy. And we were always adaptable so that we could change things if they weren't going to plan. With so many talented players we could afford to play that way. If nothing was happening for me, Bobby would come in; if Bobby wasn't creating anything, George would come in. It was a system, and it worked well because most of the time you're not all going to be playing well together at the same time. Our game plan allowed for us to slot in here and there, but it certainly wasn't off the cuff. Yes, freedom of expression was encouraged, especially on the ball, but it's not true that we ignored tactics. Then again, any team with aspirations to be good or even great has to have individuals who can do something on the day that's just that little bit different, and I have to admit it was made a whole lot easier for us by having a certain individual named George Best in the team. He made anything possible.

George made his first appearance for Manchester United at Old Trafford on 14 September 1963. The space was created for this slip of an Irish boy by the sale to Leeds United of Johnny Giles, whom we didn't think would make the grade as a winger. I was out injured for George's first game and sat with Matt Busby in the dugout watching this skinny, pale-faced lad going about his business. There was no doubting his skill, which he had in abundance, but he looked so weak and frail I could not see how on earth he was going to survive in the hurly-burly of English League football. I said as much to Matt, wondering out loud how much stick he would be able to take and commenting that it was a good job he was out on the wing where at least he could be assaulted only from one side at a time. But contrary to appearances, George was as brave as a lion. I immediately noticed that as well as being comfortable off either foot he didn't mind going in for a tackle or challenging for a header. He was up against a really tough, experienced defender that day in Welsh international Graham Williams, a left-back who was a hard player, and I mean hard. He tried to kick Bestie, but George kept skipping over him or sending him the wrong way, and at the final whistle I had to salute the little Irish boy because he had survived and won his battle on points.

Even so, I had my doubts whether he could stay on that path, and, sure enough, after that first game he was left out of the side until just after Christmas, when again I witnessed the real George Best from the dugout. We had lost 6–1 at Burnley on Boxing Day, but now here we were, just two days later, thrashing them 5–1 at Old Trafford. George scored and was a revelation, and from that day onwards he was a first-team regular. I'd actually first clapped eyes on George when he was only fifteen, so perhaps I should have remembered the determination of that skinny, bespectacled lad with a squint from Aberdeen! He certainly disproved my theory about being too weak to succeed.

I loved playing with George. He was, without doubt, the most gifted player I played with or against. He had buckets of talent, but he also had his faults. Apart from the nature of his lifestyle, he also developed a tendency to hang on to the ball for too long. That's one of the reasons why I believe that George was an even better player than the one we saw at Manchester United. He did not fulfil his talents. Had he done so, where would we have placed him? Probably above Pele himself! What's more – and it may surprise some to hear this – he was one of the best, most dedicated trainers I came across. I hated training, really hated it, so he had my respect for that as well. I never minded training with the ball, that wasn't a problem, but all that running! I always thought pre-season training was awful. Give me short sprints every time, fifty- or sixty-yard runs, not all that long running. When it came to fitness, the more games we played, the better I felt. I wanted to be playing on a Wednesday and a Saturday every week – which is why injuries and suspensions were purgatory for me. I didn't want long gaps between games because then you had to train to get back to match fitness, and that was the boring part of the profession as far as I was concerned. But George got through with no problems when he was a young man, and although he looked to be all skin and bones he was built like a whippet.

Funnily enough, the hardest trainers when I was in Italy were the goalkeepers. They trained when we trained, and after we finished they would still be there. Now, the goalkeepers' union won't thank me for saying this, but when you think about that philosophy, it has to be the right one to a certain extent because goalies aren't getting any football, are they? They don't play football. They are goalkeepers; they have to stay in their box. When I was at Turin, the reflex-work exercises our two top-class goalkeepers did by themselves looked like real killers, and I steered well clear of them. Back home, though, goalkeepers trained like normal players. Most of them wanted to play out and score goals in practice matches, and invariably they were useless. I used to say to them, 'You can't play, you're a goalkeeper. Stay there, keep out of the way.' But goalkeepers never took any notice of anyone. We would do a bit of shooting and taking penalties as much for ourselves as for them, but in a way they didn't train. As the years went by they turned to specialized guidance, and that was much, much better, but it took them and the managers an awful long time to discover the obvious.

I had, of course, to do more training during the first couple of weeks of 1965 because of my latest suspension, and when I returned to the side in mid-January I promptly scored both goals in a 2–2 draw away to Nottingham Forest. I must have been uplifted by my recent European Footballer of the Year award. Winning it had certainly been a nice way to close out 1964. The tradition behind the award was what thrilled me most. It had only begun in 1956, when Stanley Matthews won it; after that came names such as Alfredo Di Stefano (twice), the Frenchman Raymond Kopa, Luis Suarez of Spain, Omar Sivori of Italy, the

Czech Josef Masopust and, the year before me, the great Russian goalkeeper Lev Yashin. It has retained its prestigious stature over the years since I won it: I have watched keenly as the likes of Eusebio, Bobby Charlton, George Best, Johann Cruyff, Franz Beckenbauer, Kevin Keegan, Michel Platini, Ruud Gullit, Marco van Basten, Ronaldo, Rivaldo, Figo, Michael Owen and Zinedine Zidane have claimed the prize. Talk about a *Who's Who* of fine players; I genuinely feel honoured to be among them.

I was awarded the trophy before United's game against Strasbourg in the Inter Cities Fairs Cup, as the UEFA Cup was called then. We were going well in the competition – after, that is, a tame first-round 1–1 draw in Sweden with Djurgaardens IF. In the return at Old Trafford on 27 October we thrashed them 6–1 after another poor first half, and I helped myself to another hat-trick. There certainly seemed to be plenty of goals about in those days, and in the second round we exploded against Borussia Dortmund with Bobby Charlton, having been left out of the England side by Alf Ramsey, scoring three and still being matched and overshadowed by the eighteen-year-old George Best who also scored three. Matt Busby described that 6–1 win in Germany over a team that had beaten Benfica 5–0 the previous season and reached the European Cup semi-final as the club's greatest performance in Europe for years. To rub it in, we scored four without reply in the home leg.

We were unfortunate to draw Everton, a powerful side that had won the League in 1963, in the next round and were held 1–1 at Old Trafford on 20 January 1965 thanks to a sparkling display from Everton's England goalkeeper Gordon West. I was just back after my usual suspension and very rusty, and we were serious second favourites for the second leg at Goodison Park. But we went two up and then held on in the face of a terrific Everton onslaught, goalkeeper Pat Dunne our hero with several top-class saves including one which rolled along the goal-line, hit the post and bounced back into his arms. After that, we felt our name was on the trophy, especially when we swept aside Racing Strasbourg 5–0 on their own ground with me contributing two headers to the total, but we were brought down to earth somewhat in the return at Old Trafford when the French team held us to a goalless draw in front of a baffled and angry 34,000 fans who had come for the execution. Then, with the final beckoning, we once again stumbled at the last hurdle, this time in a play-off with the Hungarian side Ferencvaros in the Nep Stadium. We had won the first leg at home 3–2 and lost the return 1–0, Pat Crerand getting sent off fifteen minutes from the end. We lost the play-off 2–1, and I had a last-minute effort blocked on the line. At least Ferencvaros beat Juventus in the final in Turin.

That was our second semi-final defeat of the season, because a couple of months earlier we'd lost to Leeds in the FA Cup. That had also gone to a replay after the first had been drawn 0–0 in an awful game the highlight of which was my flare-up with Jack Charlton when he ripped the shirt off my back – not the first (or the last) time we'd had a little spat. In fact, several players were involved on both sides, again not for the first or last time. Leeds were very good at putting pressure on referees with their mass protests, and went on to earn a reputation for it. They were a professional and ruthless side that pushed the envelope as far as it would go, and we were not the sort of side to roll over on our backs at the first sign of trouble. Conflict was inevitable. There were one or two in that Leeds side over the next decade who could have started a rumble in a telephone box, but Big Jack was not one of them. Clumsy he might have been, but dirty, no – and I should know because we played against each other often enough for club and country. A little while ago, Jack brought memories of the incident flooding back when he sent me back my shirt, framed and signed with his good wishes! My biggest complaint about Jack had nothing to do with his football; rather it was to do with the fact that he never bought any cigarettes but always had one in his mouth. He was forever poncing mine. The replay came four days later at Forest's City Ground, and although we did everything but score we eventually lost to a very late goal off the back of Billy Bremner's head.

Leeds were beginning to become a bit of a bogey team for United. They'd already beaten us at Old Trafford, but in April, with them three points clear of us, we gained a little revenge with a win at Elland Road to go within a point of them. Two days later we were back on top after a good 4–2 win over Birmingham City.

We were not to realize it at the time, but these were the beginnings of the great, tough, cynical Leeds team. They stuck the ball about, and although they had a nasty side they also had quality with the likes of Norman Hunter, Johnny Giles, Billy Bremner, Big Jack, Peter Lorimer, Eddie Gray, Jimmy Greenhoff, Mick Jones and the rest. Don Revie had an inventive nature, and Leeds came up with all sorts of new ploys, particularly in dead-ball situations. The one that stands out for me is Big Jack standing in front of the goalkeeper, right on his toes, to block his move off the line. Nobody had ever done that before, but plenty did it afterwards, and still do. Revie brought in several things like that, legitimate but right on the borderline. The worst aspect of it as far as I was concerned was the surrounding of the referee whenever a Leeds player had done something wrong. The official would become so distracted that he would invariably forget the initial offence. But for all their quality and inventiveness, they failed to win as many trophies as they should have won. They were often foiled at the death with offside goals and suchlike, and sometimes you wondered whether it was because they had antagonized so many referees. The worst incident was when they lost the

European Cup final in Paris in 1975 to Bayern Munich. Peter Lorimer scored a stunning goal from all of twenty yards but the French referee disallowed it for no reason I or anyone else could see. The match was generally badly officiated, and the crowd reacted strongly to what they saw as biased refereeing.

Of all their tough players, the one I had the most trouble with was Norman Hunter. Norman was the one who liked to get it in first. He did a few players over the years just to let them know he was there, and he was effective: often you didn't see his immediate opponent a great deal during the rest of the game. He sorted them out, and made sure he did it early so that referees would just warn him. Of course, I played directly against Norman for Manchester United and for Scotland, and I too would be trying to ensure that Norman didn't get away with anything. My attitude was the usual one: if you're going to kick me, you're going to get a kick back. I wasn't going to change my philosophy for Norman. We used to talk about it on the pitch while the game was going on, as I did with most of the players I had battles with. I would say to them, 'If you're going to kick me, kid, you're going to get the same back somewhere along the line, so don't even think about it. Do me, and you're going to get it back with interest.' Norman still kicked as hard as he could, and I kicked him back. Thus it went on until eventually we stopped out of mutual respect. He went looking for somebody else, and so did I! Mind you, get rid of Norman and the next thing you knew you had Billy Bremner crashing into you. Wee Billy was exactly the type of guy you wanted in your team at the time. He was so hard I still wince when I walk past his statue at Elland Road. Our answer at Old Trafford was Nobby Stiles, but Leeds had a few more than we did.

The battle between Leeds and Manchester United for the 1964/65 League Championship went right down to the wire. On

26 April our penultimate game was against Arsenal, while Leeds had to travel to St Andrews just five days before they were due to play Liverpool in the FA Cup final. I thought I was going to miss out on the big climax as I had gashed my knee at Liverpool the previous Saturday after a clash with man mountain Ron Yeats. Half a dozen stitches were holding the wound together. I was about to hobble home that Monday after treatment when Matt Busby stopped me and said, 'Where are you going?'

I answered, somewhat bewildered, 'What do you mean? I'm going home.'

'No you're not,' the boss countered. 'You've got a game tonight.'

I was taken aback. 'I can't play,' I said, 'I've got six stitches in my knee.'

'No way, we need you to play up front,' Matt insisted.

By now totally bemused, I said in all sincerity, 'You *are* joking, aren't you?'

He wasn't.

They strapped my knee up, I played, and the night could not have worked out better. The stitches stayed intact and I scored two goals in a 3–1 win. I had never even given a thought to playing in that game, but I'm grateful for Matt's intervention because it proved to be the victory that won us the League. We were kept constantly aware of the situation from St Andrews. At one stage, Birmingham were leading Leeds 3–0, but throughout the second half we kept hearing the score creep up, 3–1, 3–2, 3–3. That was how it finished, and their final whistle was greeted with a great roar when the crowd at Old Trafford heard the result. Leeds' League programme was finished and they were level with us on points but behind on goal difference. It didn't matter what we did at Villa Park in our last game of the season, we had won the title.

The joy at Old Trafford was unconfined; it was, after all, only seven years after Munich. We were, of course, fully aware of this, and still everything revolved around the catastrophe. We were all wrapped up in our own emotions, really. It's very difficult to say what each of us felt, but everybody was obviously highly delighted. The club had spent quite a bit of money for those days, and now came the rewards. The celebrations were huge after the Arsenal game.

It was certainly a great triumph for Matt. The League Championship was the hardest thing to win; as Shanks always used to say, it's a marathon, not a sprint, and anything can happen. The big surprise was Leeds' draw at Birmingham because the Blues were not highly rated and were expected to lose. It had been terrific to win the FA Cup, but the League title was different, something very special. The great difference is that when you've won the League, every ground you travel to for the whole of the following season you arrive as champions; an FA Cup victory lasts for only a few days, and then everyone's off for the summer. And there's another big bonus, too: you're back in Europe, the real Europe, not the Cup Winners' Cup or the Fairs/UEFA Cup but the one that matters, the European Cup. You could certainly sense that for Matt Busby the European Cup was the biggest prize. It was Busby who had first taken English teams into the European Cup; Chelsea won the League in 1955, but they chose not to enter the competition and the Football League frowned on their decision. As for Busby, he'd always insisted this was the way forward; he could see the value in it. Nowadays everybody takes that for granted, but it had been a big step to take in the 1950s, and quite controversial, too. He could have proved the point had United won it in 1958 with the team he had at the time, but it was not to be. Now, however, he was back.

10 ALL IN THE HEAD

PLAYING IN EUROPE WAS DIFFICULT IN THE 1960S. IT WAS A definite problem when you were so good as a club side that you went for everything, because it invariably caught up with you. For a start, England's top division was much bigger than its equivalents in the rest of Europe. Top overseas clubs were playing only around thirty League games a season, while we were into the forties with our FA Cup games on top of that; also, in Italy and Spain they were not concerned about domestic cups at all, unless there was nothing else to win. And before long we had the League Cup as well! The only reason the League Cup took off in those days after several years drifting around without some of the top teams was because it provided an entry into European competition. Neither Everton nor ourselves were interested in the early days. It was just too many games. In fact, our domestic programme was so severe that they used to laugh at us in Europe. And many of the players at clubs like Liverpool, Leeds and Manchester United had international duties to cope with as well, so with small squads, being successful in Europe was not easy for

English teams. Nowadays, of course, big squads are the norm as managers have had to adjust to having five substitutes on the bench and, if you're in the upper echelon, an entire season of European games in the Champions League. In Italy in the 1960s, clubs didn't bother with a second team; they had a big squad of first-team players and no reserve football. Teams like Real Madrid and Juventus did well because they didn't have as many games, and for their cup teams they used the back-up players from 12 to 18, players coming back after injury, or players who were out of form. Because of the way we went about our football in England, the way was left relatively clear for Celtic to make the British breakthrough in the top European competition. But once Celtic made the break, we followed them, because other clubs could then clearly see the value in winning at that level. Gradually, the top sides began to increase the size of their squads.

Knowing about European club sides was also difficult because you didn't have the sort of television coverage you have nowadays and we just didn't know the personnel of any team in depth, other than what we could glean from publications like *World Soccer*.

There were no mini leagues then, it was a knockout right from the start, and to win any European cup you knew you had to play well throughout the year. Duff teams could easily knock you out if you had a bad day.

We should have won the European Cup in 1966. It was special then to play in Europe's top competition because the Champions Cup meant what it said: you had to win your domestic league to be admitted. And, as I said, playing in a League like the English First Division, that represented a huge effort. We had cracked it at last, we were champions, and 1965 was the start for Manchester United of a glorious spell that should really have been longer, for there is no doubt at all that you do become better players when you're playing against the best the world has to offer. Certainly we were all looking forward to the European Cup, the thought of jetting away here and there and playing the cream of Europe in their respective stadiums.

But the memory of Munich lingered. Whenever we travelled to Europe in those days it was a bit of a nightmare because Matt Busby refused to go by charter aircraft after what had happened in February 1958 after the Red Star Belgrade game. We had to fly on a scheduled airline, and that created its own problems. Manchester International airport was not as well developed then as it is now, so a typical trip would see us flying to London, then to Amsterdam, then to Madrid. That represented a full day's journey, whichever way you looked at it. A day there and a day back, with two, sometimes three, aircraft in each direction. It was not until many years later that United reverted to charter flights once more, but in those days there was an understandable fear of them. We could understand that Matt and Bobby in particular were nervous fliers; experiencing a plane crash would, I think, make the strongest man wary of flying again, and of course such feelings rub off easily. It had been exactly the same in Turin, even over a decade after their team's 1949 crash. Of course, charter airlines were as safe in Britain as scheduled aircraft, but you can understand the attitude in the circumstances, and no-one could argue with the bad logic even if it did make travelling so much more difficult and tiring before big games.

But I had more to worry about than flying in that 1965/6 season after I took a blow on my knee, the same knee I'd had an operation on during my playing days at Huddersfield, during a mid-October World Cup qualifying game at Hampden Park against Poland. I didn't know it at the time, but that injury was to affect me for the remainder of my career. To make things even worse, Poland beat us – the defeat that indirectly cost us our place in the World Cup finals in England. I was back at Old Trafford on the Friday morning after the game and the damaged knee was still painful. I didn't say anything and continued to train, then played at Spurs the next day in a 5–1 defeat, but the knee was so painful that I didn't make it out onto the pitch for the second half. Had such a problem occurred today I would have undergone immediate keyhole surgery to rectify it; instead, as a result of bad diagnoses as much as anything, I carried that injury for over two years. It's another area where football has improved beyond all imagination. I can recall, a few years ago now, Ally McCoist playing for Rangers in Romania against Steaua Bucharest. He had a knee operation on a Tuesday, the game was played on the Wednesday of the following week, and McCoist played. Eight days! Unimaginable when I had my knee problems. I was out there with BBC radio, and we attended a training session when we arrived. McCoist, a key player for Graeme Souness at the time, had not been considered and had not even brought his boots with him on the trip. I watched him walk around during that first session not really doing anything, but in the next session he was running about, and then, incredibly, playing in a little five-a-side. I couldn't believe it; we used to be out for months whenever we had similar problems. I turned to my commentator, the late Peter Jones, and remarked that I thought Ally would play. Few others, apart from one observant journalist, even considered the idea, and there was much mocking in the press box before the kick-off as Ally didn't come out for the warm-up. But just before kick-off he appeared, stunning all but a couple of us, and played his part in the game.

In contrast, I had a lot of trouble with the medical staff at Old Trafford, with the physiotherapist, the doctor and the surgeon all at odds. The surgeon kept saying it was my cartilage, to which I responded, 'It can't be, I've had it out!' They were baffled, and eventually they tried to insist it was all in my head. They kept telling me there was nothing wrong and to try to put it out of my mind. But I knew I could feel pain, real pain. I did a lot of my passing with the inside of my foot, which entails turning your knee; now, when I turned the knee and kicked the ball I could feel it catch me. It didn't happen every time, but regularly enough to worry a professional sportsman. I soon became irritated by their attitude and commented one day, 'Well, if it's in my mind, I assume you're going to operate on my head somewhere along the line to relieve this pain!'

But United were already well into a tough season, so I had to try to put all this to the back of my mind. It was particularly tough because when you are champions every game you play is like a cup tie; all your opponents want to do is beat the champions, and since the advent of European competition it had become increasingly difficult to retain the title. Indeed, some of our worst results in the League that season came immediately after a midweek European Cup fixture, when we were doing all that travelling. The proof of the pudding is in the results: we lost to Arsenal at Highbury in September 1965 after jetting back from Helsinki, to Chelsea after a trip to Benfica in March 1966, and to Sheffield United after returning from Belgrade. I believe this demonstrated not only the difficulty of pursuing the League title as well as the European Cup, but that, if only subconsciously, the European Cup was our main target that season.

Certainly for me, playing in the European Cup had been a dream ever since I'd watched on television that wonderful Real Madrid side beat Eintracht Frankfurt 7–3 in 1960 in front of 135,000 well-behaved fans in Glasgow. I was enthralled by the quality of play, the goals, and everything about this fascinating spectacle. The game opened my eyes to the possibilities of football outside our own sceptred isle, and injected into me a powerful urge to be involved. As I was a thin and somewhat callow youth at the time, playing in a European Cup final looked extremely remote to say the least, but my ambitions were beginning to flourish as I settled into First Division football with Manchester City and international football with Scotland, and anybody can dream.

The 1965/66 season gave me my first chance to realize the dream, and we certainly started our campaign well, sweeping aside HJK Helsinki (9–2 on aggregate) and ASK Vorwaerts (5–1 on aggregate). It was a truly disciplined display in East Berlin against Vorwaerts as I scored the first and John Connelly added the second for a 2–0 win. My goal in that victory was a fairly typical header after a return pass from David Herd, and I laid on the second for John despite suffering with a dreadful head cold. David's hat-trick in the second leg against the East Germans gave us a plum quarter-final draw against former champions Benfica.

Those two games against Benfica in February and March 1966 marked Manchester United out as one of the best teams in Europe. Few gave us a chance after the first leg at Old Trafford when, in front of a crowd of over 60,000, we scraped a 3–2 victory with goals from me, David Herd and Bill Foulkes, because the star of the night was undoubtedly Eusebio, who made Benfica's first goal and scored their second. Still, Davie and I hit the woodwork too in what was a pulsating game. But it was the return leg on 8 March that will be long remembered by the Manchester United faithful, not to mention football fans around the globe, who realized that night in the Stadium of Light, as we already had, that United had unearthed a genius in the long-haired nineteen-year-old Belfast boy George Best. Don't forget that Benfica were rightly considered the cream of European football. They had reached the European Cup final in 1961, 1962, 1963 and 1965, winning it twice; they were unbeaten in the Stadium of Light for seven years, and were by the mid-1960s rated even higher than Real Madrid. Consequently, we'd been given little chance in front of 80,000 Portuguese fans, especially as Sporting Lisbon had torn us apart two years earlier at their atmospheric home stadium.

The atmosphere in our dressing-room before the game was electric. Nerves were twangling as Matt Busby announced his tactical plans for a conservative start so that we didn't concede an early goal and with it the initiative. Imagine, in those circumstances, what it was like when Pat Crerand kicked a ball against the dressing-room wall and shattered a mirror. To put it mildly, it didn't ease our nerves. I would like to be able to say that everyone burst out laughing and the tension dissipated, but that didn't happen. It wound us up an extra notch.

Despite Matt's orders to be cautious, we went out and were three up within fifteen minutes. That quarter-of-an-hour spell remains the best European club performance in my memory, a true team effort, and it was fabulous to be involved in such a game. If there was a star, it was George. He scored the first two goals and made the third for John Connelly; then Pat Crerand accepted my pass for the fourth, and Bobby Charlton weighed in with the fifth. Everything came off for us that night, and quite rightly we were installed as the favourites to win the trophy, with everyone talking about El Beatle – George Best. The Portuguese press were very generous to United, *Seculo* describing it as a notable exhibition but adding that, after all, wasn't it the British who invented football?

At the same time that spring we were flying in the FA Cup. We'd beaten Derby County 5–2 at the Baseball Ground, Rotherham on the second attempt at Millmoor, Wolves 4–2 away in the fifth round and Preston North End 3–1 in a replay at Old Trafford to reach a record fifth successive semi-final. But the price was high: in the first game against Preston at Deepdale we lost

George Best when he was tackled from behind and damaged his cartilage. How strange we should both be suffering with the same problem at the same time – although in my case of course no-one realized it at the time. In fact, even George's problem was first diagnosed as a strained ligament!

April turned out to be a bad month for us, particularly for me, because on 2 April Scotland were no more than warm-up material for England in their World Cup bid, and we were lucky to get away with a 4–3 defeat in which I scored one of the goals. Then came a collapse for Manchester United, once again because of too many big games in too short a time. On 13 April we were effectively dumped out of the European Cup, surprisingly beaten 2–0 by Partizan Belgrade, George playing his last game of the season on his dodgy knee and me missing the easiest chance of the game. We won the second leg by a Nobby Stiles goal, but it wasn't enough. George's absence had proved critical, and we had gone out to a relatively poor European side. What a huge dis-appointment that was, probably my biggest in my eleven years at Old Trafford. Then, just three days after that second leg, we met Everton at Burnden Park in the semi-final of the FA Cup. We were deflated, but Everton had prepared for the game by playing their reserves against Leeds United the previous Saturday and giving their first team a rest before facing us. Colin Harvey scored the only goal in a scrappy game, and Everton went on to win the FA Cup, beating Sheffield Wednesday 3–2. To cap that, Liverpool won the League, and with it the right to contest the European Cup in 1966/67, beating Leeds and Burnley by five clear points, and although we finished the season well we could only take fourth place.

What sort of summer did I have to look forward to now, with no winners' medals in my hand and with England at home in the World Cup finals? To add to my woes, just before the start of the tournament I was transfer-listed by Matt Busby after asking for a rise.

At the end of the season I had written him a letter asking for a signing-on fee and more money when my new contract came up, adding, rather foolishly as it transpired, that I would want a move if I did not get what I wanted. I was in Aberdeen playing golf and waiting for the birth of our second child when Busby announced to the world that I was available, adding that 'no player will hold this club to ransom, no player'. He said he didn't care who it was, Denis Law or anyone else. The first I knew of it was when a horde of pressmen came over the hill at the golf course; they'd heard the statement and were coming to get my opinion. The reporter from the *Aberdeen Evening Express* told me, 'You've been put on the transfer list!' The big hit record at the time was the Beatles' 'Yesterday', and the words 'Yesterday, all my troubles seemed so far away' seemed very apt in the circumstances. In fact, the press interest was so bad that I had to go into hiding for a couple of days to avoid the glare of the publicity. Then I flew down to Manchester, sat with Matt in his office for an hour or so, sorted it all out and was taken off the transfer list. I didn't want to leave, and Matt didn't want me to go.

And how much extra had I asked for to provoke this drama? A tenner a week! One ten-pound note! Premier League players light their Cuban cigars with those these days!

I quickly found out the true story behind Matt's reaction: he had used my letter to make a point to the rest of the squad. He wasn't after me specifically, but my letter suited his purposes, and after the fuss nobody else came in for an increase. Still, it was me who had to come back, apologise and grovel. When I went into his office, he pulled out a drawer and there was my written apology already prepared for press and public consumption. All it required was my signature. That was the very public side of the unfortunate affair, but what no-one knows (until now) is that Matt paid me everything I had asked for. He just wanted to make an example of me.

A week after I signed my new contract, Andrew was born, one of my few successes that season. I'd scored only fifteen goals in thirty-five League games, and then, on top of my knee injury and the transfer row, England went and made it even worse by winning the World Cup. For the next four years I knew I would have Bobby Charlton and Nobby Stiles ramming their success down my throat, and it wasn't something I was looking forward to, particularly as I was convinced Scotland would have done well had we been there. That was even more annoying than England doing well.

I, for one, had been determined not to suffer in front of my television and watch the World Cup final from Wembley just in case England did beat West Germany. A while earlier I had played golf with a friend, a big fellow named John Hogan, and lost to him. He was a truly awful golfer, but nonetheless he'd beaten me, and to rub it in he'd said, 'Any time you want a return game, just give me a shout.' So on the day of the World Cup final I remembered his gloating mug and challenged him to play golf. Now, John was a football fan and an Englishman, and he was all prepared for his afternoon in front of the television, but I reminded him about what he'd said. 'You said a return match any day, you name it,' I said. 'I will name it now: today.'

'But it's the World Cup final today!' he spluttered.

'Well, you said it,' I pointed out reasonably, and I arranged to meet him at our local club.

So there we were on the golf course, and I was trying to concentrate on my game knowing that some of my mates were playing the biggest match of their lives. It was a typical summer's day in Manchester, pouring with rain, and again my mate gave me a thrashing. I lost my £25 bet, and as we rounded the corner from the last, heading towards the clubhouse, all the members were standing outside with their drinks waiting to tell me the result. England had won the World Cup. They were holding up four fingers for the four goals with one hand, and a pint in the other.

I have still never seen the entire game, though I have seen the goals. Hurst's goal was never over the line. I was in Germany the week after the game with Manchester United. I saw all the German papers, and not one of the photographs showed the ball over the line. I said as much to Liverpool striker Roger Hunt, who'd been standing right in front of the goal at the time, but he replied it must have been a goal because if it hadn't crossed the line he would have stuck it in. 'You were just too slow,' I remonstrated. 'You were six yards away and it would have taken you half an hour to get there.' But Roger was convinced he would and could have reached it had it not already gone over the line. I, as a Scot, continued to disagree with him.

Putting all that nationalism to one side for a moment, I still believe it was a bad result for British football at the time. Football people are great copycats, and after the England victory lots of teams switched to a 4–4–2 formation. It was a step backwards in my opinion. It was too defensive, and it took wingers out of the equation, removing the people who crossed the ball into the box to create goals for us strikers. The claim was that you would have six attackers, but in fact it didn't work out that way; it worked the other way, with only two up front and the two wide men unable to support for much of the time.

It may be said that it's very cynical of me to be so critical when Ramsey won the World Cup with it, but it is my humble opinion that he put British football back a little bit and not forward that day. To me, it's just not the way to play football. I thought

England became more defensive as a nation then; the team now had two guys up front battling against four defenders, whereas previously the wingers had stretched defences by getting the ball into danger areas. Wingers were typically tricky players, often fast, but in their place now were midfield players who weren't often in the position to get that sort of ball to the strikers. Teams wanted to, and still do, play like Real Madrid, but there is no doubt that teams all over Europe copied Sir Alf's system, and I felt that football was pretty boring as a result. There wasn't enough excitement, and little or nothing came into the penalty area. Even Matt Busby tried to follow the trend, but thankfully it didn't last very long and fizzled out. I think he got as bored with it as we were. It was not the way we played football at Old Trafford.

But, again, Ramsey won the World Cup with 4–4–2, something no other England manager had ever achieved, so how can you criticize his tactics? It was a system whereby a good team rarely conceded, but at the same time you weren't scoring the goals you would normally. To be fair to Ramsey it was a needs-must situation: he didn't have any good wingers, but he did have a strong midfield. He had powerful players and plenty of grafters, with little Alan Ball, in particular, up and down that right line.

I'm not against any of the English lads who played in the World Cup, a lot of them have become very good friends of mine over the years, but to think that Jimmy Greaves wasn't in the team makes the mind boggle. Again, it's a difficult point to argue because Ramsey brought in Geoff Hurst who scored a hat-trick in the final, something no-one has done since, but it wouldn't have been the team I would have picked. Greaves would have been in it no matter what happened. He was the best striker in the world. Alongside him as the heart of the side would have been Gordon Banks and skipper Bobby Moore. One of the great things about football is that it's subjective, and we all have our own opinions.

The other thing that disappointed me was the fact that the Queen and successive Prime Ministers decided not to honour the entire squad. Why did Alf Ramsey receive a knighthood and Bobby Moore an OBE and the others nothing? The whole team played its part, including the subs; they won the World Cup collectively. It was only much later that some of the others received recognition, George Cohen and Nobby Stiles just last year. Maybe Bobby, as captain, should also have had a knighthood, and then the rest could have been given an OBE or whatever. That would have been the right thing to do. I suppose the reason was that football did not command the same interest then as it does now, and I don't think people realized until years later, after successive England failures to recapture the crown, what an incredible achievement it was. They have been near a couple of times, though, particularly under Bobby Robson in 1990, and those were away from home. Can you imagine, if England had won the World Cup in Japan and South Korea, how many OBEs and CBEs would have been awarded? Probably not many, because they would all have been knighted!

Yes, it was an unhappy summer for me, but at least I had time to have a good rest. My knee was still flaring up, but I was able to work on it all summer at my own pace, getting ready for what everybody connected with Manchester United was expecting to be another critical assault on the League Championship. We felt we just had to get back into that European Cup, now the unspoken target for all.

11 CHAMPIONS!

THE BIGGEST CHANGES AT THE CLUB FOR THE 1966/67 SEASON were the departure of John Connelly, who went to Blackburn Rovers, and, later in the season, the arrival of former Millwall and England under-21 goalkeeper Alex Stepney, who joined us after a brief stay at Chelsea for a relatively huge fee for a goalkeeper of £55,000. Hopes were high for another big campaign, but we could not have made a worse start that summer. A really bad pre-season suddenly posed all sorts of questions. We lost 4–1 to Celtic in what was a battle royal. I am Scottish, but it made no difference and I was clobbered as well. We were all caught up in the middle of the Scotland–England war in the aftermath of England winning the World Cup; Celtic treated the game as though it were the European Cup final. It certainly set them up for the season, for that was when they went on to win the European Cup, beating Inter Milan 2–1 in Lisbon in that famous match which left jubilant Scotsmen littered all over Portugal for the next few years. They were highly delighted when they beat us, too. We suffered another World Cup backlash from the still bitter Germans when we travelled to Munich to play Bayern. That 4–1 loss was quickly followed by a 5–2 thrashing at the hands of FK Austria. United had conceded thirteen goals in just three pre-season friendlies.

The reaction to this was predictable. According to the pundits, Manchester United were over the hill; we weren't doing anything, and everybody was writing us off. Munich survivor Harry Gregg shouldered much of the blame and was replaced by David Gaskell, who in turn was replaced by new boy Stepney when in December he joined the injury list; Harry left us later in the season to join Stoke City. Once the season began, there was little ammunition to fire back at our detractors: in August and September we suffered reverses against Leeds, Stoke, Spurs and Nottingham Forest, this last heavy defeat dropping us to eighth place in the table. Alex Stepney must have wondered what he had joined when he and I sat together in the stand at Bloomfield Road and watched United get clobbered 5–1 in the League Cup by Blackpool.

But a good team does not suddenly become a bad one. Personally, I was going well, having scored a dozen goals in eleven League games including my hundredth for the club against Everton in August in only 139 games. A nice little run however you look at it, and then, from 8 October, the team joined in: we went eight games undefeated and took fifteen points out of the sixteen available before losing 2–1 to Aston Villa, a useful team at the time.

It was a significant game in more ways than one, for not only did our undefeated spell come to a close, I began again to experience serious problems with my knee. I limped on, though, and the team went from strength to strength, making nonsense of our early-season form. Things went so well, in fact, that Boxing Day 1966 was the day of our last League defeat of the season, away to Sheffield United. This form did not carry over into the FA Cup, though, which was strange because we fancied our chances in the competition having reached the last four for the past five seasons. We started well enough on 28 January 1967 with a 2–0 win against Stoke, a game in which I scored the first goal to give me an FA Cup total of thirty-one, a record that didn't include the six I'd had wiped out at Luton. I scored another against Norwich in the fourth round, but they beat us 2–1 in what was probably the shock of the season, as Norwich were firmly planted in the lower half of the Second Division at the time. It was our fault for being too casual and taking too much for granted, but there was, of course, a benefit: with three and a half months of the season remaining, for once we could concentrate solely on regaining the First Division title.

In the middle of March we went top of the table after a goalless draw with Newcastle United at St James's Park, but a week later we suffered yet another injury when David Herd broke his leg against Leicester as he scored his sixteenth goal of the season. He chased a through-ball and was in the action of prodding it home when Gordon Banks came charging out, somehow managing to get his legs underneath Davie before Graham Cross tumbled on top of him. I knew it was broken straight away; the noise seemed to resound like a rifle shot. I was right next to Davie when it happened, and it was sickening. It was the first time I'd been on the pitch when something like that had happened. I'm probably exaggerating, but that horrible noise is something I will never forget. It was a bad break, too; Davie's leg looked as though it was hanging off, just flopping about with the bone sticking through the sock. It was awful. It also had terrible repercussions, as broken legs often did in those days: having been top scorer twice and second to me on four occasions in his six years at Old Trafford, Davie returned only briefly the next season before being sold to Stoke City. He had a fine record for United with 144 goals in 263 senior games, but for some reason he'd never been a great favourite of the fans, and a certain section had barracked him from time to time. But we played well together, and he was a good foil for me with his strong running and accurate shooting.

Davie was replaced by the versatile David Sadler, which drew some of the sting from our attack, but we stayed in front and finally clinched the title in the penultimate game of the season with a 6–1 win at West Ham – our biggest of the season. We knew that if we won at Upton Park we would win the title, no matter what the other results were, so far in our wake were Nottingham Forest and Spurs trailing. Everything went our way, and virtually every shot finished in the back of the net. It was a tremendous win because West Ham had a good team at the time. They not only had England skipper Bobby Moore but what seemed like half the England team as well. They were always a nice side to play against because they played good football, very much like the Spurs side of the time who always seemed to give us a thrashing at White Hart Lane while we returned the compliment at Old Trafford.

The championship was, to say the least, good, but the highlight of that season for me had to be beating the world champions England on their own patch just nine months after their triumph against West Germany.

Special moments, certainly, but I have no doubt now that playing with Manchester United during those years shortened my career. The care and medical treatment at Old Trafford simply did not compare with what I'd experienced at Torino. Perhaps I'm being a little unfair, because it wasn't just Manchester United, it was the entire set-up in England and Scotland at that time. We simply didn't put the same emphasis on the medical side as they did in Italy; there just wasn't the same medical expertise available to players as there was in Turin five years earlier. Torino looked after their players as though they were high-class athletes. We were really mollycoddled, right down to a massage every day. In England we never had a massage unless we were injured, and then they'd just rub your ankle or whatever bit was injured. At Torino they would test your heart, your pulse would be taken, and you would be checked over on a regular basis. They had all the equipment they needed, and they were always looking after you. When I came back to England it was back to the same old same old: a bit of heat on the sore spot if you were injured, rather like the bucket of cold water and the ubiquitous sponge. That sponge in English football has got to be the greatest invention ever because it sorted out all sorts of injuries. When that physio-therapist came over with his sponge and bucket of cold water in the middle of January you were up and running before they could reach you. Ice-cold water and a sponge cured everything from concussion to pulled thigh muscles. In England, racehorses received better medical treatment than we did.

Football's idea of curing an injury was to use cortisone injections. Cortisone was the common choice to 'cure' injuries back in those days; when injected into your body it disguised pain for three or four hours, converted into cortisol and influenced the nutrition and growth of connective tissues. The advice now is not to have more than one a month, with a maximum of three or four during the course of a year, and to avoid excessive movement or stress on the joint for about a week, but we were injected and told to go straight out and play. During those years I seemed to have one every week. If I had to do it all over again, I wouldn't have them. It doesn't happen today, thank goodness, but in those days everybody was getting injections. I used to come into the dressing-room at half-time with my knee aching and throbbing and I would sit in the big bath with a hosepipe spraying cold water on it in an effort to deaden the pain. That was the extent of my treatment. Then I would get out of the bath and go out and play. The most expensive player on United's books, and that was how I was treated. And not just me, I hasten to add, everybody was treated the same. Do that for a season or two seasons, just to deaden the pain, with regular cortisone injections, and it will begin to take its toll. It was and should have been unacceptable, but we put up with it without demur.

I just didn't think long-term when it came to my career. The culture at that time was to be ready for the next match whatever the problem, but because of the severity of my knee injury, this was not lengthening my career, it was shortening it. By deliberately deadening the pain month after month, I was doing long-term damage. Everyone would be delighted because I had got through another game, and then it was back on the treadmill, not training but having treatment for another week, then back onto the pitch for the next match – and this was the pattern for over two years. George Best was into all that as well for a long time with his bad knee: injections, hot and cold water, and aspirins. Looking back on it now, it's hard to believe. Nowadays clubs have realized how valuable their playing assets are; the training ground at Manchester United is just phenomenal, with physios, doctors, medical equipment, ultrasound – everything a finely tuned athlete needs. Physios in my time were just former football players who'd taken a short course in physiotherapy. I remember in the 1970s when we had the three-day power strike. Without electricity our physios were virtually knackered because they couldn't use the heat-pad machine, on which they relied heavily. It's at times like that when your real physio comes into his own, using his fingers, but our physio's only answer was a tube of red-hot Ralgex. If you missed and dropped it between your legs, you knew about it. You had to be very careful where you rubbed it, and make sure to wash your hands thoroughly afterwards.

Every man knows what I'm talking about. Just think of after-
shave, which stings for half a second when you slap it on; with
Ralgex I am talking about two hours of agony. The problem was
that often you did get it in the wrong place.

My knee problem got much worse in 1967. At the time I was
having trouble with both the club doctor and the team physio
because I was seeing my own osteopath, Mr Millwood, to whom
I'd been recommended by a friend of mine. I'd gone private
several months earlier because nothing seemed to be easing my
pain, but in those days an osteopath was not deemed to be a
legitimate man; in fact, he was considered to be something of a
witch doctor. They were so wrong. Mr Millwood looked after me
brilliantly and gave me what the others couldn't. He was so helpful I used him for several years, paying for it myself. When the
club found out what I was doing and expressed their anger, my
attitude was: 'It's my knee, it's my life, it's my career, it's my live-
lihood, and if you're not going to do anything about it then I've no
choice but to go and get someone else to look after me.' Mr
Millwood, in contrast, was a voice of reason to whom I listened
carefully. When he told me that I desperately needed a week off
training, I pretended I had a cold in order to follow his advice.

I wish, too, that I'd followed his advice to miss the 1967
summer tour to Australia and the USA – in more ways than one,
as it turned out, for during a match against a team from Sydney I
was guilty of losing my head. They had a very vicious little Scot
playing for them who seemed determined to earn himself a reputation against us as a hard man. He eventually caught Paddy
Crerand with a particularly nasty tackle, and Pat was carried off
with an injury bad enough to prevent him playing for the
remainder of the tour. I was livid because the guy had gone over
the top and caught him on the knee with the sort of challenge that
can end a player's career. And all this in a flag-waving friendly! I

told the little Scot exactly what I thought of him, and when he thrust his face into mine to respond I gave him the infamous Glasgow Kiss. I thought I had hardly touched him, but I caught his cheekbone and he hit the deck. He was stretchered off, and after the game I discovered he had been taken to hospital with a fractured cheekbone.

Word of the incident quickly got around, and by the time we had showered and changed the atmosphere outside the club was quite ugly. The people waiting outside the dressing-room were quite agitated. As I stepped out, this old dear came rushing out of the crowd with her brolly and started whacking me over the head with it. I quickly discovered that it was the injured player's mother, and she was yelling at me, 'You bastard! You nutted my son!'

And the backlash didn't end there. The following week we returned to our base in Sydney after another game away and Sir Matt wisely left me out of the team because of the follow-up stories in the press. It was gold dust for the Aussie journalists, who were pretty awful over there at the time; they had printed what they wanted and had stirred up so much trouble that Matt was worried I might be at physical risk if I played in the scheduled game.

I watched the game pass without incident, and afterwards I felt relaxed enough to go out when we were invited to a party some-where in the Sydney suburbs. It was a good party – the Aussies know how to let their hair down – and we had a great time. Before long, though, we decided we should be getting back to our hotel. John Fitzpatrick, another Scot, and I said our farewells, then this big guy came up and offered us a lift, a typical Australian gesture we were only too delighted to accept. We jumped into the back of the car, but within a few minutes we realized that we were being driven out of the city. I looked at John, he looked at me, and we both thought, 'Oh shit.'

We were halfway to the middle of nowhere when the big guy stopped the car, turned round and said, 'You know that little guy you did last week?' I gulped and nodded, and he added ominously, 'He was my best pal.' The big guy and his equally large mate told us to get out of the car, and we were about to be well and truly battered when, to our astonishment, instead of getting out with us, they just started up the car and drove off into the distance, leaving us in the bush.

I said to John, 'You do realize we've just got away with murder, don't you?'

That much was true, but then we hadn't a clue where we were, it was pitch black, and we were absolutely frightened to death. It was two or three o'clock in the morning, and we had to walk back along this dark road to our hotel. We didn't arrive back until about three hours later, relieved to be safe after our horrific ordeal. I'm not so sure that had that happened today we would have returned safely.

Strangely, that wasn't the only scary incident while we were in Sydney. We had just been out at another function with the club – it was just that sort of tour, and we did a lot of these social gatherings with as much good grace as we could muster. After this one particular event we returned to our hotel, which had corridors outside running in front of the rooms. I was walking up the stairs to our floor with John and Paddy when we realized Fitz's door was wide open. He had been burgled, very recently as it proved, as someone suddenly burst out and ran past us. Without thinking, we started to chase the guy down the stairs, but as we rounded the bend we saw that the burglar had stopped, was now facing us, and had a gun in his hand, pointed in our direction. 'If you come any closer, I'll shoot you,' he said. We froze, Paddy at the top of the stairs and John and I halfway down them. Fortunately, the guy then left.

In both instances, we sobered up remarkably quickly.

But it was perhaps as a result of all the games I played on that tour with my dodgy knee that throughout 1967/68 I played only twenty-three League games, many of them when I wasn't properly fit. Moreover, I scored only seven goals in the League and three in nine games in Europe. I had more treatment in that one season than a player should have in a career, and I ended it in a hospital bed. It was pathetic, really, and it should never have happened. I wasn't fit, full stop, and I should never have played until I was properly recovered. Occasionally I'd complain, but the club would continue to insist it was all in my mind. What was worse was the fact that I was one of those players who had to be fit for the sake of my confidence; if there was anything niggly about me it preyed on my mind and affected my performance. On top of that, to be at my best I had to be playing lots of games.

As professionals, we should be fit. The people who pay to enter the stadium expect you to be 100 per cent fit. Once you cross the touchline you are deemed to have declared yourself fit, but unfortunately in that era many players turned out when they were far from fit. Everybody played while carrying injuries; it was just what happened. I don't think it happens on a regular basis today, though there are still the odd one or two who escape the net, as evidenced by David Beckham playing in the 2002 World Cup. No way was he fit when he took the field, but who wants to miss a World Cup? You only had to look at his performances to know the truth: he was shying out of tackles and not playing to his usual high standards. I can understand it because as a player you never know if this might be your last World Cup, but it was Sven Goran Eriksson's job to decide. That's why he is paid so much money. The classic example of a managerial cop-out had come four years earlier when Ronaldo played in the World Cup final after being ruled out just half an hour before the kick-off against France. I mean, was that a joke or what? The man wasn't even half-fit; thirty minutes before the game he wasn't even on the teamsheet handed to the broadcasters and journalists in the press seats. Managers have said to me in the past, 'Maybe you're not fully fit, but your presence on the field is important.' That was their way of getting round it; you might make the opposition afraid, tie up a marker or two. But there was nothing Ronaldo could have done that day. He wasn't ready for that final either mentally or physically, and he could have done himself some permanent damage. It was awful, because it affected him for a couple of years afterwards.

My knee injury was not helped in the early rounds of the European Cup. We played Hibernians of Malta in the opening round on 20 September 1967 and were expected to score a hatful of goals. We managed four, of which I scored two, but it was considered a bad performance and a bad result – though not nearly as poor as the goalless draw in Valetta that followed in front of a Manchester United-daft crowd. The local fans, all of whom seemed to support us rather than Hibs, turned out in their thousands, outside our hotel and in the ground. Naturally they wanted to see all our stars, but with the game won surely that was an opportunity to rest players like George and me who were carrying injuries? Not a bit of it, even though the pitch was like an unmade road. Neither George nor I should have played. What a joke it was. Four goals up, playing a bunch of amateurs on a lethal pitch with a bad knee. I still don't know to this day why I played. Needless to say, the experience did my knee no good at all.

The best spell I managed that season was when I played thirteen games in a row, including one for Scotland, between September and the end of October. Every evening when I returned home from training, a match, or a day on the treatment table, I put hot kaolin poultices on my knee. The club had initially prescribed this, and I ended up using them every day, but even this backfired. You had to apply these poultices, filled with fine, soft, white china clay, when they were very hot, and gradually they tenderized my knee. It must have been rather like slow-cooking a chicken leg, and it made a hell of a mess of the sheets. My other home-developed treatment was alternate hot and cold water, which certainly eased the pain and allowed me to get some sleep.

It was a nightmare. All I seemed to be doing was playing, having treatment and playing again. Eventually this sort of routine becomes a mental problem as well as a physical one. Nobody likes to be injured, but when you're injured for that length of time and you're watching the others training and playing five-a-side, it begins to prey on the mind. You're part of a team, but you're not involved. Then, all of a sudden, you'll play a game and get your hopes up only to find that the pain is still awful and you can't turn sharply. That first yard was so important to my game. You've got the ball and you're away, hopefully with half a yard on the defender. That was my game. I was quick, and I had to get in there fast, but suddenly I found I couldn't do it in the same way any more. And all the time the club was saying they couldn't find anything wrong, it was all in my mind. It was enough to drive any professional sportsman mad. Nowadays I'd probably be sent to America or wherever to see the best specialist in the field, and I'm sure that would have happened then if I'd been Italian. They were light-years ahead in terms of diet, training and treatment. Italy was only just across the road in global terms, but nobody in England bothered to find out what they were doing for ages.

Still, for a sport that generated so much interest and so much cash, it is amazing that we weren't looked after better. It often felt like that Jane Fonda film *They Shoot Horses, Don't They?* about dancers who danced in competitions until they dropped. The same could have applied to footballers. You could have looked at many teams and found that they all treated their players the same: you played until you dropped. There might have been some clubs worse than others, but they'd basically all adhere to the same culture because no-one knew any better, medically speaking. What other country regularly turned their players into physios, and sometimes their physios into managers? Bob Paisley was the physio at Liverpool, and Bertie Mee held the same position at Arsenal; both became double-winning managers, but they were the exceptions. The physio when I was at Huddersfield was Roy Goodall, a former full-back who'd had the distinction of being captain of England when they lost for the very first time on foreign soil, beaten 4–3 by Spain in Madrid back in May 1929. I remember Roy leaving me on the treatment table once at Huddersfield and never returning. He just locked the ground and went home while I lay there on the table thinking that things were becoming bloody hot. I was nearly fried when I got up, took off the heat pads and went to find him. He had totally forgotten me, though I suppose he was knocking on a bit.

The odd thing during 1967/68 was that although everybody knew I had problems with the knee because it was always in the papers, the opposition never once targeted me deliberately. That was one of the reasons why I managed that thirteen-match sequence in the autumn of 1967, and after all that it wasn't my bad knee or any other injury that ended the run, but suspension. It had been a few years since my last sending-off, and in all that time I had collected only a couple of yellow cards. Sir Matt had worked hard on me in his office, lecturing me about the importance of not retaliating, of leaving things to the referee to sort out, but on 7 October I was banned for six weeks after a tussle with Arsenal's Ian Ure for responding with one foul to every four of his. The sending-off came in the 82nd minute when he kicked me again as

I lay on the floor; I took a swing, and referee George McCabe ordered us both from the pitch. The disappointing bit for me was that I missed Ian with my effort. I should have made the ban worthwhile. I was still relieved, though, because despite my recent good conduct the newspapers were predicting a much worse punishment of up to six months. I think it was nine games I missed altogether this time, and I felt aggrieved because I still didn't feel that referees were giving me any protection from late tackles with studs showing. If I was playing today, I'd be very happy: your marker has only to kick you once and the next time he's in the book or even on his way. In fact, watching the game and seeing how it has changed today, I think it's easier to play up front now. The referees are far more protective – and so they should be. People come to watch good footballers. Was it good for football when Pele was kicked out of the 1966 World Cup, Diego Maradona out of the 1982 tournament in Spain?

The funny thing was that a couple of weeks later I was asked to share a room with Ian Ure when we were both selected for Scotland for a home international in Belfast against Northern Ireland. Not so funny was the fact that we lost 1–0 and I took another kick on my damaged knee. I spent the whole six weeks of my suspension having treatment and was then told to carry on playing by Mr Glass, a private consultant who was widely used by football clubs at this time. I did as I was told and played seven more games, but by the end of January 1968 it was worse than ever. Mr Glass, too, speculated that the problem might be a piece of cartilage left over from the operation I had undergone while I was in Huddersfield.

After our 2–2 draw with Spurs at Old Trafford in the third round of the FA Cup on 27 January, Matt Busby decided that while the team was in London for the replay I should visit the Harley street specialist Mr Osmond-Clarke. So, while the rest of the team prepared for the match, I visited the highly rated orthopaedic surgeon who later treated the Queen and received a knighthood. The visit produced this rather damning report:

> The behaviour of the knee is a powerful indictment of its competence to stand up to professional football, especially in the years since late 1965. There may indeed be a tag of external semi-lunar cartilage still in the joint, and it might help to remove it. But the fact will remain that this is a degenerating joint and that nothing and nobody can prevent further deterioration, be it slow or fast. My own view is that this knee has reached a stage when it will handicap Mr Law in top-flight play, and I very much doubt whether it will stand up to it for more than a season or two. Even then I suspect the knee would give rise to many complaints and periods of unfitness. My conclusion is that if Mr Law and the club are agreeable, a chance should be taken on further exploration of the knee to prolong the life of the knee in first-class professional Association Football. I feel it would be reasonable to take a chance, but I cannot confess to being optimistic myself about the possibilities of a successful outcome.

At least for the first time the medical staff at Old Trafford were aware there was something genuinely wrong and that the guy who had done the operation in the first place had botched it. It seemed the guy who did that first operation in Huddersfield had not succeeded in extracting the whole cartilage and had left a piece in there which, at some early stage, had obviously been lodged until it was knocked loose. Still, although I didn't see the report until some years later, it was decided, would you believe, that I should continue full training while having Faradization treatment – the therapeutic use of an interrupted current to stimulate the nerves and muscles – and taking aspirins, with the position to be reviewed after four weeks.

During this period I managed to play two more League games, both with the help of cortisone injections, but the knee just got worse and worse. At the end of February, Mr Glass put me on the painkiller Protocain. For some reason, the knee blew up and I became delirious. That night United were due to play a European Cup match against Gornik Zabrze, and I was going to be playing, so I went for an injection at the Jewish Hospital in Manchester in the morning and then went back home to have a sleep. Because I was going home to sleep before a big game, Di had taken all the kids out so that I wouldn't be disturbed. It wasn't long before I woke up to see that my knee had blown up again, this time to about four times its normal size. It was as though I had elephantiasis! I couldn't walk, and there was nobody in the house to help me. I had to get off the bed, crawl down the stairs to the telephone and call the club to say that I was flat out and couldn't move. They had to send somebody round; I was too far gone to remember who it was. I was in a real mess, and the next day they had to syringe the knee, explaining that it was quite a complicated procedure and that they had to be very careful. So much fluid came out that they had to pour it into a bucket.

If February was a month of pain, March was no better when I came out of hospital after five days. With Di having gone to Scotland for the birth of our third child, it was a miserable time I spent living on my own and travelling to the ground every day for treatment. I played in just one game that month, on the 27th, when we were beaten 3–1 by Manchester City who were coming up on the rails as we stumbled with three successive home defeats and frittered away a five-point lead at the top of the table. Robert wasn't born until April, so I ended up on my own for eight weeks, cooking, cleaning and worrying about my ongoing injury. It was just an awful time. The only light at the end of the tunnel was the regular visits to my osteopath, Mr Millwood, who manipulated my leg and relieved some of the tension and pain. He was a huge help.

I recovered enough to play in the last five games of the season, including the first leg of the European Cup semi-final against Real Madrid on 24 April, but I missed the game in Madrid in mid-May having failed a fitness test. I wanted to play, but I just felt that I wasn't going to be able to give a proper performance because I was nowhere near fit. In a match of so much importance, the team could not afford to carry a passenger. I watched the game in the dugout with Sir Matt. I was so disappointed. Don't forget, I was captain then as well, so it was a hell of a blow not to be playing in this massive game in the Bernabeu. To make matters worse, Real Madrid were fantastic. By half-time they were leading 3–1 in front of 120,000 passionate fans, erasing our 1–0 lead from the first leg, and it could have been four or five more. Real players had scored all four goals – Pirri, Gento and Amancio for Madrid, and Zoco for us with an own-goal – with the little inside-forward Amancio their outstanding player. Sir Matt and I feared the worst, but it was Busby who undoubtedly changed the pattern of the game by telling the team, 'We must go out and attack. If we are going to lose, it might as well be by six goals.' When the Madrid players emerged for the second half, for some reason they stopped playing. I turned to Matt and said, 'I'll tell you what, we've got a chance here, they've jacked it in.' They were killing us, then all of a sudden they sat back on their lead and started to, not exactly fanny about, but just to sit back thinking they'd done enough to reach the final. But we weren't finished. David Sadler pulled back another goal, and we began shouting at centre-half Bill Foulkes, who wasn't a particularly good footballer but was one hell of a good defender, to get back.

Whenever he went driving forward, we yelled at him. Then he scored. They had this dugout at the Bernabeu which was like a sheet with iron bars, and when Bill scored I jumped up and accidentally hit the iron bar with my hand. The next day it too had swollen up to twice its size, black and blue.

We were in the final thanks to George Best's goal at Old Trafford in the first leg which few of us, if we were honest, had thought would be enough. After the game our coach was stoned on its way out of the stadium as the Spanish supporters reacted angrily to the defeat of a team that had been strolling into yet another European final. But what price me making the final at Wembley on 29 May? Sadly, I had no chance. Sir Matt suggested I went with the team to London to watch the game and have an operation afterwards, but I just wanted to get it done as quickly as possible and opted to go straight into Manchester's St Joseph's Hospital.

It was only supposed to be an exploratory operation, but they pulled out the piece of floating cartilage, put it in a jar and gave it to me. The surgeon made a great show of it and said to me, 'This is what came out, and your problem is over. It's just a matter of building your leg back up now.' It was an inch and a half long, and I must admit I had doubts it was mine. A whole cartilage is only about that long, and I'd already had mine removed! It crossed my mind that perhaps they had done another cartilage operation just before mine and got things mixed up. It would certainly be interesting to check the records to see whether there had been a similar operation that day.

One thing I had no doubts about, and that was that I was going to miss the European Cup final, the greatest disappointment of my career. I felt sorry for myself lying there in my hospital bed during the final. This wasn't just the European Cup final, it was at Wembley as well; it was like playing at home. I was traumatized, but I had to hide my emotions. At least I wasn't as devastated as I would have been had I just been injured the previous Saturday. Sadly, I'd had plenty of time to get used to the idea. I'd been there at the start against Hibernians of Malta, but had been suspended when United edged nervously past Sarajevo of Belgrade 2–1 on aggregate, and then debilitated when they defeated the Poles Gornik Zabrze by the same narrow margin in the quarter-finals. I was ring-rusty against the mighty Real Madrid in the semi-final first leg, a magical night, but I ran and ran and helped United to what turned out to be a valuable 1–0 win. Our reward for the brilliant fightback that followed in the Spanish capital was a place in the final against our old rivals Benfica.

I'm not a great watcher of football, certainly not when I was playing, but this was different. This was the European Cup final, and all the nurses at St Joseph's were Manchester United supporters. A few of my pals came in too, and along with the nurses we watched the match in my room and got bladdered together on a case of McEwan's. It was a great, emotional night for everyone. Benfica forced the game into extra time, Graça replying to Bobby Charlton's goal, but then United took over and ran riot in just seven minutes. George Best proved once again that scoring goals is really quite a simple thing, Brian Kidd added another, then Bobby added his second and United's fourth. I took the congratulations from my friends, the nursing staff and other patients, but it wasn't about me; it was about Sir Matt, a decade after he'd lain on what he must have thought was his deathbed. The cheers were soon mixed with tears as Matt Busby finally held aloft the European Cup.

12 A GRADUAL DECLINE

THE VICTORY AT WEMBLEY WAS THE GREATEST POSSIBLE TRIUMPH for Sir Matt Busby and Manchester United, but little did we know then that it was all going to be downhill from there. Having won the European Cup once, we really should have gone on and done it again, but I suppose at least we broke the mould and opened the way for other English clubs: Liverpool, who won it four times and finished second once; Nottingham Forest, who won it two years in succession under the magical touch of Brian Clough, who had almost taken Derby County there as well; and Aston Villa, who beat Bayern Munich in the 1982 final in Rotterdam.

Still, in the summer of 1968 the club and its players were on a high. I was finally declared fit to resume training on 11 July, which was a relief because it had been a long time, even though I had to build up my leg muscles again before I could contemplate playing. The match I was really determined not to miss was the notorious World Club Cup final; as champions of Europe, United had earned the right to take on the champions of South America, Estudiantes of Argentina. This annual meeting had been started in 1960, when Real Madrid (who else?) had thumped Peñarol of Uruguay 5–1 in the second leg to take the first World Club Cup, but the final had by this stage acquired a bad name as a result of the 1967 game when Jock Stein's Celtic were kicked to pieces by the Racing Club players. The Argentinians were venting their anger at some of Jock's pre-match comments and, of course, those of Sir Alf Ramsey a year earlier. For it was at the 1966 World Cup that Argentinian tactics were really shown up for what they were. They were absolutely disgraceful, and it was a joke because they were good players and didn't need to do that. They could have beaten England fair and square that day if they'd just played football, certainly if skipper Antonio Rattin had not got himself sent off. But they decided to resort to thuggery – Ramsey famously branded them 'animals' – and thuggery on the pitch cannot be tolerated. Much of it could be put down to weak refereeing, and we're still seeing plenty of that. For his part, Jock Stein vowed he would never play in the competition again if his club were in a position to do so.

Ours was, as usual, a two-legged final, with the first leg away. We departed for South America on Saturday, 21 September 1968, straight after beating Newcastle United 3–1 at Old Trafford, and it took the best part of a day to get there. Because of Celtic's problems and other experiences of European clubs there were some doubts over whether we should go, but Matt, despite his own reservations, decided that as the arrangements were already in place we should make the trip. We had been forewarned of a hostile reception at the other end, especially because of the presence in our side of Nobby Stiles, who had played in the England–Argentina World Cup game and had been branded 'El Assassin' by the Benfica manager Otto Gloria. His quotes to the local journalists were a disgrace, describing Nobby as 'brutal, bad intentioned and a bad sportsman' after his marking of Eusebio in the semi-final, and in our European club games.

With my injury problems, it would probably have been a good idea for me to pass on the trip, but having missed the European Cup final and so many other matches I was loath to pull out of any game, particularly one as glamorous – or supposedly so – as the World Club Cup. But it was a long and uncomfortable trip for me. I was sore after playing against Newcastle, and then I had to face this monumental trip to Buenos Aires via Amsterdam. It wasn't even as if we could stretch out in business or first class as we were all dumped in economy, crowded and with little leg room compared with the space up front. It was just horrendous, and when we arrived we discovered that they'd put us up not in a high-class hotel but in a place called the Hindu Club. I don't know how many floors high the accommodation was; I think it was about six or seven, but it could have been more. During our entire stay the lifts never once worked (though we were told that whenever we weren't there they miraculously began to function normally), so we had to climb up and down a dozen or more sets of stairs just to reach our rooms in these private apartments. Sounds good? Forget it. They were basic, and I mean basic: two wooden beds and very little else. Everything was done to upset us and create a bad atmosphere, even down to a reception an hour and a half's drive outside Buenos Aires where we waited and waited for the Estudiantes team to turn up. We went because Matt saw it as an opportunity to improve public relations and to develop some rapport with our opponents. We were continually told they were on their way but held up in traffic, so we waited for two hours. They never did turn up, nor did they ever intend to. In the end, there was nothing we could do but go back to the Hindu Club – another hour and a half's journey. And whenever we were at the Hindu Club there always seemed to be plenty of traffic moving around the perimeter, regardless of what time of night it was, all of them beeping their horns and revving their engines.

Imagine such tricks being pulled *before* the game and it can be easily worked out what it was like once the match started in the very atmospheric and intimidating Boca Juniors Stadium, known to all and sundry as the 'Chocolate Box' with its steep, almost vertical stands and enclosed arena. I had played all over the world, but I had never played in anything like that atmosphere, or against a team as dirty as Estudiantes. Within minutes I found myself agreeing with Ramsey's conclusions, probably for the first time in my life. These guys were animals. Take every trick and underhand ruse ever used by the Italians and double, no, treble it. They were kicking us off the ball; they were spitting; they were treading on our feet; they were using their elbows and fists; they were even, would you believe, picking us up by the skin or the hairs under our arms after knocking us down, making it look as though they were helping you to your feet. In the first minute, someone ran past and pinched me, and the next thing I knew someone had hold of my hair. And what did the referee, Señor Sosa Miranda of Paraguay, do? He offered us no protection, cancelled out a perfectly good goal by David Sadler, and sent off Nobby Stiles who had been butted in the face by Bilardo. Poor Nobby was hounded out because of his reputation. Every decision went against us, and we did well to keep our tempers in the face of extreme provocation. Nobby was not only butted, he was also punched in the face; he was suffering from cuts and double vision when he was sent off, not for retaliating or kicking but for showing his displeasure with a V sign. Bobby Charlton needed two stitches in his shin where studs had deliberately punctured his skin, and he was lucky not to have his leg broken. The rest of us suffered various bumps and bruises which we had to nurse on the long trip back home.

Looking back, that first leg was a truly frightening experience in a country where the army colonels ruled and people vanished without explanation. We didn't want any trouble in those circumstances. The real danger came when the supporters spilled over onto the pitch, aiming kicks or punches. What might have happened had one of them had a knife? It doesn't bear thinking about. It was the worst match I ever played in, without a doubt. It wasn't about football, it was about war. Football, no matter how tough and abrasive the game, tends to throw players together afterwards, and certainly later in life I got on with many a player who kicked lumps out of me, but there weren't any friendships made or banquets or anything after that Estudiantes game. As far as I can recall, we went straight back to the hotel in Buenos Aires and then flew off the next day. I think if there'd been a banquet there'd have been a fight. Certainly Pat Crerand would have had a word or two to say to his opponents.

Hooliganism, on and off the pitch, is one of the saddest sights in football. It was once rampant; it's controlled to a large degree now, but it's still bubbling under the surface. Although it is popularly labelled the 'English Disease', I think it came here from abroad, probably Italy via television sets. That's certainly where I first saw trouble on the terraces, and I'm sure a great deal of it was provoked by the actions on the field. Sure we had hard men and hard tacklers in the English game, but none of the play-acting, the rolling about and sprawling on the deck that so enrages the supporters. But children saw that sort of thing on their TVs and started to copy it. When the fans abroad began ripping up seats and throwing bottles, it was soon copied too. When I was playing in Italy there was always that undercurrent, the feeling that trouble could erupt at any time. I also felt it in places like Spain, Greece and Turkey when I was playing for Scotland, and I have to confess that some of the things that went on during those football matches could provoke the wrong sort of supporter. I was not as guilty as some, but I still had my moments when self-preservation was all that was on my mind, as in those games against Estudiantes. It has never been more important for all players to portray the right sort of attitude on the pitch.

Considering the circumstances, and the fact that we were playing for personal survival rather than a victory, we did remarkably well to hold these so-called 'Students' to just 1–0. The 'student' marking me looked more like an Apache Indian with his long hair and headband. He had a snarling face, too, which regularly came very close to mine. They were frightening to look at as well as to play against. (I met a couple of those Estudiantes players when I went back to Argentina with the BBC for the World Cup ten years later. My marker still looked like an animal.) At one stage we were wondering out loud whether or not we were going to get away from the stadium in one piece. We had come to South America to wave the European banner, play good football and make friends, but all we received was abuse and violence. We couldn't wait to get them back home and give them a footballing lesson.

But it was not to be. Estudiantes were a little better at Old Trafford but not much, and the game gradually deteriorated into another kicking match as they clung on to their slim advantage. Before long I was being carried off with a lacerated knee that needed ten stitches. Perhaps the goalkeeper did me a favour, because I was hell bent on revenge. I had made up my mind that I was going to give some of them a bit of a whack. I knew I would have to be fast to catch them, but I was ready – then I was stretchered off. The goalkeeper had caught me on the knee as we both challenged for a ball.

It all boiled over in the last ten minutes when the Yugoslav referee, by this stage really struggling to keep control, sent off George Best and his marker Medina after an off-the-ball incident.

George had been cruelly chopped down by his man after crossing the ball, and this time his temper snapped and he lashed out; Medina, of course, rolled over and over as though he had been poleaxed. It was a pity, because George had resisted all thoughts of retaliation for the first eighty minutes of the game, even when he was spat at directly in the face. It was 1–1 at the time, Willie Morgan having scored our goal, but we all thought we had taken it to a replay in Amsterdam the following Saturday when Brian Kidd scored, only for the referee to blow his whistle for full time and rule it out. Perhaps it was a good thing because we might not have had a team left had we been forced to play them again.

Many of the viewers and reporters did not see what went on in the second leg because so much of it was covert and off the ball. But take my word for it, Estudiantes were a very naughty team, and it still baffles me why they went into the games with the attitude they did when clearly they also boasted some very good players. The troubles in the competition continued until 1980, when the two legs became a single match played in Tokyo, where they were far calmer affairs in front of the staid Japanese fans.

That World Club Cup disaster was a bad start for us because we were desperate to do well for Matt who, having received his knighthood six weeks after the European triumph in his twenty-third year at Old Trafford, having built three great sides, and having won five League Championships, two FA Cups and the European Cup, had announced that he was ready to step elegantly to one side at the end of the 1968/69 season. Most of all, it was the European Cup we wanted to retain. We began the defence of our trophy in, of all places, Dublin against Waterford, and I celebrated my return to the competition by scoring a hat-trick (and missing a penalty) in a 3–1 win in Dublin. Then, at the beginning of October, I scored four more in the return at Old Trafford, which we won 7–1. Against Anderlecht in the first leg of the next round I missed another penalty, but made up for it by scoring two of the three goals in our 3–0 victory at Old Trafford. It looked to be a cakewalk, especially when we went 1–0 up in Brussels, but then Anderlecht came storming back at us and scored three times, forcing us to hold on to a victory we had taken too much for granted. European Footballer of the Year George Best grabbed a brace in the quarters against Rapid Vienna at Old Trafford in February 1969 to give us a good cushion against the Austrian champions, but sadly I had to sit out the return leg with injury as we drew 0–0 to ensure a semi-final meeting on 23 April with Italian champions AC Milan.

The San Siro in Milan is an intimidating place to play football, and our idea was to contain. But we were always a better side when attacking, and when Nobby Stiles was carried off with a locked knee our best-laid plans suddenly began to look rather ragged. Hamrin and Sormani scored either side of the break to leave us with a mountain to climb at Old Trafford. It didn't help on the night having young full-back John Fitzpatrick dismissed for retaliating against Hamrin. The Italians are at their best when protecting a lead, and on 15 May at Old Trafford they packed their defence and resorted to all their old tricks on the blind side of the referee. As bad as anyone that night was my old Torino friend Roberto Rosato, who was set the task of marking me any way he wanted. I warned him again and again, but he ignored me, and in the end I was forced to take my own form of retribution, again on the blind side of the referee. I confess I punched him straight in the mouth after a particularly bad assault, and he lost two front teeth as a result. Worse than that, however, was the missile that was thrown from the Stretford End; it hit Milan goalkeeper Cudicini, father of the current Chelsea goalkeeper, and knocked him out.

But I remember that night particularly for some seriously

dubious decisions. We had put ourselves back in the game with a goal from Bobby Charlton, brilliantly made by George Best, and were looking for a second to carry the game into extra time. At one stage I scrambled the ball over the line, but a defender quickly emerged from the pack and hooked it out of the goal. The French referee waved play on. I couldn't believe it. Neither could Willie Morgan, the nearest of the other players, who could easily have made certain of the goal by rapping the ball into the back of the net, but he was as convinced as I was that the ball had crossed the line. Indeed, television replays proved it. Had that goal counted we would have been favourites to reach the final against Ajax, even if it had gone to a replay in Brussels. Ajax were not yet the force they were to become in Europe, and AC Milan demolished them 4–1 to win the cup. Some years later, the *Sunday Times* pointed the finger at several Italian clubs that had been guilty of offering gifts to referees, and AC Milan were one of them. The article listed quite a number of games involving Italian teams during which strange decisions had gone against the opposition. Had the referee awarded my goal against Milan, I'm convinced we would have won the tie, and the final against Ajax. I really felt bad about that one, especially as I'd had to sit out the European Cup final the previous year, but once the referee's made his mind up, what can you do?

We'd all been hoping so much to give Sir Matt a tremendous send-off in his last season, but it wasn't to be. Our League form throughout the season wasn't good enough either; by March 1969 we had slumped as low as sixth from bottom, though we pulled ourselves together and rallied to finish the season in eleventh place. During these months, though, we had suffered a catalogue of injury problems. It had soon become evident, for instance, that my knee had not been fully cured by the operation I'd undergone in May 1968 and I was forced to miss a dozen games. At least I was more fortunate than John Aston, who broke his leg as early as August, forcing Matt Busby into the transfer market to buy Willie Morgan. Bobby Charlton was suffering with knee ligament trouble and was missing from the side for over two months, both Nobby Stiles and Francis Burns had cartilage problems, and Tony Dunne broke his jaw – and on top of all that we had the usual little niggles and absenteeism.

At the end of that frustrating 1968/69 season, Sir Matt, suffering from ill health and a bad back, retired and the critics lashed us for being an aged team, even though we'd come within a whisker of retaining the European Cup. It was a cruel, hard world. The reporters had begun to say 'This is the end of the team' after that Milan semi-final, but would they have said that had we won the European Cup for a second successive season, as we should have done? I doubt it very much. But after the defeat everybody started to think the same way; I think we even started to believe it ourselves at times. We weren't that old as a team – I was twenty-nine, roughly the same age as Pat Crerand, Bestie was considerably younger, and Bobby was just thirty – but because we hadn't won anything that year suddenly we were written off, and, indeed, we started to go. I am certain that happened as much as anything as a result of the psychological effect of everyone telling us we were on the wane.

The most important change of the season came in April 1969, which was when an ailing Matt Busby sensibly moved himself upstairs to become general manager, and our reserve-team coach Wilf McGuinness was promoted to first-team coach with responsibility for running the team from the start of the 1969/70 season. Wilf's appointment came as a surprise to just about everyone, inside and outside the club. Clearly, though, it was going to be difficult for anyone to take over from a giant like Sir Matt

Busby, and under the circumstances Wilf did a good job, but it was perhaps a case of the right man at the wrong time. The job came too soon for him, and at just thirty-one he was too young. The other problem he had to contend with was that he was too close to many of the players. He'd actually played with some of the players in our first team, which made his job even more complex.

It's a problem the club will have to confront again very soon when Sir Alex Ferguson finally steps down. There will always be somebody to take over, but not necessarily the right man. The club has to be big and decide how to do it properly. They have to ask the question of whether to bring in a stopgap before a major appointment, or go for the big name straight away, and there are, of course, no guarantees. Take Bob Paisley at Liverpool. He was a stopgap after Bill Shankly, and what a stopgap he was! He turned out to be one of the most successful British managers of all time with even better results than Shanks. Joe Fagan did exactly the same thing when he took over from Paisley; he didn't just keep things going, he made changes then left a good team for his successor, just as Paisley had done. But Wilf was introduced when the team was on the slide, and he didn't have the experience of a Paisley or a Fagan to hold it together, let alone improve on it. The players backed him, as you would back any manager to see how he gets on, but there were doubts, not just because of his tender years but because we felt he was still one of the lads.

He'd always been at the club joking with all the senior players, then all of a sudden he was the boss. It was not an easy adjustment for us, nor for him. We knew one another too well. We'd been out drinking as a group. You can't just change your relationship with someone overnight. If the boss of a club knows the players like that, knows our haunts and has even been out with us, does he now turn a blind eye or does he crack the whip?

I firmly believe it was the wrong appointment, if only for that reason. Wilf was too young, too close to us. Had he gone away somewhere, put in his time with another club and gained a bit of experience, he could have come back a few years later. He was undoubtedly a capable coach, had even been part of the coaching squad under Sir Alf Ramsey when England won the World Cup, a good entry on anyone's curriculum vitae. He came in with lots of new ideas, too, but while the finger of blame was pointed at the senior players for not fully getting behind Wilf, the truth of the matter was that he tried to change our entire philosophy in an instant, switching from what was basically an attacking side to a much more defensively minded unit.

Moreover, because Wilf had been one of the boys, he seemed to feel the need to prove himself, to show how strong he was. Certainly he had to do something, because after opening our 1969/70 League campaign with a draw at Crystal Palace we lost two successive home games against Everton and Southampton, the last by four goals to one. Ron Davies, the powerful Welsh international centre-forward, exposed our defence that day, and it wasn't surprising that the now ageing Bill Foulkes, still playing at thirty-seven, was dropped for the visit to Everton along with goalkeeper Jimmy Rimmer and defender Shay Brennan. But the biggest shock was the axing of me and Bobby Charlton. I was absolutely stunned, and Bobby was very upset. It was the first time either of us had been dropped by United. The changes were unsuccessful: we lost 3–0 at Goodison Park, and consequently both Bobby and I were restored for the goalless draw with Wolves, along with our new signing from Arsenal, my old international colleague and sometime sparring partner Ian Ure. I felt at the time, and I still feel the same way now, that Wilf only dropped us to show that he was the boss. I mean, he only left us out of one game, so there couldn't have been any other reason, unless someone upstairs had had words with him. He'd also, of course, picked two of the biggest names in the club. I'm convinced it was a token gesture, as if to say to everyone, 'I'm not afraid to take tough decisions, and everyone has to work hard for his place.' I couldn't work hard for my place after that Wolves game because I strained my groin and was out of action for twelve weeks.

The other dramatic change Wilf introduced was the dressing-room blackboard, on which team tactics could be demonstrated. But we just weren't that sort of team. Matt had never got a black-board out. All of a sudden it felt like we were back at school, and it was a bit embarrassing. You don't need to tell senior inter-national players the sort of things Wilf would tell us to do on his blackboard: who to pick up here, what to do there, how to put that situation right, etc. It reached the unfortunate stage where we were taking the mickey out of his system. Wilf had these magnetic players to attach to his board, and when he was away we took to slipping an extra player on. We would then set him up by asking questions about who was picking up who until he dis-covered he had one too many defenders or attackers. Perhaps it was a bit childish, but at least it helped to hasten the departure of the despised blackboard. We also used to ask him difficult questions on tactics, which he found hard to answer. I just think we were too experienced as players to be told how to play football like that. In another walk of life the senior people would have taken Wilf to one side and passed on some advice, but footballers don't do that. They tend to wait and see what happens. You don't interfere; you listen, and maybe ask some questions, though we would never have asked questions of Sir Matt.

Injury kept me out of action for much of the season, and players like Pat Crerand and Willie Morgan found themselves out of favour as Wilf brought in some of his youth and reserve-team players who were more attuned to his defensive demands. My direct replacement was a young ginger-haired striker with a strong Italian background by the name of Carlo Sartori (it was Carlo who had come on for me during the second leg of that World Club Cup final at Old Trafford when I had to go off with a lacerated knee). He still lives in Manchester, and he sharpens my knives. I leave them at the fishmonger's and pick them up the following day. It's a job his dad used to do. I seem to remember, too, Carlo going 'home' to Italy for a long holiday. He'd lived in Manchester since he was a little boy, but the Italians kept him because he hadn't done his National Service. He had to serve for something like six months. He played for Bologna, probably at the same time as he did his National Service, but eventually came back to Manchester. Carlo was a player of promise that he never fulfilled. He worked desperately hard on his game, but he lacked a touch of class and played only forty games all told for United.

With this 'new' side, we managed to finish eighth in the League and reach two semi-finals. In December 1969 we lost 2–1 to Manchester City in the first leg of the League Cup semi-final thanks to a disputed penalty given by top FIFA referee Jack Taylor. As we left the field, George Best angrily knocked the ball out of Taylor's hands and was subsequently suspended for a month. I missed that first leg, but played in the second and scored an early goal to pull the scores level, but in the end we went out 4–3 on aggregate, losing our way when Alex Stepney saved a Francis Lee free-kick only to parry it to Mike Summerbee, who scored. It was an indirect free-kick, too, and the irony was that had Franny's shot beaten Alex it would not have counted. A month later, on 24 January 1970, we beat City 3–0 in the fourth round of the FA Cup at Old Trafford, and in the fifth we thrashed Northampton Town 8–2, George scoring six on his return from suspension. I missed that game too – in fact I was constantly in and out of the side through injury – but we kept moving in the right direction, beating Middlesbrough 2–1 in a replay to set up a semi-final clash with our old friends and reigning champions Leeds United. We drew the first game at Hillsborough, and when the replay too went into extra time at Villa Park I was sent on as a substitute, and within a minute missed an absolute sitter with my first touch of the game. If only it had come a few minutes later! That game was again drawn, but we eventually went out to a Billy Bremner header.

Once again injuries had dominated my season. I struggled all year and played in only ten League matches, scoring just two goals. In April 1970 the retained list came out and I was transfer-listed for £60,000. I was written off. Manchester United were saying they no longer wanted me. Worse than that, it seemed no-one else wanted me either, for no bids were tabled. Everyone thought I was finished, and I was not taken on a close-season tour to the United States. Finding myself with three months to spare, the season having finished early in April to accommodate the Mexico World Cup, I made up my mind I was not going to be written off and spent the summer getting fit, as I had done in 1966. I trained six days a week at the club, and three days a week in a private gym in the basement of a house five minutes away from my home, where I did weight training to build up my leg muscles. That took some mental effort on my part, I can tell you, but at the age of thirty and with my history of injuries, it was something I felt I had to do. The only break I had was when I took a couple of weeks off when my fourth son Iain was born on 5 May. I had to go through the pain barrier, but when all the lads reported back for training I was fresh and as fit as I could expect to be in the circumstances.

Before the 1970/71 season started, Wilf McGuinness was, as had been promised, officially promoted from first-team coach to team manager, but he was to be gone before the end of the year.

Nothing further had been said to me about my transfer listing, and it just seemed to die away as we moved into the new season. Again we started poorly, with just a single point to show from our opening three games, but we gradually began to pull it round and reached the semi-final of the League Cup for the second successive season, with wins against Aldershot, Portsmouth, Chelsea and Crystal Palace. We were odds-on favourites to go all the way to the final when we were drawn against Third Division Aston Villa, but then we hit a wall. Our dreadful sequence began ominously at Old Trafford on 12 December with a disastrous 4–1 defeat at the hands of our local rivals Manchester City. Four days later we drew with Villa in the semi-final first leg, again at Old Trafford; six days before Christmas we were thumped 3–1 by Arsenal; and then came the final indignity, a 2–1 Villa win in the second leg, despite our taking the lead through Brian Kidd. The writing was on the wall for Wilf when Andy Lochhead and Pat McMahon scored those goals to put Villa through to Wembley. On Boxing Day we battled to a 4–4 draw with Derby County at the Baseball Ground, but it wasn't enough to save our manager, who was sacked three days later.

Sir Matt Busby returned to take charge until the end of season, and the first thing he said was, 'Let's get back to playing football and enjoying what we are doing.' We were eighteenth in the League that Christmas, but Matt brought back some old faces and dragged us back to eighth, though we still went out of the FA Cup at the first hurdle to Boro in a replay. Matt's first League match of 1971 was away to Chelsea, and although we won 2–1 – only our third away win of the season – it was notable for the absence of George Best, who missed the train for London. George had already been in trouble for failing to turn up for training on Christmas Day, and for arriving late at an FA disciplinary hearing that January. Matt, who had been a great supporter of George over the years, finally ran out of patience with him and sent for John Aston to take his place at Stamford Bridge. That was the start of two traumatic years which eventually led to George quitting the club and the game for a while.

I remember that day when George failed to turn up for training. It's one thing you just can't do in the football world and expect to get away with it. No manager worth his salt would stand for that type of behaviour; if he didn't take action, the players would lose all faith in him. This was the time when George really started going on the blink. He blamed it on his disappointment at the fact that no new players had been bought by United, and that we were getting old, but I think that was just an excuse for his lifestyle at the time. Certainly some of the players were getting a bit old, though. Bill Foulkes, for instance, was a veteran. I know Sir Matt had tried to buy Mike England, but Blackburn had refused to sell him, although eventually he left Ewood Park to join Spurs. He could have made a major difference to our side because he was an excellent player, but he didn't come and went on to have a wonderful career at White Hart Lane.

Anyway, we weren't playing badly in 1971. Sir Matt's win against Chelsea on 9 January began a run of nine points out of a possible ten and included a satisfying win over Spurs on the thirteenth anniversary of the Munich disaster, our first home win for a startling three months! There were a few stutters, but by the end of the season we were playing with our old freedom, and on 5 May we even managed to avenge our defeat by Manchester City when we beat them 4–3 at Maine Road by throwing everything into attack as we used to do, with a forward line of me, Alan Gowling, Bobby Charlton, Brian Kidd and George Best, who was briefly back in favour. George scored two while Bobby Charlton and I scored the others. What about the old boys now? But there was a sad end to the season for my old buddy Pat Crerand, who was sent off against Blackpool in the penultimate match of the season. It meant he started the 1971/72 season under suspension, and he never regained his place in the side. Still, having started the season on the transfer list, I was very pleased with the way things had finished, and despite the ongoing injury problems I scored fifteen goals in twenty-eight League appearances.

But perhaps we'd been inspired by Sir Matt Busby's return. He had not wanted to come back in January 1971, but he'd felt he had to when Wilf McGuinness was sacked. It was a turbulent period for the club. There was unrest within the camp and a lot of dissatisfaction with George Best not turning up for games. It could not be tolerated, but Matt didn't really have the stomach for a fight any more. There had been a lot of unreasonable expectation on his shoulders too; everybody assumed success would follow him wherever he went. It was a big burden to carry, and he was never going to continue with it into 1971/72.

Having gone in 1969 for a young, inexperienced manager in Wilf McGuinness, the board this time decided they would plump for someone with greater maturity and experience. I'm not at all certain he was the first choice, but in the end they went for Frank O'Farrell, who arrived at Old Trafford from Leicester City via Weymouth and Torquay, and with him he brought former West Ham United player Malcolm Musgrove from the so-called Academy of Science. For a while it looked to be an inspired choice. Because some crazed fan had thrown a knife onto the field during a game with Newcastle the previous season, we were ordered to play our first two home matches away from Old Trafford, but despite this handicap we started really well, drawing at Derby and winning at Chelsea, and then beating Arsenal at Anfield and West Bromwich Albion at Stoke in our 'home' matches. In fact, so good was our start that we lost only once, against Everton by a single goal, until we were beaten by the same score at Leeds on 30 October. By the end of the year we were top of the division with a five-point cushion and the goals were flowing, George having scored seventeen and me a dozen. But doubts were already being broadcast by some of the top people in the game, Manchester City boss Malcolm Allison in particular saying out loud that we would not finish in the top three.

Sour grapes? No. The unpalatable truth. Throughout 1971 we played above ourselves; it was a case of individuals doing the business against the odds. Certainly our outstanding start to the 1971/72 campaign had little to do with Frank O'Farrell. I don't mean this disrespectfully to Frank, but he did come to Old Trafford as a stranger and he left as a stranger. We never got to know him, never really found out who he was or what type of guy he was. He remained very aloof from the players. In the time he was with us, from June 1971 to December 1972, we hardly ever saw him; it was Malcolm Musgrove who did most of the speaking, and certainly most of the training. They might have learned this way of going about things at another club with different traditions, but at times it was as though they were from another planet, such was the lack of communication and understanding.

There's always a dodgy transition period when a football club changes its manager. Wilf was brought in at the wrong time, and now, it seemed, Frank was the wrong man. The difference was that I liked Wilf. I felt sorry for him and had nothing against him. Frank O'Farrell was a different ball game. Malcolm Musgrove was all right, but he was just a basic coach, not a manager. Frank just sat in his office, and the players never got to know him. Sure he gave a few team talks, but even then he appeared aloof. With Musgrove, there was too much fannying around. He was always a West Ham man, just like John Bond, Noel Cantwell and others who became managers from that club. They all had the Hammers way of thinking: very technical, very orderly in their approach to

A young me and an even younger George.

ABOVE: This was the dream squad that won the European Cup for Sir Matt Busby just ten years after he had almost been killed in the Munich disaster. My only regret was that I missed the final itself.

Empics

LEFT: A typical pose, right arm raised aloft to salute a goal as I share the moment of pleasure with George Best. He was to become a much better friend long after we had both finished playing.

Mirror Syndication International

OPPOSITE: Fit? I should say so as George Best and I show off our torsos in pre-season training.

LEFT: How do I get in these positions? This time my contortions lead to a goal against Crystal Palace in March 1974. *Action Images*

BOTTOM: Moment of despair! Have I sent Manchester United down with my last kick for Man City in league football in April 1975? *Action Images*

OPPOSITE TOP: Signing for Manchester City for the second time in August 1972, watched by directors Robert Harris and Eric Alexander and manager Johnny Hart (*right*).

OPPOSITE BOTTOM, LEFT: Denis at the Beeb!

OPPOSITE BOTTOM, RIGHT: Ready for Argentina – but not until I've changed out of the kilt!

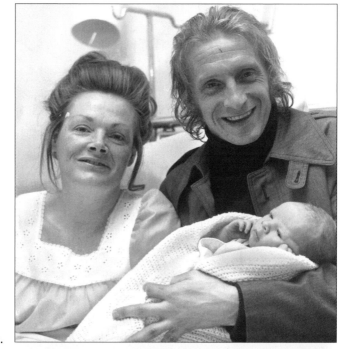

OPPOSITE, TOP: The Law family (*left to right*) Iain, me, Gary, Robert, Di and little Di, and Andrew.

OPPOSITE BOTTOM: Dad and Gary playing football – there's a surprise.

RIGHT, TOP: Now we have enough for five-a-side! My daughter and her mum.

RIGHT, BOTTOM: Who's that in the background? The twelve-foot-high statue of yours truly at the Stretford End, with (*left to right*) Iain, Andrew, me, Robert, little Di, Gary and Di.

Rod Stewart – our biggest fan!

the game; they liked to coach their players well, some might say overcoach them. It might have worked for some teams, but it certainly didn't work for us. It was the blackboard style of coaching again, without the blackboard this time.

Allison and others were soon proved right. After our scintillating start, the bubble burst and we started slipping down the table, eventually finishing eighth after a run of seven League defeats in a row. Our bad run had begun on New Year's Day 1972 when we lost 3–0 to West Ham. This was followed by successive losses against Wolves, Chelsea West Bromwich Albion, Newcastle United, Leeds (a fearful 5–1 thumping I happily missed) and Spurs. It was that thrashing by Leeds at Elland Road on 19 February that brought home the reality of the situation to us. We just weren't good enough, and we were getting worse.

Money was made available to O'Farrell, and with it he made one brilliant signing – Martin Buchan from my old club Aberdeen for £125,000 – and one disaster: Ian Storey-Moore for £200,000 from Nottingham Forest. Ian was an outstanding player but not a good signing because, quite simply, he wasn't fit. He'd been high on the list for a place in England's World Cup team in Mexico in 1970 but had pulled out through injury, and he'd continued to have problems. His track record should have rung the warning bells, but it didn't. Fast and with a powerful shot, Ian briefly looked the answer to our prayers when he scored a goal in each of his first three games for us, but then he was laid low with injury. We knew there would be problems from his very first day in training when he strapped up both his ankles. Clearly there was a weakness there, and he was also having knee problems, which eventually forced him out of the game. The laugh was on United, for Forest had earned a big transfer fee; Derby County, who had thought they'd signed him and had even paraded him on their ground before a match, were lucky to escape.

During this time we threatened another run in the FA Cup by beating Southampton, Preston North End and Middlesbrough, but in the sixth round we lost to Stoke after a replay. We'd also been drawn against Stoke in the fourth round of the League Cup, and that tie had required two replays. In fact, in seven League and cup meetings with Stoke that season, we beat them only once. They weren't a bad little team in those days. They had a lovely manager in Tony Waddington, who was relaxed and laid back and who could get all sorts of players who seemed to be at the end of their career to play out of their skins for him. He was at Stoke for seventeen years and guided his team of veterans to a couple of semi-finals in the FA Cup and the Football League Cup in 1972, when they beat Chelsea 2–1. That season he had players like Gordon Banks, Mike Pejic, Harry Burrows, Peter Dobing, my old friend George Eastham, Jimmy Greenhoff and Jimmy Robertson, and there were others like Dennis Violett, Harry Gregg, Maurice Setters, Geoff Hurst and Alan Hudson, to name just a few, who played for Waddington when bigger clubs overlooked them at the end of their career. They were never averse to a drink after a game, usually at the Railway Hotel opposite the station. Tony brought a bit of joy back into the game, and his players played good football for him. Everyone was delighted when they won the League Cup – except Chelsea, of course.

Team spirit might have been high in the Potteries, but at United we had George to contend with, and he was becoming more and more unpredictable as he struggled to combine his lifestyle with his football. At the tail end of the season he went missing again, this time from the Northern Ireland side that was due to play Scotland in Glasgow. A few days later, shortly before his twenty-sixth birthday, he turned up in Spain and announced his retirement from the game, but within three weeks he was back with us and, incredibly, was offered and signed an eight-year contract, which was unheard of at the time, particularly with such an uncertain soul as George. I still find it hard to believe today. It was Frank O' Farrell who offered him the deal, with the proviso that George moved out of his home and into digs with Paddy Crerand and his family. Everyone hoped this extraordinary action and even more extraordinary contract would get George doing what he did best.

The warning signs for United had been posted in the spring of 1972, but they were ignored, and we began the 1972/73 season in dreadful fashion. In mid-November we lost 3–0 to Manchester City at Maine Road and hit the bottom of the table. There were no grounds for complaint because we had opened the season with three straight defeats at the hands of Ipswich, Liverpool and Everton; we didn't record our first win until 30 September, when we beat Derby County 3–0. Before that match we'd hit the back of the net a measly four times. I had scored in that first game of the season at Ipswich, my lucky team, but I didn't record another League goal all season.

O'Farrell's response to that was to bring in two strikers, Wyn Davies from Manchester City and Ted MacDougall from Bournemouth, but it changed nothing as we crashed out of the League Cup to Second Division Bristol Rovers. Things went from bad to worse when George went over the wall again in November and was transfer-listed. On 16 December we were thumped 5–0 by an average Palace side, and three days later O'Farrell and Musgrove were on their way. It was hard to argue with the decision reached by the board as in forty-two games in charge O'Farrell had seen his team win only ten, draw eleven and lose a staggering twenty-one. The same day they sacked O'Farrell, the club also announced that George Best would stay on the transfer list and would not play for the club again. This was truly the end of the road for the old boys.

13 SHIPS THAT PASS IN THE NIGHT

I HAD GOOD CAUSE TO LIKE TOMMY DOCHERTY. HE WAS A BIG help when I won my first cap for Scotland at the age of eighteen, and while I was still at Huddersfield and he was with Arsenal he invited me out to dinner in London on a Saturday night after we had both played in London, and then we travelled up to Scotland together for an international. He showed me round Highbury, too, and years later he picked me to play for Scotland when I thought my international days were long gone. He even made me captain. He was a colourful and extrovert figure who had enjoyed his life in management, not only with Scotland but also with Chelsea, Queens Park Rangers, Aston Villa, Rotherham United and Porto in Portugal. I was particularly impressed by the Doc's management skills during a 1972 summer tour of Brazil with the Scotland squad, and I told Sir Matt all about his abilities and adaptability when I got back. Once, we'd found it too hot to train at the prearranged time, and when the Doc was told he immediately called it off and rearranged the session. He was very good with the lads in ways like that. He also showed his grasp of selection strategy and onfield tactics; in the match against Brazil on 5 July we only lost in the last few minutes when Jairzinho scored from nowhere.

When December 1972 came around and the problems with Frank O'Farrell became apparent, Busby called me in to talk again because he remembered me coming back from the tour and saying how well Tommy Docherty had done. I repeated to Sir Matt right away that the Doc was as good as anybody I knew, that I felt he could get United out of the hole we were in, and that there was the possibility that he was available. So it was pretty much on my word that Manchester United went and got him on 29 December, and he brought with him his old pal from Hull City Tommy Cavanagh, who coincidentally had been a player at Huddersfield when I was there.

It seemed to be a good appointment, too. The Doc did indeed get United out of trouble and we moved up the table as high as thirteenth place before losing our last two games of the season against Sheffield United and Chelsea. Because of injury, I had played only a couple of games for him, but our relationship was, I thought, good and I was looking forward not only to the 1973/74 season but to a long-term future at Old Trafford as the Doc had talked extensively about my joining the staff when I finally hung up my boots. It was often a subject of discussion over dinner on a Saturday night, when Di and I would go out for a meal with Pat Crerand and his wife. When Doc appointed Pat to the staff, Pat invited the Doc to join us on our Saturday evenings. That was when he assured me I had a job for life at the club.

The Doc had come into the club with all his usual gusto and made an immediate impact with his motivational skills. He also brought in some of the Scots he knew so well, like George Graham, Lou Macari, Alex Forsyth and Jim Holton. I was of course delighted with the way he had hauled us off the bottom of the table – my first concern was always Manchester United – but my impression of him gradually began to change as I got to know him better. It soon became apparent that Docherty was not a popular figure at Old Trafford, basically because the players did not trust him, and therefore felt insecure. The resulting bad atmosphere at the club was blamed on the old brigade disliking change, but that was a load of rubbish because football players go out and try to play their best every time. Obviously you play for the manager, but you're also playing for the people who pay to come and watch you. That's where pride comes in; you never ever go out and give anything other than 100 per cent. The difference is in the mind, not the body, for when you are discouraged or dispirited, no matter how hard you try nothing ever seems to work – and the cultivation of team spirit is down to the manager.

Four months after I had helped ease him through the front door, the Doc was easing me out of the back door. I wasn't in the team for the final game of the season against Chelsea at Stamford Bridge on 28 April 1973, so as two of my youngsters were in Scotland I thought I'd go up there and bring them back. Before I left, I popped into the office to see Docherty and he told me, 'Denis, we've decided to give you a free.' It was a total shock, I can tell you; I was totally unsuspecting after our previous conversations about my future with United. Di was expecting our fifth child at the time, we were about to move into a new house, and suddenly I was as good as out of work. I know I hadn't been playing, but I was only thirty-three, I still had a year left on my contract and I still felt fairly fit. I decided not to shout and scream. Instead, I sat down and had a discussion with the Doc, reminding him that I had a testimonial the following year that the club had arranged for me. He suggested we rearrange the testimonial for some time in September so I had only August to play out, and then we agreed I would announce my retirement on that night. He then gave me permission to travel up to Scotland.

It was while I was up there in my local with one of my brothers and two of his pals watching television that the lunchtime sports bulletin announced the news that Manchester United had given free transfers to Denis Law and Tony Dunne. After our conversation a couple of days before, I was gobsmacked. I had to phone Di and tell her that that wasn't what the Doc and I had agreed two days earlier. Tommy Docherty denied my version of the story in the press, saying it was the board not him who had insisted on going ahead with the free transfer. Naturally I went to see Sir Matt to ask him what had happened, because he knew of the arrangement that I was going to retire after my testimonial against European champions Ajax at Old Trafford. But Sir Matt was an old man now and he didn't want to become involved in internal battles.

I felt badly let down. For me it was an abrupt thank you and goodbye, while the club I had served for so long tried to make out it was doing me a big favour by giving me the chance to play out my days with a new club. I never got a chance to see Docherty to quiz him on the dramatic change of events because the League season had ended; when I went back to the ground to collect my boots, the place was deserted. I gathered my bits and pieces and cleared out my locker. There was nobody even to say goodbye to. I even missed out when the testimonial was finally played. The game had been billed as Denis Law meets Johann Cruyff, but not long before the match Ajax sold him to Barcelona, and I had to sit out the game as well with an injury. Despite the fact that the two key players were missing, there was still a crowd of 46,000 at Old Trafford, which made me feel very humble and grateful. Those were the loyal fans I could count on. But still I lost out: when the deal had been done, we'd assumed that Cruyff, the European

Footballer of the Year, would be playing and we'd made them a very sizeable guarantee, but his name was not stipulated in the contract and there was no offer to return any of the fees we had paid. I'm afraid that was typical football!

A few days after leaving Old Trafford with my boots in my hand, I was at the traditional Football Writers' Player of the Year dinner in London on the Thursday before the FA Cup final. At one point that evening Manchester City manager Johnny Hart approached me and asked me if I had ever thought of going back to Maine Road. I was flabbergasted. As far as I was concerned I had finished as a professional footballer, yet here was a First Division club willing to take me on. I didn't even give myself time to think about it, we just shook hands on it there and then in front of hundreds of journalists who had no reason to realize there was a big story right under their noses. The beauty of the move, of course, was that I didn't have to uproot my family. One of the alternatives I had when I left United was to go to America to join their newly formed league. They had tempted a few old internationals from around the world, but it wasn't for a year or two that it kicked off when players like Pele and Bobby Moore were signed. It was never a serious consideration for me because of my family. It just wouldn't have been fair, so it seemed ideal when City came in for me.

I immediately went to see Sir Matt, told him that Manchester City wanted to sign me, and asked him what I should do. He replied, 'If I were you, I'd sign. You've got to look after your wife and your children first. You'll probably get a bit of stick from the fans and the press, but ignore it.' I must confess that I'd already made up my mind to accept Johnny Hart's offer, but I wanted Matt's blessing. I knew all the lads at Manchester City anyway. Although the rivalry between the two Manchester clubs was intense, it was more so on the terraces and on the pitch than off it.

The camaraderie between the two sets of players was good, and we would go out for drinks together. Happily for me, it turned out to be a lovely year. Had things gone as planned, I would not have signed off my career by playing for Scotland in the World Cup finals because I would have been retired.

There was an unhappy sequel to the Tommy Docherty episode in 1979 when I was involved in a court case; it was only then that the story behind my sharp exit from Old Trafford became public knowledge. I had been called as a somewhat reluctant witness for Willie Morgan, who was being sued for libel by Docherty for calling him the worst manager in the world ever over something that had happened at a game at West Ham. Willie called up certain witnesses to tell different stories about the Doc, and mine was regarding what happened to me in those last days at Old Trafford back in 1973. I was saved from the ordeal when Docherty admitted everything, but then his case was thrown out because he had committed perjury over the evidence he was going to be giving regarding me, which meant I had to go back to court some weeks later. I hated every moment of it. It was nothing to do with me at all, but there I was at the Old Bailey, thinking, 'Crippen's been in this dock!' Being grilled for several hours by his lawyers when I was an innocent party wasn't a pleasant experience. Moreover, I knew that were the Doc to be found guilty, he was going down, just like Jeffrey Archer not so long ago. I didn't want to be involved in sending Tommy Docherty to jail, and I was honestly delighted when he was found not guilty. I don't bear him a grudge on a personal level, though it's hard to forgive him for what he put my family through.

Back in the summer of 1973, I was once again going regularly to the gym to work on the muscles in my right leg so that I would be as fit as possible for the 1973/74 season. I was dreading my first day back at Maine Road, but the players made me feel very welcome. In fact, it was as though I hadn't been away. Manchester City were and still are a big club with brilliant supporters, whatever division they are in. They were always a happy lot. Mentally I felt really sharp, and I proved it by scoring twice in the opening game against Birmingham City and then again against Stoke City a week later. I could not have been happier, my mood was reflected in my form, and before I knew it the new Scotland manager Willie Ormond was sniffing around Maine Road and confiding in his old friend Ken Barnes that I would be in the Scotland team to play the Czechs in a crucial World Cup qualifier at the end of September. We beat them after going behind to take our place in the 1974 finals, and I returned elated to Manchester, not only with the win but also with the birth of my daughter Diana.

It was certainly good to be playing with some top-class players. Francis Lee, Mike Summerbee and Colin Bell all played a huge part in Manchester City's surge to the top and secured for themselves a reputation as the crucial players in an exciting team, thrilling not only domestic crowds but also those in Europe. They had terrific flair. Colin was probably one of the best English players for many years and would have gone on to even greater things but for a really serious injury which put him out of action for a long time. He was indefatigable, so full of running. In fact, he never stopped, and his nickname 'Nijinsky' suited him perfectly. He was such an elegant runner, too. Francis was so strong and powerful for such a small guy. He knew where the goal was, had a great right foot and was a good all-round goalscorer. Mike was as tough a winger as I ever knew. That was unusual because wingers normally were not the bravest of players by nature. Full-backs were usually looking to kick them, but Mike got his dig in first, which usually made the left-backs start to panic.

It was a good side, and for a footballer approaching his mid-thirties, it was a busy season internationally and domestically. City had made a good start to their League campaign, but had suffered a lot of injuries with players like Franny and Mike sidelined along with me. The problems this caused made poor Johnny Hart ill, and he retired that November. It was a great shame. Johnny was a lovely man who had shown great faith in me. He was replaced by Ron Saunders, a completely different type of manager, a sergeant-major who didn't go down well with the troops, who weren't used to so much hard work without the ball in training. I think Ron made a major misjudgement in deciding to come to Manchester City. He arrived with set ideas and a rigid tactical plan. City were a team of flair with some very experienced players, wise in the ways not only of domestic football but of the game at all levels. Then in came this regimental type, barking his orders and making life very boring for guys who at that stage of their career did not need to be told how to play, what to do and where to pass the ball. None of the older players got on with him because of this, and because he wanted to veer away from the type of football the players and the fans were used to, the sort of football that had brought them so much success in the recent past. Ron needed a younger group of players to inflict his ideas on, not players of this knowledge and background.

Still, under him we did reach Wembley in the League Cup final, where we played Wolves. I had taken a knock in the first leg of the semi-final against Plymouth and was out of the side until a week before Wembley, and Francis Lee was struggling with knee problems of his own, but even so, on paper our forward line of Mike Summerbee, Colin Bell, Francis Lee and me looked about as entertaining and exciting as any in the country. Bell, however, was the only one fully fit. We played as awful a game as I have ever played in that arena with 100,000 fans watching. It was a big game and a big day, but we let them down completely. It was mainly because we weren't fit, and you can't play effectively at Wembley if you're not fit. Few get away with it, and we were found out very quickly. It felt as though we'd been playing for six hours with nothing going right for us. We started as strong favourites but never looked like winning as Derek Dougan and John Richards ran us ragged.

A week after that shabby performance, on 9 March, we were soundly beaten by Leeds, and I, along with a few other big-name stars, found myself out of the side and in crisis. Not only was I playing for the reserves, but Saunders, it transpired, had agreed to sell me to a Fourth Division side, Bradford City. I would have retired there and then, but the World Cup was only a few weeks away and I was determined to regain my place in the City team and at least give myself a chance of going to my first World Cup. I told Saunders I wasn't going anywhere and set my sights on becoming as fit as possible. I was eventually recalled at the beginning of April to play against QPR. We lost 3–0, but it was Saunders who was asked to leave the next day after just five months in charge. Right or wrong? Who knows? He must soon have thought it a good thing because he went off to Aston Villa where he was incredibly successful, winning the First Division title and the European Cup.

The simple fact is that the Manchester City players didn't like or respect Ron Saunders. Indeed, there had been something of a revolt in the form of a players' meeting to discuss the situation. We weren't happy with the training and we weren't happy with the way things were going on the pitch, and when that happens at a club the only way is down unless something is changed. Still, he had taken the club to the League Cup final, so I can only assume there must also have been problems behind the scenes, not only in the dressing-room. Ultimately, it rarely matters what the players think. It's what happens in the boardroom that counts. Personally, any respect I had for the man disappeared when he tried to sell me to Bradford. I felt insulted. There I was, preparing for a World Cup, and he was getting ready to sell me to a club in the lowest division in the country.

The players' dissatisfaction with Saunders could be understood to a degree because Manchester City had only recently been a great team, the most successful team in the history of the club, under Joe Mercer and Malcolm Allison. City had built themselves a reputation for playing with flair, but that wasn't the sort of team Saunders wanted. His ideas, though, simply didn't work. None of us was happy about how we were being asked to play, to such a restrictive tactical plan, and I think there was a general sigh of relief when he finally walked out of the door and headed down the motorway to Villa Park.

There were still four matches to play, and Tony Book became our third manager of the season. His responsibility was to ensure we did not go down. Tony was a good replacement, a decent human being. He had come into the professional game very late in life but become one of the most successful players in Manchester. In fact, in 1969 the football writers hadn't been able to separate him and Dave Mackay for the Footballer of the Year award; it's still the only time this prestigious prize has been shared. Ironically, we secured our Division One status under Tony with a 2–1 victory over Ron Saunders' Aston Villa at Maine Road in our penultimate game of the season.

In another irony, our final game was a local derby at Old Trafford, and it was a crucial game for United. If they lost they would go down; even if they won they would still be relegated if Birmingham City and Southampton won their games. I must confess that I didn't want to play. For all the bad blood between Tommy Docherty and me, I didn't want to send him and his team down. United meant too much to me. But as a professional, once I had been selected I had to play; all I could do was keep my fingers crossed that it would be a draw, with honour satisfied on every side. I even had a long talk with Tony Book about how I felt.

It looked as though my wish was going to come true as we both battled in vain until minutes from the end, when a ball flashed into the box and with a reflex action and my back to goal I stuck out a heel. The ball flew into the corner of the net past Alex Stepney. The rest of the Manchester City team dived on me, but I didn't celebrate. I was feeling sick, wondering what I had done. Had I just dumped my beloved Manchester United into the Second Division? The crowd poured onto the pitch and sheer bedlam ensued. I was totally depressed, wishing desperately that the ball had gone wide, and then Tony Book beckoned me off for my own safety. He need not have worried, though, the fans weren't after me. Referee David Smith pulled everyone off with eight minutes of the match still remaining, then called it off because of the pitch invasion. Quite rightly, the Football League ruled the result should stand, and United were relegated. The strange thing was that I did not get the anticipated stick after the game. The United supporters were fine about it, and there were no fists raised or even bad language when I left the ground. There was plenty of opportunity for such things because that night I went to see Rod Stewart at the Apollo in Manchester. Had there been any animosity towards me I would surely have found out then.

When I returned to Manchester later that summer, thrilled at having finally represented my country in the World Cup finals, it was to the news that City were looking to the future. Book wanted me to stay and play only home reserve games, just to keep me fit and ready for when I might be needed for the odd League game, but I didn't come back from the World Cup in West

Germany just to go straight into the reserves. To me, that was where a player started his career, not where he ended it. I went home, thought it over, and made the decision on my own. On August Bank Holiday Monday, I woke up and decided I was going to retire. I was fairly certain I could get back into the City first team, but pride is an awful thing – I can fully understand why it is considered one of the seven deadly sins – and I just couldn't get it out of my head that I was being expected to play reserve football. A lot of good players are happy to play at a lower level at the end of their career, simply because they enjoy playing and passing on their experience, but that wasn't me. In my case, pride overruled common sense. I wanted to go out at the top.

When I formally announced my retirement, many people believed that I'd made up my mind to quit the game during the World Cup, but nothing could have been further from the truth. I had enjoyed the trip, and it had given me a renewed appetite for more top-level football – and that was the key to my decision to retire, because I wasn't being offered it. That summer, Tony Book had been mulling over what should be done after an unproductive season for the club, and he made it plain to me that reserve-team football was my immediate lot. It had been a long season before the World Cup, interrupted by injuries, and if I'd thought about it a bit more, a rest at the start of the season with a few gentle run-outs for the reserves would probably have done me an awful lot of good in terms of recharging the batteries. But as I said, the thought of going from World Cup football to reserve-team foot-ball was at the time just too awful. Funny, I thought at that moment, that my last ever touch of a ball in professional football should be the goal that beat United and sent them tumbling out of the First Division. You couldn't really script a finish like that.

I subsequently received good offers from all over the globe, from Australia, Ireland, Norway, Holland, South Africa, the

USA again, and even Scotland from Hamilton Academicals. Looking back, I should have taken more time to think about what I was doing. I accept now that I retired a year or so too soon. I wasn't as sprightly in the summer of 1974 as I had been, but I could still score goals, even though my dodgy right leg was about ten years older than me! But I really couldn't stomach the thought of finishing in reserve football, so I left the stage, without really taking a bow.

14   WHAT TO DO NEXT?

WHEN YOU RETIRE AND YOU'RE ASKED WHAT YOU MISS ABOUT the game, if you're up to telling the truth you'll answer that it's not the game you miss so much as the lads. Suddenly you find yourself in the real world, somewhere you haven't been for twenty years. For me, the hardest thing was living without the atmosphere that surrounds a football club during a League season, the camaraderie, the socializing and especially the training with the lads. It took me several years to adjust to being without those things.

It might not have been the best decision in the world at that stage to quit football and walk away from a game that had given me my living for my entire adult life, and I was fortunate that my wife Di, whom I'd not brought in on the decision process, accepted it. She'd always accepted that her life was our family of five children, and mine was football – but now the two began to overlap. Club wages in those days were good to live on – I earned around £200 a week in the 1970s with United and City – but now, what with buying houses and bringing up four boys and a girl, there wasn't a great deal of money left, certainly not enough to retire on and take round-the-world cruises. I hadn't put any money into business or shares because I was frightened of all that; I felt I needed to keep what I had for my family. My major investment was the house, and I certainly didn't want to lose that because of a failed business venture.

What's more, when I left Maine Road and quit football I hadn't a clue what I was going to do. I had wrongly assumed at Manchester United that I was going to follow other long-serving players with a place on the staff until Tommy Docherty kicked me out. Naturally, I soon began to kick myself for being so stupid as to walk out when I did, and not to have put a lot more thought into it. Had I thought about things commercially instead of personally I could easily have landed a two-year contract somewhere and banked the money. The various possibilities have run through my brain over the years, and I have to admit that for the first few months after hanging up my boots, things were not good.

I was out of work, I had no nest egg, I was only thirty-four, I hadn't a trade or a profession, and I was struggling to adjust to life without a football club.

What I would have loved to do was coach youngsters; I'd honestly thought I was going to be doing exactly that at Old Trafford until I received that spoonful of nasty medicine. I thought about taking my Football Association coaching badge, but that was another area where pride forbade me to do the sensible thing. I was obstinate about it, because in many ways I didn't agree with those coaching schemes; I was a bit like Shanks in thinking that I had seventeen years' worth of League, European and international experience and knowledge to offer, so why did I need to take a course? I know I was again being headstrong, and that I should have swallowed that pride and taken my coaching badge at Lilleshall like many other retired or retiring footballers, but I didn't.

In the end, I knew I had to pull myself together, forget about football and start feeding my family, and I managed to find a job with a friend, a Manchester United fan, who sold carpets. Those first few weeks were a real shock to the system. Suddenly I was living in the real world, having been living a fantasy life where everything was looked after and taken care of, where I was taken here, there and everywhere, where I was generally protected from the outside world. Now, I was no longer training in the morning, sleeping in the afternoon and playing football on a Saturday; I had to get up at seven and sell carpets to earn money to look after my family. My one big advantage was my name, and I unashamedly used it to get me into places where others might not have got in. Guys like to talk about football, and if you can get a deal done because of it, all the better. I still had to come up with the right price, of course, but the name Denis Law opened doors and gave me a chance. After a while, I even began to enjoy it.

Sadly, after only about a year or so the company went bankrupt, and I was fortunate to leave with some redundancy money. But then, in 1975, the lifesaver came up: the BBC contacted me and asked me to do some summarizing on football matches for the radio. I have to confess that my immediate reaction was that I didn't want to do it. To tell the truth, I'm a bit shy when I haven't got my boots laced up. But in life I was fast learning that sometimes you have to do things you don't particularly want to do, certainly that I had to look after my family. Again I was fortunate, because as soon as I started doing the radio work I found I was enjoying myself, which surprised me because I'd never been keen on watching football. It was quite nerve-racking at the beginning, but the guys I worked with, Peter Jones and Alan Parry in particular, were as good as gold and they helped me enormously.

I'm afraid I can't recall my first game for the BBC, but it was certainly an experience. I went in thinking that all I had to do was chat about football, but it's not quite like that. That became obvious the moment I noticed my fellow commentators' carefully prepared notes on the two teams. They had done their homework while I had done none. I was intending to rely on my experience and knowledge to make the odd insightful comment, but that, of course, wasn't enough, and I knew that if I was to make a fist of the job I was going to have to get into it and learn a bit more about the players I had played with and against and the new ones coming through. It sounds an easy job when you're sitting in front of your radio listening to commentary, but it isn't, I can assure you. It's live, and you can't afford to make mistakes if you want to keep your job – and there were plenty of clangers in my early days on radio. One of the earliest came during a match between Manchester United and Wolves. United were well on top, so I made it clear to the listeners it was only a matter of time before United scored. Unfortunately for United and for me, it was Wolves who scored, against the run of play. Undeterred, I kept on about a United equalizer at any moment, then Wolves scored their second. I quickly switched horses, but no sooner had I announced that it wouldn't be long before they scored a third than United pulled one back. I quickly switched horses again, boldly forecasting that having scored once, United were sure to get another. Wolves made it 3–1. You'd've thought I'd learned my lesson by then, but I carried on in the same vein. United eventually won 4–3!

But you soon learn what is required of you in terms of being professional, and not to go over the listeners' heads by going too deeply into tactics or whatever – though a broadcaster must be careful never to talk down to his audience. I was given a lot of help and plenty of rollickings for saying the wrong thing about a referee or a player; after all, it could be slanderous. Occasionally I'd get a little figurative rap across the knuckles down my ear-piece: 'Be careful what you say, Denis!' Like anything in life, it takes a little practice and more than a little effort, but the lovely thing about reporting on football on the radio in those days was that from four o'clock on a Saturday your voice went round the world on the World Service. I had, of course, tuned in to the World Service myself whenever I was abroad playing football or on holiday, and it always made you feel a little closer to home. It excited me to think that there were people around the globe catching our every word as they listened to the match commentary and the scores of their teams as they came in to us.

It did not, however, pay fortunes, and when Francis Lee offered me a job in his paper business I jumped at it. Two wages are always better than one, after all. The work I did for Franny was similar to what I'd done at the carpet company: I was just doing sales and public relations and talking to big customers, hopefully getting into places where your normal salesmen might not get in. It kept me busy and, as I said, the extra money was very welcome.

But radio was what I enjoyed doing most. The BBC were marvellous to me, and over the years took me to some wonderful places and some amazing games. I remember being in Argentina in 1978 for the World Cup when I met this Scottish guy who was the chairman of a big company over there. When we were intro-duced, I said, 'Oh, are you British?' He knew who I was and what I was doing, and he answered, 'I listen to the World Service regularly, every game on Saturday and Wednesday.' He was so enthusiastic about football on the World Service that when he'd been given a new company car the previous year he'd turned it down because the radio, which came with it, couldn't get World Service. As I said, for many people it's a valuable link. I used to get letters from all over the place, little villages in Africa, townships in Australia and British troops stationed all over the globe. It was incredible. Football-loving World Service listeners from all over the world would ask me about my own playing days and which players I liked best; they sought my opinions on managers and international teams, and even, sometimes, asked me to arrange trials for them! I still get them now, addressed to 'Denis Law, Manchester, England'. I answer as many as I can, but sometimes there are just too many of them.

I went to Argentina for the World Cup because by that time I had three years' experience under my belt and the BBC felt I had learned enough to cope with the tournament, especially as Scotland had qualified again and England had not. That was an experience, not least because I was away for six weeks – as long as the winners themselves! Being an ex-player also opened doors that were closed to others, especially with the Scottish players in 1978, many of whom I had known from 1974 as well. They made me welcome, and I got on well with them. They accepted me far more easily than they would accept a journalist who had never played the game. It meant I got privileged access to the squad and picked up little bits of news that weren't generally broadcast. At first you never think what you're hearing is important, but you quickly realize a snippet about who might be in or out of the team is a gold nugget to a broadcaster or a journalist. The Scots would tell me who was hiding an injury, who was being left out and who was coming in simply because I was one of them, albeit a former player. It wasn't only my knowledge of the game the BBC was hiring, but my contacts too. (Of course, I was always discreet, always careful not to give away vital tactical secrets or other weighty matters that might have affected the course of the game.)

It was during that tournament that I experienced my most

enjoyable game as a broadcaster, the World Cup final itself between Argentina and Holland in Buenos Aires. It went to extra time before Argentina won 3–1, making worldwide heroes of players like captain Daniel Passarella, Mario Kempes, Leopoldo Luque and, of course, little Ossie Ardiles. The match was truly electric, partly because of the atmosphere surrounding the tournament. Of course, the entire host country went delirious with delight when the final whistle sounded, but there had been considerable carping beforehand, claims that Argentina had been favoured, Juventus manager Giovanni Trapattoni expressing the opinion that they would not even have passed the first round had the finals not been held in their country. A lot of people claimed it was fixed when Argentina came through their two opening games against Hungary and France, particularly the French game during which two penalties were claimed, one given to the host nation and one refused for the visitors. Then there was the political backdrop with the Argentinian military regime of General Jorge Videla. There were many who said both before and after the finals that they should never have been held in the country. The final was a great spectacle, but it missed Cruyff, who had pulled out as a result of death threats made against him.

Still, the Argentinian manager, Luis Cesar Menotti, had certainly developed a strong, attacking team that took full advantage of playing at home in front of some of the most passionate fans in the world. It was not long after the finals that Spurs brought both Ardiles and Ricardo Villa to White Hart Lane, and that – apart, perhaps, from Bobby Robson's acquisition of the two gifted Dutchmen Arnold Muhren and Frans Thijssen – was the start of the influx of foreign players into Britain. Both were incredibly successful, especially Ardiles, whom we all thought far too small to succeed, particularly on heavy pitches during the winter. But we were all proved wrong. Ardiles showed he was capable of playing anywhere, and Villa wasn't a bad player either.

That 1978 tournament was definitely one of the best World Cups, and I thoroughly enjoyed watching the matches. It was sad that England weren't there to contribute, and that Ally MacLeod got it so wrong for Scotland. He picked the wrong teams against Peru and Iran, then suddenly found the correct formula against Holland in Mendoza. That was another great game, Graeme Souness coming back into a side that needed to beat the mercurial Dutch by a three-goal margin. The Scots, to the Tartan Army's delight, went 3–1 up after going a goal down and looked more likely to score the fourth until Johnny Rep made it safe for Holland with a twenty-five-yard shot. It was a great shame because Scotland had a nice little side with a good midfield: apart from Souness, there was little Archie Gemmill, who scored a wonderful goal against the Dutch, and Bruce Rioch. If only MacLeod had done his homework a bit more conscientiously for those opening games . . .

My next World Cup was in Spain in 1982 with Granada Television, then I went to Mexico in 1986 (again for the BBC), Italy in 1990 (ITV) and, finally, the US in 1994 (ITV) before I gave it up. I met some interesting people: commentators, ex-players who were doing what I was doing for TV and radio, and, of course, old players who were managing or doing other things for their country. It seemed remarkable to me that I hadn't got to a World Cup until the end of my career in 1974, yet here I was being paid to go round the world and watch the best players in the best teams in the world's premier competition. But the problem for me by the mid-1990s was the growth of the game; I was finding that I had to be away from my home and my family more and more. Domestically, it was no longer solely Wednesday and Saturday, suddenly it was Monday, Tuesday and Wednesday nights around the country and getting home late. I just got fed up with the travelling, to be honest. You can't just turn up five minutes before kick-off, you have to be there three or four hours before the game for the preview programmes. There were other difficulties too that you soon tire of, such as communication links breaking down and some truly awful vantage points from which to report, the stand roof at Port Vale for a cup-tie and an old bus in Moscow for a UEFA Cup game between Torpedo Moscow and Manchester United being the two that took the biscuit for me. Both were a nightmare, and both freezing cold. The bus window didn't even offer a full view of the ground; one of us would have to nip downstairs every now and then to watch the replays on the monitor. And then United lost on penalties!

It was an enjoyable period of my life, but when I was in my mid-fifties I decided that enough was enough. Radio pay, as I said, was never great, although it was a big help, especially early on, and later on it did improve. Television work got more lucrative too, but I never found it easy. I used to do some studio work for Granada in Manchester, usually on the eve of a big game or on a Friday night when I would talk about the upcoming games, giving my opinions and then talking about the games on Monday evenings. It was hard, nerve-racking work. I wouldn't exactly say I felt uncomfortable with television, but it's certainly a more intense experience than radio because you're on screen. These days producers seem to be looking more and more towards ex-players rather than trained journalists, but in my opinion a balance is necessary for it to work. You can get different perspectives on a game that way.

I'd given up my work with Francis Lee years earlier, just before I went to the World Cup in Spain in 1982. Franny wanted me to stay at the company because we were getting busy; he said I had to make a decision whether it was broadcasting or the company.

But he was very good about it, saying that the decision was entirely up to me. 'Do the one you enjoy doing most,' he said. I enjoyed both, to tell the truth, but the radio work was football-related and offered me greater possibilities, so I called it a day with Franny. My next working venture to supplement my broadcasting pay was to get into after-dinner speaking, but once again I used to get very nervous and I didn't like doing it. I still don't like doing it, but it pays well. The evening, of course, is longer than just your stint on your feet for you're expected to travel to and attend the function, dinner or whatever as well. I just talk about my career. I also did a bit of public relations for different companies, promoting this and that, and a couple of commercials for a holiday company in Scotland. Touch wood, I'm still asked to do my turn now and again.

If I have a lasting regret, it's that I quit football a year or so too early – you are a long time retired – and that afterwards I didn't take that coaching course which would have kept me in the football world. I'm sure I would have had something to offer, and salaries were improving every year. Football has changed drastically since my day, especially in the last ten years or so, and it's very much a business nowadays. It has always been a business, of course, but it never used to be run quite how it should have been run. The meat-pie men who ran the game as chairmen in the 1960s had different attitudes compared with the paid directors of today; they just did it for the glory, or the personal promotion locally. I confess that I do look back and feel a little unfulfilled, but I'm afraid it's too late now.

15 GEORGE BEST, MY YOUNGER BROTHER

I HAVE OFTEN PONDERED EXACTLY HOW GOOD GEORGE BEST might have been had he kept off the booze and not gone off the rails. George's career effectively ended at the age of twenty-six, and as footballers don't reach their prime until their late twenties, I can only assume he would have got better and better as a player between the ages of, say, twenty-seven and thirty-two, and still he's considered a challenger to the likes of Pele, Alfredo Di Stefano, John Charles and Diego Maradona as the best footballer of all time. I would certainly put him in my top ten, but I have reservations about him being the greatest because of those missing years. The other aspect that makes George's career difficult to judge is that his international experience was confined to Northern Ireland, and therefore he never got to display his talents in front of a truly worldwide audience. George would undoubtedly have achieved even greater world acclaim had he played for one of the more successful national sides; after all, players of considerably less ability have achieved greater fame simply because they played for the likes of Holland, West Germany, Brazil and Argentina.

George was a complete footballer. The only fault I can put my finger on was that he was sometimes unaware of others when in possession. When I look at other great players, like Pele, Cruyff and Maradona, they were more aware of the players around them. I remember Pele in the 1970 World Cup final passing across from just outside the penalty area for right-back Carlos Alberto to score. Pele could undoubtedly have scored himself, but his peripheral vision was so acute that he spotted his team-mate in an even better position and fed him. A pal of mine used to say that when you're in the penalty area and you have a crack at goal, fair enough; but if you feel your team-mate is in a better position, then give the ball to him, because you're all in the same team. You're passing to yourself, in a way. This was a philosophy that tended to pass over George's head. I felt sometimes that he would go into the box and have a go himself when there were maybe other players in a better position to score. On a number of occasions, all he had to do was square the ball and it would probably have been in the back of the net.

As a fellow striker, it would do your brain in at times. George would be going here and there and I'd be going in and coming back out again. I would have to say out loud, 'Excuse me, but I should be having the ball, man!' And then he would do something spectacular and it would all be forgotten. That was George Best. He had terrific skills. He was a supporter's joy, and he'd have them sitting on the edge of their seats every time he picked up the ball. He had a bit of everything. He was brave – he really did get stuck in for a lad who was the size of nothing – he was a fine dribbler, he had outstanding control and he had a sharp eye for situations. He wasn't, however, a great header of the ball. He could do it, but it was far from being his forte. But what did that matter? It was his goals – spectacular, marvellous goals – that made him a player who was feared by the opposition. He was an all-round star player with loads of talent and loads of heart, and sadly, because of his skills, he took a lot of knocks. That didn't make him afraid to go in where it hurt, though. For a forward, he was a reasonably good tackler. He got stuck in at a time when there were some hard guys about, guys who were marking him, defenders such as Paul Reaney of Leeds United and Chopper Harris of Chelsea.

George's behaviour became very unpredictable as the years passed, but he wasn't always that way. Things just seemed to get out of hand once he had achieved a certain level. We all used to enjoy a beer coming back from an away match, especially if we were on the train returning from London, and it was never a problem for Matt during a three-hour journey. It was part and parcel of football in those days, it was nothing excessive, and George would be drinking beer as well. But, of course, when most of us arrived back in Manchester we would be heading for home and our families; George, being single, would get back and look for somewhere to go. He didn't want to return to an empty house. And you can't blame him for that. Had I been single I would probably have been off too. Manchester was covered in nightclubs in those days, good nightclubs at that. There was no violence, and the players knew the guys in the clubs. That was probably where George began drinking shorts, but I have to say he never did so in front of us.

There were always plenty of stories about what he was up to, what he was drinking and how much he was drinking, but it was hard for us to believe he was on the strong stuff because few of the lads ever really drank shorts. We all liked a few beers, claiming it put back the fluids we had lost through perspiration while playing and training, but all of a sudden in the 1960s drinks like Bacardi and Coke became fashionable. It tasted like Coke and was as easy to swallow as a soft drink, but it was Bacardi, and you were getting bladdered without realizing it. Really strong alcoholic drinks like vodka, Scotch and gin were taboo, but George went from vodka to brandy, and when you got on to the brandy at that age, it really was serious stuff. It never showed, though, because he was always first in for training and he was a good trainer, unlike me. This sort of drinking went on for maybe a couple of years before we all found out. George started to miss a few training sessions, we'd be thinking, 'What's wrong with George?' and then the stories about nightclubs, booze and the rest of it would get bandied around. But still we didn't know whether to believe it or not, because George Best stories, in particular, we took with a big pinch of salt. We had all suffered from the two-beers-miraculously-becoming-six syndrome. Exaggeration was rife.

But of course eventually we became convinced of the truth of the rumours. My first thought was, 'What a shame!' Here was a nice, good-looking lad with a terrific talent, and he looked as though he was going to waste it. But George was the first real football superstar during a period when football came out of the backwoods. Although the top players were not quite of film-star status, it was quickly going that way; the famous and the fabulous were beginning to go to games, particularly in London, where Fulham and Chelsea attracted several actors and actresses. I thought it would prove to be a short-lived fad, but they seemed to love it. All of a sudden we were in the same company as these screen stars, and Bestie was as right for this type of celebrity as were the Beatles. He even had the Beatle fringe haircut. He was part of a new generation with no knowledge of war and the deprivation it brought. Footballers were suddenly cult status in a society that was rapidly becoming more liberal, and as a result there were a lot of things Bestie was doing that had never been done by footballers before. The days of the football player at the bar with his pint, just one of the lads having a jar after a game, were disappearing; now the pub was swapped for the nightclub, and the pints for glasses of champagne. And remember, George was still a very young man when this scene first exploded, and it must have been hard for him to take it all in and cope with it. The partying and drinking could only go on for so long before it began to take its toll on the field.

Still, when people talk about George Best, they tend to forget the number of games he actually played in his shortened career – not far short of the number of appearances I managed between the ages of sixteen and thirty-four. George played 466 games alone for United, plus 37 for Northern Ireland and over 50 for teams such as Stockport County, Fulham and the Los Angeles Aztecs; in comparison, I played 393 times for United, 81 times for Huddersfield, 68 times for Manchester City, 27 times for Torino and 55 times for my country. If he could reach those figures given his lifestyle at the time, what heights might he have scaled had he lived a cleaner life?

More to the point, what qualities could have helped him reach the dizzy heights he was capable of? More discipline, obviously, and perhaps marriage. I know Sir Matt would have loved to marry Bestie off, but wedlock doesn't suit everyone, and who's to say he would have settled down had he tied the knot in his early twenties? I still feel, though, that he would have had a better chance of going on to fulfil his extraordinary potential had he married instead of going clubbing. After a match, had he been going back home or meeting his good lady for a meal or something in Manchester, would that not have extended his playing career? For a rich, handsome, single lad, Manchester was a swinging place and a powerful distraction.

Sadly, George's behaviour in the latter years at United, when he started to miss training and matches, caused a split with the older players, particularly Bobby Charlton.

I would say there were a few at the club who were a wee bit envious of him and his lifestyle; they felt he was being given preferential treatment and was getting away with all sorts of things. I never felt that way, though; as long as he was doing his stuff on the field it was not for me to be criticizing. I might have occasionally passed on the odd piece of advice to him, but nothing heavier than that. It was up to the management to sort out problems like that, and when George's absenteeism really did begin to take effect in the early 1970s, Matt was past that stage. He didn't want any aggravation. Five years earlier and George would have had a few raps over the knuckles. He got a few as it was, but they weren't hard enough. Whenever I overdid it, a quiet word from Matt worked wonders.

I remember coming back from a European game once, sitting with George at the back of the plane having a drink. I'm not a shorts drinker, but on this occasion I got stuck in and had a few gin and tonics. It always sounded good in the films, ordering a G&T, but not being used to it I got well bladdered. Nothing was said at the time, but the following morning I was walking into the dressing-room from the corridor, and from the referee's room, which was right there as you went in, I heard a hiss. It was the boss. 'Come in here,' he said. I went into the referee's room. 'Don't be doing that again in the back of the plane,' Matt said. 'I don't mind you having a beer, but keep off that stuff.' As I said, that did the trick for me. I thought we had got away with it, but Matt knew, and what's more he knew what to do about it.

But Matt had to be careful with George. We could see and understand that to some extent, because here was a lad who was obviously having problems. We all had to be careful about how we went about telling him what to do and what not to do. Get it wrong, and some guys could go completely. When he was in control of his affairs, Bestie was a sensible guy and a clever lad, but as time went on it was clear he had a drink problem that was affecting his game. By their very nature, nightclubs meant late nights, and late nights are incompatible with playing top-flight football.

Looking back, there are a lot of things you think could have been done for George, but at the time there wasn't the back-up at clubs, with the Professional Footballers' Association and what have you. And we were all young men at the club, friends of George but with little experience of life beyond the club. He certainly had plenty of pals in the team. David Sadler, John Fitzpatrick and others of that age group, those were his friends, and they knocked about together. George and I were never close when we were playing because he was six years younger than me, and that's a big gap when you're young. If one guy is thirty-two and another is thirty-eight, there's very little difference, but there's a chasm between, say, a nineteen-year-old and a twenty-five-year-old. And don't forget I was married and in the throes of fathering children. I was with another group altogether, older players like Pat Crerand and Alex Stepney; Bobby Charlton tended to socialize with Seamus Brennan and Nobby Stiles. The only time we did muck in together was when we were on tour, or after away matches in Europe, but even then the guys would eventually splinter into little groups and go their separate ways.

But as the years went on George and I grew close. Indeed, we became better friends after we had finished playing. He even came on holiday with the Law family a few times because I always felt like, not exactly a father figure to George, but more his elder brother. There were similarities between us. We were both away from our native land, for one, and anyone in that situation needs a bit of help every now and then. When we were on holiday together, I knew what he was like and I accepted it. He was always as good as gold, but by about ten o'clock in the morning he would be having his first glass of wine. I have seen him in a state. He tended to reach the stage where he couldn't speak. I've been to several functions over the years where George has got to his feet but been unable to perform as an after-dinner speaker (on those occasions the elder statesman had to help out). I'm not saying this happened frequently, but every now and then he would have just a wee bit too much to drink. Fortunately, George was never a problem when he over-imbibed, he was never a violent person. In fact, the man is very gentle, soppy even. It was other people who got involved with him who caused the trouble; more often than not it was nothing to do with George whatsoever.

But, boy, he could get bladdered. I was supposed to meet up with him in the summer of 1994 after the World Cup in America. Some of my family were coming over too, as was George's girl-friend at the time, Mary, and we arranged to meet in Tampa Bay, Florida. I flew in from Dallas, my family flew in from London with Mary, and we all arrived together – except there was no Bestie. All we knew was that American television had flown him to Pasadena for the World Cup final and he was due to meet us the next day in Florida. At first we assumed he'd caught a later flight, but by the end of the next day he still hadn't turned up. We started panicking a wee bit. A few more days passed, and then, out of the blue, he appeared. He never batted an eyelid. 'Hi, how are you doing?' he said. We were gobsmacked. Bestie was only five days late! What had happened, apparently, was that he'd been found on a beach in Los Angeles with no passport, no money, nothing. I never heard the full story, but that was George. He'd go on a bender and then he'd be perfectly OK when you next saw him a few days later, as though nothing had happened.

Things couldn't continue like that, of course. I went down to see him in hospital when he was due to have a liver operation, and he didn't look well. They were only monitoring him at the time, but he looked so ill. I went back about a month later to see how he was getting on, and he was still in hospital and was due to be released in about a week's time. He still didn't look well to me. I was really concerned for him, but I still told him he looked good. It was hardly surprising he looked like that considering he had gone through this huge operation, ten hours under the knife or whatever it was, and had had something like forty pints of blood pumped into him because they could not stop the bleeding.

George is a sportsman and a fighter, and it is great to see he has turned the corner and looks so much better. As long as he keeps off the drink then he has a chance with his implants to stay off the booze permanently. He shouldn't drink at all now, whatever the temptation, and when we go out and we're all having a glass of beer or a nice bottle of wine, he has to have a cup of tea or a glass of water. That's the killer, the biggest test. If you're strong enough to come through that you're going to be all right.

But I remember a holiday we had in Portugal during one of his dry periods. I recall feeling a bit guilty when we were out because I was having a few drinks. That's what my holiday is all about. I don't drink a lot at home, but when I'm away I like to have a few beers, then a nice glass of red wine with my meal. I did feel guilty, but George said, 'Hey, no problem. Don't worry about it.' I certainly drank less when I was with him than I would have done had he not been there, and to be fair, he was as good as gold. When we returned, as far as I know he went back on it for a short spell, and that's when they had to take him into hospital. We realized he had a severe problem because he needed a new liver. His old one was shattered, and the doctors told him he had to wait until somebody died before he was able to have his transplant. That, I know, was a problem for him. He could go nowhere in case they suddenly called him. Happily, they found a donor, and after those tough first few months he became as feisty as ever. He even started writing a weekly column in the *Mail on Sunday*.

I was over in Ireland a while ago as a surprise guest when George was given the Freedom of Castlereagh. He looked superb. They had put up a plaque in his honour on his father's house, and he was delighted. It was a nice award, and we had dinner afterwards. The usual Irish drinking was going on, but George was on tea or lemonade.

I was dreadfully sorry to hear George had recently fallen off the wagon. I spoke to him a few days afterwards, and he was very remorseful, saying to me he had just had a blip and it was going to be the only one. I hope he is right, but, of course, neither he nor I knows. It's just a shame it happened.

We all have to accept that he is an addict and it is a problem. It's easy for the rest of us to sit on the fence and shake our heads at his behaviour. I don't want to be judgemental because we don't know the mental anguish he goes through. I do not believe you blame an alcoholic for their illness any more than you would someone who has cancer. Let's all hope day by day he copes with it. He needs our help, not our condemnation.

I'm sure it's the luck of the draw with alcohol. I can think of people I knew who drank as much as George, and still do, with no apparent problems. George's problem might be hereditary, because his mother had a problem with alcohol and she died quite young, in her forties I believe. But his father looks brilliant. He must be in his eighties, and although he takes a drink he is not a big drinker by any means, happy with a glass of wine or a beer. The real problem with alcohol is when you start wanting to drink it first thing in the morning. If somebody showed me the dregs of a bottle of wine from the night before and said, 'Would you fancy a glass of wine with your bacon and eggs?' I'd be in danger of being physically sick. Not even at lunchtime – only with dinner.

In the end, for me, it all comes down to this: if only George Best could have progressed to that very top level. Maybe if he had played for England or Scotland he would have done. Northern Ireland had come good in 1958 when they reached the final stages of the World Cup in Sweden alongside Wales, but players like Danny Blanchflower and Harry Gregg were getting a wee bit too old by the mid-1960s. When Bestie first came on the scene they still had a decent team that could hurt you, but it was on the wane. Apart from the European Cup final in 1968, there were no big stages for George to show off his talent and his charisma. Just imagine if George had exploded on to the scene as a teenager in the mid-1990s with Manchester United. With TV coverage as it is today, he would have been a sensation.

16 THE PLAYERS

IN ADDITION TO THE ONE AND ONLY GEORGE BEST, I HAVE BEEN fortunate over the years to play with and against some of the greatest footballers of our time, the sort of people who left not only other professional footballers with happy memories, but those who followed the game too.

Ray Wilson was one of the first professional footballers I came to know, and we are still close friends. We still see each other and speak regularly, which I appreciate after all these years. In fact, there's a group of us who meet once a year, although we enjoy it so much we're going to increase that to twice a year, some time in the summer and then again just before Christmas. It's always good to go back to Huddersfield and see them all. The others who join us are Gordon Low, who came down from Scotland with me when I was fifteen; Les Massie, another Aberdonian; and Jack Connor. We were the original five, though John Corrington, who played with Middlesbrough, recently joined us. We have a good old chat, and it's lovely to reminisce and talk about old times, particularly about Bill Shankly whom they knew far better than I did.

Ray was special as a player, an excellent defender, probably the best left-back I ever played with. He was classy, and not many people beat him because he was so quick. He had a lot of footballing qualities because he began as an inside-forward then moved to the back – a clever move by Bill Shankly as it transpired. He was a good passer of the ball, wasting very few and never hitting long balls; it was always something nice and short for the midfield player or the winger, and then he'd make himself available. He got stuck in as well; Ray was a real little tiger. He went on from Huddersfield to reach the very top after moving to Everton, who had an outstanding team at the time and well into the mid-1960s. He and Alan Ball had very good careers with England as well as with their club.

On a personal note, I will never forget how he and Jack looked after Gordon and me when we arrived as young kids from Aberdeen, helping us, looking out for us and passing on their experience. Without them it would have been a lonely life at times. Instead, they were happy times. It was all very matey, helped by the fact that nobody had a car. We all went on the trolleybus together to the game with all the punters. Can you imagine that happening today? This was only an hour before kick-off, too, but the supporters were never intrusive and would say banal things like, 'Are you playing today?' We would nod, and they would reply, 'Oh, good.' And that was the end of the conversation. The only two at the club who had cars were the manager and the physiotherapist Roy Goodall. We were all amazed that Roy had a car, an old Minor Morris he could never get into gear.

When Ray Wilson stopped playing he went into the undertaking business. I bumped into him some years ago when I happened to be in Huddersfield because my then agent Ken Stanley lived over there. I hadn't seen him for a while because it was well before we started our annual get-together.

'Denis, nice to see you,' he said when he spotted me.

'You're looking really happy today, Ray, what's happened?' I responded.

Ray grinned. 'I've just passed my embalming test.'

He was so overjoyed he looked happier than he did when he won the World Cup. Ray had taken over the family business when his father-in-law retired and he had to learn the trade, but an embalming test? Stuffing dead bodies was not for me, but he was over the moon. I thought he was going to say he had won the pools or something! Later, he used to tell us stories about the trade, always starting off with 'You won't believe this . . .' Of course people die, it's normal, but Ray was telling us tales about road accidents that had ripped people apart, people with an arm or a leg lopped off or half their head missing. It's a job I could never do. I couldn't even look at a dead body never mind take an embalming test. But that was Ray, and he was as happy as Larry.

Another favourite player of mine was John White, the brilliant Spurs and Scotland inside-forward who was tragically killed in the prime of his life and with a glorious football career beckoning. I don't know what the odds are of somebody being killed by lightning, but they're obviously into the millions. People do get hit by lightning and survive, but unfortunately John didn't. It was a tremendous loss, not solely for his family, but for all his team-mates at club and international level. He was a super player and had still to reach his peak, even though the old saying of 'an old head on young shoulders' fitted him perfectly. He read the game very well as he drifted around the midfield almost unnoticed, so much so that he was known as The Ghost because the opposition didn't spot him until the damage was done.

He was wonderful to play with. If you were in difficulty when on the ball there was always a shout and he would be there on your shoulder to get you out of trouble by taking over possession.

He was always round about you, always following you. It's around players like John that good teams are built. The Brazilians play that way, and in many respects John was a Brazilian-type player; he would have graced even their best sides. When a Brazilian player has the ball there are always three or four of his team-mates following up in case the move breaks down. John White was like that. When you got the ball he was always there with you, on your left-hand side or on your right. You were rarely isolated on the pitch with John in your side. He also had a lovely touch on the ball.

It was so sad when he went. We will always be left to wonder how good he might have been, just like Duncan Edwards, the young Englishman killed in the Munich crash. All the signs were right with John. He wasn't a drinker or a late-night boy, and he worked hard to keep in condition. He was ambitious, too. He stood well and didn't slouch, in fact he looked every inch a professional athlete, and he was indeed a very elegant player. Had he lived, I'm sure Scotland would have made it to the 1966 World Cup finals. A group of us came on to the scene at the same time and developed a spirit and an understanding. We had an excellent team with huge potential, and John was just beginning to make his mark when he was struck down.

Dave Mackay was a member alongside John White of both the Spurs and Scotland sides, a giant of a player and first class as a guy as well. He didn't receive the caps he should have won, mainly because he moved down to England. He, like me, felt there was a bit of anti-Anglo feeling back home, and he was usually the one to suffer if anything ever went wrong. He also lost caps when he was out of football for more than a year after breaking his leg twice. I wasn't always totally convinced by the Scottish team selection in the 1950s and 1960s, and I repeat, Dave should have won far more caps than he did.

Way back in 1958 he was captain of Scotland, probably the youngest the country has ever had at the age of twenty-three. He was imposing and commanding, and he'd progressed through the ranks with Scotland as a schoolboy and an under-23 international. He won the Scottish Cup and the League with Hearts, then with Spurs he won the FA Cup three times, the League and the European Cup Winners' Cup, and with Derby County the League Championship in 1971/72. That was Dave, a general in the army commanding his troops to victory. He was skilful, too, more skilful than many people imagined, because most thought of him as a hard man – which, of course, he was. He could keep the ball under control with either foot. He was certainly one to have in your team, to drive you on and give you that bit of steel. The best teams have always had someone like him at their heart. We had little Nobby Stiles at Old Trafford, Billy Bremner was the key at Leeds, and Graeme Souness at Liverpool. Mackay was in that category, and he'd always be the first name on my teamsheet.

I know people have different opinions on players, and I know Dave wasn't the greatest player the world has ever seen, but he gave everything for his team and his team-mates, and by doing so could influence matches. Other guys could come in and have either a great game or a rubbish game, but with Dave Mackay you knew exactly what you were going to get every time. He never gave less than 100 per cent, he would never avoid a challenge, and he would fight for the cause until the last second – and he expected you to do the same. A football team needs a leader, a great captain, not someone just to toss a coin. They have more influence on a game than with their footballing abilities alone, and when you come across one – and they are quite a rare breed – they are invariably part of a winning side. Their value to the team is not always obvious from the terraces. It was no surprise to me that he did well as a manager. He won the League

Championship in 1974/75 at Derby County, and went on to follow in Brian Clough's footsteps at Nottingham Forest, also managing at Swindon and Walsall and coaching in the Middle East. He was sadly let down by some of his senior players at Derby, and I always thought he deserved better from a club he served brilliantly as a player and a manager.

He was very much a personal friend, too. He looked after me when I was first selected for Scotland in the late 1950s, and after playing for Scotland in Glasgow we would always head for his home town Edinburgh where we used to have some good nights out. I went to his sixtieth-birthday bash not long ago in Nottingham, and our two families have remained good friends.

Jim Baxter was a bit like Bestie, a really talented player good enough to be up in the top-ten bracket with his natural ability. I felt he went to the wrong team when he left Rangers to join Sunderland; I think he would have fitted better into the Spurs team. London would have suited him perfectly. He would have loved it because he was always dapper was Slim Jim, and a really good-looking guy as well. He also had that cockiness which you must have if you are his sort of player. He would have slotted into the London scene without a worry. But why did he leave Rangers, a huge club where he was an idol, in the first place? I don't know. The pull for him at Roker Park was manager Ian McCall, who had been the Scotland manager, and the two had played for Rangers and Scotland as well. But Jim was a big-stage player, and he needed a high-profile club to strut his stuff. He had great panache and lovely control with his left foot. He played a large part in the memorable victory over England the year after they won the World Cup. His quality can be gauged by the fact that he was selected to play for the Rest of the World in that game against England at Wembley. He went back to Rangers after spells at Sunderland and Nottingham Forest, but it's never easy to go back. It doesn't always work out, and it didn't for him.

Then again, he was a little on the wild side. He became known as Bacardi Jim, for obvious reasons. It was the start of the Bacardi era, when people used to go on holiday to Spain and come back having discovered Bacardi and Coke. It was a couple of quid for a litre bottle over there in those days, and there was always more Bacardi than Coke in there.

While he was still playing Jim was running his own pub, something that was allowed in Scotland but not in England. It sounds like fun, but I imagine running a pub is hard work and scarcely good preparation for playing football on a Saturday – not to mention the constant temptation to put your feet up and have a drink. And I can't imagine that Jim passed on the opportunity too many times! We all liked to have a drink, but for most of us it was a beer or two; Jim, like George Best, preferred his spirits. I went drinking with Slim Jim, of course, after games, and he was known in all the bars.

He passed away not long ago after two liver transplants failed to save him. He'd always been talked of as a George Best type of player, but in the end he only followed him in one way, onto the operating table. When I went to his funeral in Glasgow, the turnout was fantastic, unbelievable. The streets were lined with people, and the service was held at a huge church in the centre of Glasgow. Several players spoke, and it was all very moving.

You couldn't help but love the man, even if he was sometimes infuriating to play with, especially in that memorable game against England in April 1967. We had a laugh about that over the years, how he started playing keepy-uppy with the ball on the far side of the field and taking the mickey out of the English. Every time he touched the ball there was a huge cheer from the travelling hordes. It was stupid, really, because sometimes cockiness can rebound on you; all it usually takes is for a goal to be scored and you're back on the rack. It's best just to be professional and get the job done. I kept on at him, 'We must keep playing and try to get some more goals,' but good old Jim kept on juggling the ball and taunting the English. It would have been a disaster after that had we let England back into the match, but we won, and despite everything I'd still say that Jim was man of the match that day.

Jimmy Johnstone was another terrific Scottish player, part of the European Cup-winning Celtic side, a little dynamo and a tough little beggar as well. He was only five feet tall, but those who tried to intimidate him invariably failed. If there was a problem with Jimmy it was that he was never easy to play with, because more often than not he didn't know where he was going himself, though he usually got there anyway. Jinky, as he was known, was a good player, and a good singer, and like many players of the age he liked a few drinks. When I spoke to him recently, though, he was on the wagon because he has motor neurone disease. As soon as I heard I phoned him because I thought immediately of Don Revie, but he reassured me he was fine, telling me he had been fortunate because they'd caught it early and they could treat it successfully.

I have kept in touch with Jimmy because we were good pals. We often trained together, and I loved his sense of humour. He was always up to mischief, and was always optimistic. I shall never forget one night on the Clyde prior to the England game before the World Cup in 1974. We played three internationals in a week, against Northern Ireland, Wales and then England, before leaving for West Germany. After the Wales game on the Tuesday we returned to our hotel in Largs and our manager Willie Ormond told us he could see no reason why we shouldn't go off for a drink to relax and enjoy ourselves. We didn't get back to Largs until late, probably around eleven o'clock at night, but we knew a couple of hotels where they served late drinks. We had worked hard, played two internationals in a short space of time and had four days before the England game, so we decided to take up Willie's offer.

It was an extremely convivial evening, and gradually the lads began to disappear off to bed until there were only five of us left: me, Jimmy Johnstone, David Hay of Celtic, and Sandy Jardine and Pat Stanton from Hibs. For those who don't know Largs, there are hotels along the front, a pebbly beach and a narrow channel. In the early hours of the morning we decided to cross that channel. We crossed over and were having a little chat when Jimmy decided to board a rowing boat. All of a sudden it began to float out, and we started to shout, 'Hey, Jimmy, you'd better come back, man, we're going.' But Jimmy didn't hear us, or didn't want to hear us; he was singing 'Scotland the Brave' at the top of his voice. The boat had soon drifted about fifty yards out, so I called to him again to come back. Nothing.

When the boat was about a hundred yards out, we started to panic. A few hotel windows had begun to open, guests leaning out wondering what the fuss was about. We were shouting at Jimmy, but the only response we got from out on the water was another chorus of 'Scotland the Brave'. Soon, Jimmy was just a dot on the horizon, so Davie Hay and Pat Stanton rushed back to raise the alarm at the hotel while the rest of us ran off to alert Willie Ormond and the coastguards, who immediately set out after our errant winger who by now had disappeared over the horizon.

It was fully an hour later, maybe even an hour and a half, when they came back with him. There were no oars in the boat, so had he not been rescued he would have been a goner. If Celtic supporters had seen him they would have shot him because all he had on was a wee vest and he was as blue as a Rangers shirt with cold.

Naturally the press got hold of the story and there were

questions galore at the press conference at our hotel in Largs. Quite reasonably, they wanted to know why Jimmy Johnstone had been out in a boat in the Clyde without any oars at three o'clock in the morning. Jimmy had to answer for himself. As he went to sit in front of the gathered media, he leaned across to me and said, 'Come and sit beside me, Denis.'

'Excuse me, Jimmy,' I replied, 'but this has got nothing to do with me. You were the one in the boat, not me.'

But Jimmy was adamant. 'Come on, Denis,' he said, 'just give me a bit of help.'

He knew I was his big pal and wouldn't let him down, and he wanted me to play the elder statesman.

The very first question put to Jimmy was straight to the point. 'Right, Jimmy, what was you doin' on the boat?'

'Well, Denis and I decided to go fishing,' Jimmy replied.

For heaven's sake! He'd roped me straight in when I was supposed just to be keeping him company! There was nothing I could do about it. I wasn't worried about the press so much as about my wife Di. She knew I couldn't swim, and it was for sure a very odd time to be out fishing, even if it was with Jimmy. 'Fishing?' she said in an incredulous voice when we finally spoke about it, and I had to say yes because it had been on national television.

Jimmy was apparently the luckiest boy in the world that night because the area where he was was exactly where the Clyde goes out and the sea comes in, creating a tremendous whirlpool. He was very fortunate, according to the coastguard, not to have drowned. His luck continued that Saturday against England, because I was dropped but Jimmy went on to have the most fantastic game you've ever seen. Such was the euphoria after we beat the English 2–0 that everyone soon forgot the fishing expedition on the Clyde, yet before the game they were saying we should be banned from the team for ever.

He was a bit daft, was Jimmy, but he had the capacity to wriggle out of most situations, though he didn't play in West Germany because Willie Ormond was getting a little tired of the wee man after he gestured to the press box at Hampden. Then he was almost sent home from a World Cup warm-up match in Oslo at the beginning of June after an incident with Billy Bremner, another Scot who enjoyed a little bit of a bevy.

Billy Bremner lived hard and played hard. He would always be the first guy in there, battling it out, despite his size. But he wasn't simply a fiery little competitor and tackler, he was also a very good passer of the ball and a good lad. I had some scrapes with him. When we played against each other it was often a bit of a battle but always fair; we had too much respect to kick each other. Billy would pick and choose whom he battled with, whom he kicked and whom he would have a drink with afterwards.

He certainly wasn't a guy to upset or rile. I remember him giving the Czech left-half a right whack in autumn 1973 during the game when we qualified for the World Cup, hard enough for him to be carried off and put in an ambulance. Billy's opponent must have thought he had an easy touch when he first saw him; maybe he should have taken more note of his red hair. Billy did the guy well and truly. As he was being carried off he told Billy what he and his mates were going to do to him when he went to Prague for the return leg. It wasn't nice, but as it happened Billy didn't play in the return game. When we arrived in Prague the player was shouting, 'He has not come, has he? He has not come.' So the guy got me instead! I presume he took me out because I was standing next to Billy when he did him. It wasn't important for us to have Billy as the game was no longer a live match in the qualifying competition. Leeds players did not always turn out for international duty; they had their doctor's notes when they wanted them as Don Revie gave them the choice whether they played or not. So Billy had his doctor's note and I took the stick. Thank you very much, Billy, lovely.

Revie and Bremner were well suited because they were both incredibly ambitious and didn't mind how they won. You always knew what you were going to get with Bremner. He was truly a good little player, and it was so sad when he passed away. I was delighted when they erected a statue in his memory at Elland Road because he deserved it. He was the very essence of the Leeds United team and image.

Talking of icons, Bobby Charlton has to be one of the best players England has ever produced. I know because I played with him many times. Like George Best, he was one of the world's top players; he did it for England and for Manchester United and was feared across the globe for the ferocity of his shooting and his raking crosses. His importance to the game can be gauged by the fact that he remains as well known as ever after all these years and was even selected to head a British bid for the World Cup and help launch the J League in Japan. The world also respects the fact that he was one of the survivors of Munich and somehow came back from the nightmare to become a star player. He tried and failed as a manager, but he has always remained close to Manchester United.

He was a lovely mover of the ball and will always be remembered for his spectacular goals. He was also a fine reader of the game. As a person, he was always intense, and still is. People tend to think of him as a little dour, but behind the scenes, away from the public, he has a terrific sense of humour; he was always good pals with Nobby Stiles and Shay Brennan and they used to have a good laugh together. Whenever he was on television he always seemed to come over a bit too serious, but as I said, that wasn't the real Bobby; he always seemed to put a front up when he was appearing in public. And what a marvellous ambassador for

United and the game in general at all levels he has been, both while playing and afterwards. I can't remember him ever being sent off, though he probably was booked because he could be a bit of a moaner on the pitch!

My worst moment with Bobby in all the years I have known him was when we went on that tour of Australia at the end of 1966/67 and we were flying from Sydney to Perth, a long flight. The pilot suddenly asked us to fasten our seatbelts because there was severe turbulence coming up. I was sitting next to poor old Bobby and I immediately wished the pilot had said something a little softer. The sky was an azure blue with not a cloud in sight, but we were 30,000 feet up and soon the plane started to rock and shudder. I had Bobby by the arm and we sat there holding on to each other silently for well over an hour while the plane bounced all over the place. We honestly thought we weren't going to make it. When we eventually pulled out of it I had purple marks on my arm where Bobby had grabbed me, and I'm sure he had the same. Nobody spoke about it, nobody said a word, but that was the worst flight I've ever experienced. Sitting next to Bobby, a man who had already survived an air tragedy, had made me even more stressed and nervous than I think I would ordinarily have been. It was a frightening experience.

And still on the subject of icons, it would be wrong to miss out Kenny Dalglish, who I played with a handful of times for Scotland. Kenny was a fine player, and the real beauty about him was that if he wasn't scoring goals his actual play was still as valuable. He was a good reader of the game and a good passer of the ball with an outstanding all-round game, and there aren't many players who also score goals you can say that about. Dalglish was a team player and a goalscorer, and one of the best without a doubt. Unlike Kenny, Johnny Haynes of Fulham didn't gain the recognition he deserved as a footballer. He is best known today for being the first £100-a-week footballer. But there haven't been many finer passers of the ball in the game than Johnny, especially inside the full-back for the winger coming in. I thought he was an excellent player, and he didn't get the plaudits other lesser players received at the time. Sure he was captain of England, but maybe if he had played his club football at Spurs or Arsenal he would have been an icon. Fulham were a decent side, but they were never going to win anything. Still, I have played against Johnny at both club and international level, and he always impressed me with his cultured style of play.

When it comes to goalkeepers, there weren't many better than Pat Jennings, even fewer who were nicer or more amenable. The big Irishman had huge buckets for hands and one of the biggest volleyed clearances in the game. In August 1967 he scored a magnificent goal for Spurs against us at Old Trafford in the Charity Shield, and what's more he did it more than once. I remember watching the ball sail through the air and bounce in front of Bill Foulkes and over his head; Alex Stepney had come out of his goal, and he watched in vain as it bounced over him and into the net. The game ended 3–3, thanks to Pat. He had a spectacular career and, unusually, won honours with both Spurs and Arsenal without rousing the anger of either set of supporters. They all loved him and his maverick style, notably catching crosses one-handed. He won over a hundred caps for Northern Ireland, was a regular with them for over twenty years, and was loved by everyone because he was a genuinely nice guy. Bill Brown was another outstanding Tottenham goalkeeper, and probably the best goalkeeper Scotland has ever had. He played his part in the double-winning Spurs side, playing 222 times for the north London club between 1959 and 1965, but unlike Pat he did not win the international caps he should have won. Scotland were never as well blessed as England for goalkeepers; at one time they had Peter Shilton, Ray Clemence and Joe Corrigan – spoilt for choice. I've played with a few other good keepers too, including the ex-German prisoner-of-war Bert Trautmann at the end of his career at Manchester City, a fine and brave goalkeeper who was lucky to live after playing on when he broke his neck in the FA Cup final against Birmingham City in 1956. Then there was the great Russian Lev Yashin, the Black Panther, who many believe was the greatest and who passed away in 1990 with stomach cancer.

But the best in my experience was Gordon Banks. And don't take my word for it, or even Pele's; Banks was recognized everywhere as the best in the world, until a car crash gave him an eye injury that all but finished his career. I loved to play against him because to score past him was very special indeed.

During my career I was also fortunate enough to play with some legendary overseas stars. To me, Alfredo Di Stefano was the best, and that includes Pele. He was my type of player, the one I would have loved to emulate. Though he was a prolific goalscorer, he was not a centre-forward as such, more of an inside-forward cum centre-forward cum midfielder. He was always running and playing, always involved in the game. He first won me over when Real Madrid thumped Eintracht Frankfurt at Hampden in 1960, when he and Real were in their prime.

I had the good fortune of playing with him for the Rest of the World, and we stayed friends for years. The members of that side were all in Paris about ten years ago; we hadn't seen one another for years. We and some journalists formed a panel to select the greatest ever European player. Di Stefano won it handsomely, and I was happy to be in his corner. I was still starry-eyed in his presence all those years later. He couldn't speak a great deal of English, but nevertheless we became good friends in the few days the Rest of the World squad had together before playing England, and I saw him many times through the years when I was commentating on European Cup finals, especially when Real Madrid were involved.

What an influence he and the side he played for had on the game! In those days, everybody wanted to be like Real Madrid. The kit alone was worth having. A lot of people fancied the Brazilian kit, but for me the white of Real Madrid was the special gear. Clearly Don Revie felt the same, because he changed the Leeds strip to all white.

Considering we had never played together and spoke different languages, it was incredibly easy to slot in with him that day. The only words we needed were 'Alfredo' and 'Denis'. I would shout, receive the ball from him, and then I'd link up with Puskas, who came on in the second half. Yes, suddenly I was playing with two of my heroes. I knew everything about Ferenc Puskas, the Real Madrid side he played with and the great Hungarian team that had thrashed England twice in 1953 and 1954. I will never forget at Wembley how he pulled the ball back with his foot and just whacked it into the back of the net. The great Billy Wright didn't even get to him. He did it with no backlift at all. During that Rest of the World game, whenever I called for the ball with a 'Ferenc!', it came to me like an arrow. One of his passes allowed me to score against Banks. 'Nice pass, Ferenc,' I said, 'thank you very much!'

What a left foot he had! Puskas would stand on his right leg because, like Jim Baxter, he was so good with his left he didn't need it. He scored eighty-three goals with it for Hungary in eighty-four appearances before switching his allegiance to Spain. Not only was he one-footed, he didn't look or act particularly like a player either. He was always a bit on the chubby side, and he liked a drink, as did most of his Hungarian colleagues. But he was sublime and could hold the ball and play it, as well as score goals for fun.

Di Stefano, however, was the best player on the park that day. Yes, for me, he was the perfect player. He could do everything, although he would admit he wasn't great with the left foot. He scored a few goals with it, mind, but it wasn't cultured like his right. Perhaps that was why he and Puskas complemented each other so well, because Ferenc was all left foot. The perfect balance. Alfredo was a good header of the ball too, despite not being particularly big, and he got stuck in as well. But perhaps his greatest asset was that he was incredibly sharp. Everything was one, two, getting it back, and one, two again to split a defence apart, and you never knew what he was going to do because he was also a canny dribbler, although he much preferred the ball to beat the opponent. If you come up to somebody, flick the ball to the side and then get the return, the defender is out of the game.

I modelled myself on Alfredo, but when I came back to England to play for Manchester United I wasn't allowed to be like him because Matt said they were struggling up front to score goals and I was warned not to come back over the halfway line, which wasn't really my game. For Manchester City and Torino I'd played all over the park. Torino hadn't been too happy about it either, they too wanted me sticking the ball in the net, but I couldn't play up there in Italy because you'd never get the ball. Much better to play in the Di Stefano way.

The pair of them, Puskas and Di Stefano, fascinated me; in fact they fascinated everyone in football. It was an honour and a thrill to play with Alfredo, and Ferenc was a bonus.

Franz Beckenbauer was another quality player I played with, for the Rest of Europe, and of course against, whenever Scotland played West Germany. He first came to everyone's attention during the 1966 World Cup when he was a young lad, but he really came to the fore four years later when Bobby Charlton was subbed by Alf Ramsey and Franz was given the freedom to go forward and orchestrate one of the great World Cup comebacks of all time. Everyone blamed goalkeeper Peter Bonetti at the time, but it was Beckenbauer who changed the match, aided by Alf Ramsey's decision.

He was an excellent player through the years, as good as a mid-field player as he'd been in those early days as a centre-half. He was quick, he scored goals, and he was a tough guy who could look after himself – as I found out to my cost. In April 1969 I played for Scotland in our World Cup qualifier against the Germans at Hampden, and we were in direct confrontation. He had a plaster on an obviously broken wrist and had to receive permission to play with it. I licked my lips, thinking I would take advantage and get stuck in early to test his courage. Five minutes into the game I gave him a whack, and before I knew it he had whacked me back with his plastered hand. Boomph! What a crack it was, and there was me thinking he was a soft player, like some deluded fools thought Bobby Moore to be a soft touch.

Beckenbauer was a world-class player in his position, probably the best. He was always so cool. He would just come up to you, pass the ball, and he was gone like a Mercedes. He was a lovely player, and I liked the guy too.

But it wasn't so much the forwards who impressed me over the years as the defenders, and there were several who were very difficult to play against. Whenever I saw their names on the teamsheet before kick-off, I knew I was in for a battle. They roll off the tongue: Norman Hunter, Billy Bremner, Tommy Smith, Ron Chopper Harris, Jimmy Gabriel and Tony Kay at Everton, and Dave Mackay, the hardest and fairest of them all. Some of them were not only hard, but a bit naughty as well. Chopper

Harris was one of those. After we'd finished playing I met up with him again and you couldn't meet a nicer guy in the world, but he would kick his granny from one end of the pitch to the other if he thought it would help his team to win the game. He knew he was a tough player, and he took the blows as well, didn't bat an eyelid. You couldn't intimidate Ron.

Big Ron Yeats at Liverpool was a bit tasty to play against too, as was Jack Charlton, who was awkward but largely fair. He was all elbows and knees, climbing all over you for every cross. It was tough and tiring. Ron was so big that when Bill Shankly signed him for Liverpool he invited the press to take a walk around him! Mike England was another tough but very fair player, an out-standing centre-half for Wales and Spurs, while Bobby Moore, the great West Ham United and England captain, was excellent at reading the game and hard to get around. In fact, he read the game so well he hardly had to make a tackle – which was fortunate, for he wasn't the greatest tackler in the world, despite the famous one he made on Pele during the 1970 World Cup; he would just predict the situation, get in and intercept before the tackle was needed. You have to be a really good defender to be able to do that.

Another defender I liked was a guy called Joe Harris, who played for Sheffield United. He was only five feet nothing in his socks, but he still played centre-half because he read the game and controlled it so well. He was never a big star, but the Sheffield United fans loved him and they had a reasonably good side around him.

As for the toughest, they were so hard I still have to be careful what I say about them! Norman Hunter was as hard as any I ever played against (in fact, Leeds had more than their fair share: Paul Reaney, Terry Cooper, Jack Charlton, Billy Bremner, Allan Clarke, they all liked a dig), with Peter Storey of Arsenal close and his Highbury team-mate Peter Simpson not far behind. He could dig a bit, could the quiet man, but, as with Bobby Moore, referees rarely spotted his excesses. Arsenal were never short of a few who could put the foot in. Irish full-back Sammy Nelson, another hard boy, could do a bit of digging too.

They were tough men, yes, but they could all play, and that is what made them special.

17 AND THOSE I MISSED

I MIGHT HAVE BEEN FORTUNATE ENOUGH TO PLAY WITH AND against some of the greats of all time, but there were those I missed out on, players I had no contact with other than as a fan, and they too feature in my mental scrapbook of a lifetime connected with the beautiful game.

Pele was a player I would certainly have loved to play with, or even against, just to have seen him in action. He is rated the best of all time by many people, and he was clearly a special player. I remember him scoring in the 1958 World Cup in Sweden at the age of just sixteen. It really doesn't matter how old they are; if they're good enough, they're old enough. He wasn't a big guy, but he was very fast and strong, and he struck the ball superbly. We even saw from him a few attempts from the halfway line at a time when a lot of the leading players wouldn't even have dreamed of trying. As well as being a marvellous player, he has also been a great ambassador for football, travelling all over the world. With the possible exception, now, of David Beckham, he's almost certainly the most famous footballer in the world, definitely the best-known ex-player, and he'll remain so for a long time, even after he's gone, as we now seem to live in a world of heroes and nostalgia.

Had Pele played in today's game, without the tackling from behind and other violent measures, I'm sure he would have been a sensation. Imagine what Brazil might have done to add to their already phenomenal record had Pele not been kicked out of the 1966 World Cup. It was much the same for many of the skilful players of that particular era, but Pele took more stick than most. I'm convinced he would have been an even better player under today's interpretation of the laws of the game, and one wonders what he might have been worth.

As I said, he wasn't alone in being marked and kicked out of games, particularly in Italy and South America, and that's why Diego Maradona has my respect as an excellent player. He had to learn how to survive, how to ride potentially crippling tackles. He had his much-publicized problems, but there's no rule that states you have to be a good guy to be a great player. I suppose you could say he did it despite his poor upbringing in the slums of Buenos Aires, the drugs, the gangsters and everything else that blighted his life. He was five foot nothing but built like a tank. Defenders just could not get the ball off him. He shielded it like nobody's business, he had a good shot, he was a magical dribbler and had an excellent football brain to go with it.

I fear for his future now that the football has gone. The last time I saw him he had shaved his head and was sporting a yellow-striped beard. Oh dear, hallelujah! Pele he is not. But how difficult to come from his background and be thrust into football when it was dripping with money. Barcelona paid £4.8 million for him, Napoli a then world record of £6.9 million, and even after his drug abuse, his heavy drinking, his criminal shenanigans and his arrest, when he was a ravaged man in his early thirties, Sevilla still shelled out £4.8 million! For a player like him, the skill side of things was never going to be an issue; it was off the field where his problems multiplied. Settling into a new environment – a different culture, a different language, a different way of life – is never easy for anyone. I remember when he first went to Barcelona, and there were sixty thousand people watching him training. Sixty thousand! At most at Torino we had something like five thousand watching us training, and even that was a strain because you had to do your best at all times. You can't fiddle or fanny about when a crowd's watching. And he had sixty thousand. Imagine the pressure. When he went to Italy, despite similar difficulties including an even more intrusive media, he turned Napoli into a championship-winning team. They were nothing before Maradona and nothing after him. But the media attention on him was horrendous. They were just as football crazy in Argentina, of course, but at least then he was in his own country with his own people talking his own language. When a player of limited education and intelligence moves to another continent and has to put up with what Maradona had to put up with, things are bound to get difficult. We thought George Best's boozing was bad, but with Diego, apparently, it was drugs. I have never seen a social drug in my life, and I wouldn't know what to do with it if I was given one, but of course we knew they were in society. It was no way to prepare for football, and neither was mixing with the Mafia, as the stories suggested he was doing. In the end, there was no way out for him.

I remember seeing Maradona at Hampden Park for the first time. He was only a young boy then, and I thought his was one of the best performances I'd seen for a long time. He was marvellous that day, and I said to commentator Peter Jones that he was the best prospect I'd seen for a long time – and then they didn't play him in the World Cup in Argentina because at eighteen he was too young, even though Pele had proved that if you're good enough you're old enough, as had others like Duncan Edwards. More recently, the young Everton striker Wayne Rooney has proved the adage, though he has yet to prove himself worthy of joining that elite group of players.

Johann Cruyff was another terrific player with a really good footballing brain, though there is a measure of opinion against him. George Best was one of those who didn't rate him that highly, but I felt he was a very influential player. The Dutch team of which he was a crucial part was unlucky not to win the World Cup in 1974, and despite getting to the final again four years later, they missed him. I just thought he was one of the best, and he performed wherever he went. He was a god at Barcelona for many years, both as a player and a manager. I wish I had played with him, because he was a thinking player.

Dutch football came from nowhere in the 1970s, as did Cruyff. They were semi-professional nobodies when we used to play them, we didn't even bat an eyelid; not quite your Third World country, but poor compared to the likes of the Italians, the Germans and the Spanish, even the Czechs, the Poles and the Hungarians. They were never in that class at all. Then, suddenly, they produced a stack of outstanding players, introduced total football and threatened to dominate the world, in club football as well. Ajax, Feyenoord and PSV Eindhoven all made their assaults on Europe, Ajax reaching three European Cup finals. Cruyff was the first Dutchman to be voted European Footballer of the Year, in 1971, and he went on to win it three times. He quit the game after missing the 1978 World Cup because of a death threat but came back later to play in America and then in Holland after a wonderful career with Barcelona.

He had great vision and scored a lot of goals from his midfield position. I rate Cruyff a better player than Michel Platini, who tended to stand out in winning sides and who owed his European Footballer of the Year award to the players around him who gave him his platform. Don't get me wrong, Platini was a good player, but I never thought he was the player people made him out to be, and he certainly wasn't the same standard as Cruyff. I would have worried far more if I'd seen Cruyff's name on the opposing teamsheet.

Another player I'm sad not to have played with was John Charles, who surely deserves a place on anyone's list of great players. I met John for the first time in the early 1960s when I was playing in Italy, and he was marvellous to me when I was having problems settling down in a land he had totally conquered. He was equally at home as a centre-half or as a centre-forward. If his team was struggling, Big John would be sent up front and was more likely to score a goal than the man who was already there. Even when he was approaching his forties his clubs still wanted him to play up front and score goals. He was an excellent player, and he wasn't called the Gentle Giant for nothing: when he tackled you, you stayed tackled, but he was a lovely man who would hurt no-one. Proof of that lies in the fact that he was never booked or sent off in six years of playing in Italy. He was a good football player, and one of the best headers of the ball the game has ever seen. He headed that ball solidly, whether it was to clear his own goal or to attack the other. I rate him so highly that I would pick him as the greatest centre-half I have ever seen and one of my top three strikers.

Imagine the impact he would have made in today's game with such versatility. Imagine him alongside someone like Ole Gunnar Solskjaer; what a devastating pair they would make! He was far from a selfish player, but he still scored a goal a game during the era of *catenaccio*. That's why he was 'The King' over there. He was just a lovely man and a fabulous player. Times have changed and things have changed, but John Charles remains for me a giant among players.

Another attacking player I admire greatly from that era is Luis Suarez, one of the best inside-forwards the game has produced. He also won the European Footballer of the Year award, when he was with Barcelona; then he moved on to Inter Milan where he really blossomed, winning three Scudettos, the European Cup and the World Club Championship. I thought he had a bit of everything in terms of ability. We didn't see him a great deal on television, but he was world class.

When it comes to modern players, right up there for me is Zinedine Zidane of France and Real Madrid, who I think is a better player than his team-mate Luis Figo. I'm not saying Figo's not a good player, but Zidane is a class above, an outstanding player in anyone's estimation, terrific with both feet and so skilful when dragging a ball, which not many players can do well. He has a good step-over too. You never know whether he's going to go this way or that way. He has tremendous touch on the ball. The goal he scored in the 2002 Champions League final at Hampden Park must be one of the best ever scored in a huge game like that. The perfect volley. Zidane's a player I can sit and watch and enjoy. He doesn't roll about on the deck either; he gets tackled, he gets back up. There are very few top European stars you can put in that category. There are very good players in Britain, but there's not one to touch him.

Then there's his team-mate, the Brazilian striker Ronaldo, who looked to be finished after the disastrously late decision to play him against France in the 1998 World Cup final in Paris, but he's still shining, even among a firmament of stars at Real Madrid. After a few years practically out of the game, he came storming back and had a marvellous World Cup in 2002. He was possibly the difference between the two sides in the final against Germany, the reason why Brazil were crowned champions again. His goals came out of nothing, absolutely nothing. I fancied him to score every time Brazil attacked, even though as a team they didn't play particularly well. But rarely has a team been able to shackle Ronaldo. He's a star, no doubt about that.

The nearest equivalent we have here is Michael Owen of Liverpool and England, another striker who, if he receives the ball in front of goal, is a natural predator. I believe he does a fine job for both club and country, though the proof will lie in his final tally of goals for both. His main asset is his electric pace, particularly over the first few yards, but he is also developing his game in other areas. He burst on to the scene as a teenager during the 1998 World Cup in France, displaying his pace, intelligence and finishing ability with a spectacular goal against Argentina. I thought that for one so young he played really well. It could not have been easy. He has followed that up by helping Liverpool to win three trophies in a season, and he's consistently scored goals at all levels.

Over the years, Liverpool has either been very fortunate or very clever in finding top goalscorers. To win trophies, you have to be able to score goals. Good management or good luck? It has to be a bit of both. Look at Ian Rush. He was taken from Third Division Chester, pinched, I can reveal, from under the nose of Manchester City. Ken Barnes recommended him to City well before Liverpool, but for some reason they were too slow to respond and Liverpool stole in. Rushie went on to have a productive relationship with Kenny Dalglish which led to many goals and trophies. Then they found Robbie Fowler, a prolific marksman, even though at the end of the day he didn't fit in with Gérard Houllier's plans. Before that there was John Toshack and Kevin Keegan, and before them Roger Hunt. Every team with ambition needs players like that, players who aren't necessarily strikers but who still score goals. When Liverpool had their great runs, they had midfield players like Graeme Souness, Terry McDermott and Ray Kennedy who would knock in half a dozen goals or more apiece.

The current Arsenal squad is blessed with several world-class players, and of them all I like Thierry Henry the most. I first saw him when he played for Monaco against Manchester United, when he was on the wing, and I knew instinctively he was an outstanding prospect. In fact, I was surprised Sir Alex Ferguson didn't go straight in and buy him there and then. How much is he worth now? Henry is certainly a player I would have liked to play with, and the same goes for his team-mate and fellow French international Patrick Vieira, a top player and a good tackler of the ball. I can offer no higher praise than that he reminds me of Dave Mackay. He's a big, tough lad who gets himself into a bit of trouble with referees, but he's a fantastic passer of the ball, and when he's released from his holding role in midfield he likes to get forward. Even a skilful team like Arsenal needs somebody to get up and down, to fetch and carry, to defend and then get the ball up to the front men, and Vieira's that type of player. A ninety-minute, 100 per cent player. Just look at Arsenal's achievements over the last few years while he and Henry have been the main cogs in their machinery. That tells you how good they both are, and what a good talent-spotter Arsène Wenger is.

There's another Arsenal player I would have loved to play alongside, and that's Dennis Bergkamp. (Folklore would have it that his father was a fan of mine and named him after me. I'm very flattered, but where did the extra 'n' come from?) Like Vieira and Henry, Bergkamp came to Highbury via Italy and immediately settled into English football. What I like about him is that he doesn't fiddle about; he's a fine one-touch player who is quick, and he's a natural goalscorer. He can score spectacular goals or he can tap them in from close range, he doesn't mind how he gets them. He can, however, sometimes be a bit spiky, and like me he has had his share of suspensions for the occasional word and the odd kick. But even in today's game you have to be prepared to look after yourself up front; if you don't, you're still likely to be kicked from pillar to post, or to have your shirt pulled. Sometimes you've got to be a bit up front to play up front. It's easy to be a destroyer; it's more difficult to be a creator. You need something a bit special, and Bergkamp has it, even though his best playing days are surely behind him. I also like Robert Pires, but though he won the Footballer of the Year trophy he was injured the next season when we would have seen what he was made of, and even in 2002/03 he did not scale the same heights. The jury's still out on him.

Gianfranco Zola is probably the best of the rest, although at the time of writing he has left Stamford Bridge for Cagliari. I liked him when he was playing in Italy, and he was outstanding for Chelsea. He's a terrific ball player, small but strong with good vision, and he scores lovely goals. He also takes a wicked free-kick with a real bend on the ball. I think he's a lovely player, and a really nice guy too. When he's on the ball you always think something is going to happen, whether it's a nice pass, a clever move or a goal out of the blue. As a spectator, you get that feeling of excitement, and that to me is always a sign of a great player. I doubt, though, if you'd find him on many people's top-ten lists. The world did not see as much of him in an Italian shirt as they might have done, but then a lot of really good players don't get the recognition they deserve for some reason or another.

In terms of teams, the best club side I ever saw was undoubtedly the Real Madrid of the Di Stefano/Puskas era, and the best national team the Brazil World Cup-winning side of 1970. We are now more than thirty years on from that tournament, but

I still reckon they are the best team the world has ever seen, and if they were playing now they would still be the best. I don't buy the argument that modern teams would slaughter the old teams; if you've got the skill, you've got the skill. You can always make a footballer fitter, but the best coach in the world cannot hand out talent, and these guys had talent in spades. They benefited from an innovative training regime and a huge back-up team of doctors and psychiatrists, but what made them great was their skill from back to front. It's worth remembering the team that crushed Italy 4–1 in the final that summer: Felix, Carlos Alberto, Brito, Piazza, Everaldo, Clodoaldo, Gerson, Rivelino, Jairzinho, Tostão, Pele.

Real Madrid were their nearest equivalents at club level. Several sides have come close – the Torino team of the late 1940s; Juventus with Charles, Sivori and Boniperti in the 1950s; the Spurs double-winning team; Ajax in the 1970s; the Liverpool teams when they were winning European Cups; AC Milan in the 1990s; Santos in South America; even several Manchester United teams from the side that was decimated in 1958, through ours in the 1960s to the treble-winning side of 1999 – but that Real Madrid team of the late 1950s and early 1960s is my choice for the best of all time. Dominguez, Marquitos, Pachin, Vidal, Santamaria, Zarraga, Canario, Del Sol, Di Stefano, Puskas, Gento – in 1960 they murdered that Eintracht Frankfurt side. It doesn't get any better than that.

This brings us rather neatly to the current Manchester United squad. The Dutch striker Ruud Van Nistelrooy has impressed me immensely. When he first came to Old Trafford I thought he was an excellent player. He's another I would have liked to play alongside because he gives the team everything. He chases lost causes and balls that are really going nowhere, and he always seems to do something with it once he has chased it down. I like Roy Keane too. He's built in the same fashion as Dave Mackay, a fierce competitor and a winner. You'd always prefer to have a player like Keane in your team rather than playing against you. How he copes with injuries will dictate his future. Paul Scholes is another smashing player in the current squad. He can do two jobs for United. He can play midfield quite easily or play behind the front strikers, score goals and put his foot in. He's the size of nothing but he punches his weight. I like that kind of player. Another player who has always impressed me since his arrival at Old Trafford is Ole Gunnar Solskjaer, another natural goalscorer, a good player and a wonderful clubman who has been uncomplaining throughout his United career despite spending so much time on the bench. Teddy Sheringham also did well for Sir Alex when everybody thought he was past his best. He was a fine provider and also came in with some goals, as did Andy Cole and Dwight Yorke, who worked effectively as a pair for a while.

The big question now is how much United will miss David Beckham. Well, only time will tell. There's no question he was a wonderful provider of crosses, whether from open play or from free-kicks. I know I would have enjoyed his service. Beckham was worth his place purely in that sense; his steady flow of corners, free-kicks and crosses always seemed to move into the critical areas, swinging away from the keeper. In that respect David will be missed, but probably United sold him at the right time. As far as I'm concerned, his move to Real Madrid was good for both the player and the club. As an outsider looking in, I felt that David was becoming bigger than the club, and that, of course, cannot be. I think there were many at Old Trafford who were fed up with reading about him, his wife and his social exploits. He was in every part of the newspaper whatever he did, and I believe it was affecting both him as a player and the team. Sir Alex Ferguson has always been one to put the club before everything else, as he did when he sold his own son and when he moved on other top players. David is now at a club where there are many superstars; certainly he can't be put on a pedestal above a player of the quality of Zinedine Zidane! It may do him a lot of good, and he could become an even better player because he will have to get away from the showbiz side and back to the real world, his real world, of football. He will have to work hard and fight for his place. With so many great players around him, I have the feeling he can move on. As for Manchester United, well, players come and go, as do teams. Even so, only by the end of the 2003/04 season will we be able to judge whether or not it was a shrewd manoeuvre.

18 THE MANAGERS AND THE GAME

ON MY LIST OF TOP MANAGERS IN MY LIFETIME, SIR ALF RAMSEY sticks out like a sore thumb. My favourites, and the most successful, are easy to name – Sir Matt Busby, Bill Shankly, Jock Stein, Bill Nicholson, Brian Clough, Bob Paisley and Sir Alex Ferguson – but how can you leave out the man who won the World Cup for England? He also won the First Division title with an unfashionable club, Ipswich Town, without the finances and the support of big city clubs, so he is impossible to ignore. But I still don't agree with the style of football he played to win the world's premier trophy, and I still believe he and England set our game back in this country because of it.

The others on my list are different: all their teams played attractive, attacking football and they were all a joy to watch. Forest was not a big city club, but under Brian Clough they were superb. I was lucky enough to cover their progress in the late 1970s and early 1980s through my media work. I saw all their triumphs, and I can confirm they were a very good and very exciting team to watch. One of the key players for them was a

Scottish lad on the left-hand side who didn't look like a football player. He was a bit chubby and boasted a bit of a beer belly. He was hardly a male model, but, boy, could John Robertson play football! A little chip here, a little pass there; what a good midfield player he was, and he weighed in with his share of goals too. He was a funny bloke in every respect, and reportedly once turned up for an away match with just a toothbrush in his back pocket. I didn't know him well enough to pass judgement on his lifestyle or character, but he was clearly a different personality from John McGovern, who was not a queen bee but a worker bee, the sort of player every team needs. Together, they made a nice balance. That was what Brian Clough was good at, picking square pegs and fitting them into round holes for very little outlay. Clough did incredibly well, not only in the domestic competitions but in Europe as well, twice winning the European Cup.

At his height, Brian Clough should have been the England manager. For me he was the obvious choice in 1977 when Don Revie left to go to the Middle East. He was the popular choice too, but everyone felt that because he wasn't a yes man when it came to the FA, he wouldn't be offered the job. Clearly it went a little deeper than that; they'd tried out Clough and his assistant Peter Taylor with the England under-21 side, so obviously something had happened to convince the men at Lancaster Gate that they shouldn't appoint him. But looking at it from the public perspective, it should have been between him and Bob Paisley, for there was no-one around more successful than those two, even though neither of them had a coaching certificate. The fans hoped for Clough because they knew Bob didn't want it, not in a million years. He was not that type of manager, and he hated the spotlight. Joe Fagan, the final successful manager of that Anfield dynasty, was another who definitely would not have had the slightest interest in leaving his beloved club to work for what he saw as stuffed shirts at Lancaster Gate.

Bill Nicholson at Tottenham Hotspur was another who could spot a quality player at a distance, and he built a superb double-winning side when winning doubles was something that belonged to the previous century. Jock Stein did the same with Celtic, confounding everyone with his home-built style and homespun philosophy. He won nine titles on the bounce at home as well as prising open the Continental grip on the European Cup. The similarities in background of Jock Stein, Matt Busby, Bill Shankly and Alex Ferguson, all Scots from around the same area, is remarkable. They were hungry managers who knew how important it was for the fans to enjoy their football. They knew these were the people who were paying the wages, that you had to give them something back, and every one of their sides gave nothing less than 100 per cent all the time. If they didn't, the manager would get stuck into them, telling them it wasn't good enough. The players knew they were good guys but hard as nails when it came to making a decision to let someone go or to bring in a player from outside who was better than the one they had in their own team. There was no sentiment and no favouritism, but the teams they produced played attractive football; they scored goals and were exhilarating to watch.

Sir Alex Ferguson, of course, has spanned the generations with his teams, as has another footballing knight, Sir Bobby Robson. Now back home in his beloved Newcastle, Bobby has turned the club around from the wrong end of the Premier League to challenging for the title and competing in the Champions League. Like Alex, Bobby loves to see his teams attack and regularly takes to the field with two genuine wingers. It is bold and it is adventurous, but for two seasons in succession he has guided Newcastle into the top four and brought packed houses and an awful lot of pride to every game at St James's Park. Bobby, of course, has a wealth of experience to call upon: after his quiet but successful start in the backwaters of Ipswich he went on to manage England for eight years, at the worst possible time with the European bans on English teams, before moving on to great adventures with club sides in Holland, Portugal and Spain.

I'm sure no-one would begrudge Bobby success in his remaining years in charge at Newcastle, but he has plenty of competition, and not solely from Sir Alex Ferguson and Manchester United. Everyone has to admit that Arsène Wenger has done a brilliant job at Arsenal. It can't be easy for a foreign manager to come to our little island, win over the fans and win big trophies, but the unassuming Wenger has done it, as has his compatriot Gérard Houllier at Liverpool where, not many years ago, they were suspicious of anything foreign. Houllier also seems to be a lovely guy, always the gentleman. He comes over well on television and earned nationwide sympathy in 2001 when he was rushed to hospital after a heart attack in the middle of a tense game. He is an Anglophile and has settled well in a city he knew from his youth, while Wenger is equally cosmopolitan, having worked in Japan's J League.

What's so good about the top managers in England today is that they enjoy playing the attractive, attacking football patented by their illustrious predecessors. Arsenal are certainly in that group with players of real flair and excitement. They've always been a hard team to beat, but they haven't always had the flair they have now. Wenger has brought it to them by nurturing and signing players like Vieira, Henry, Pires, Kanu, Jeffers and Wiltord. That type of player can fill a ground every week, home or away.

But you still have to know how to defend, a point Shanks always liked to hammer home. 'The thing you've got to get right in your team is your defence,' he would say. 'You can't be conceding goals all over the place because there's no point scoring four if you concede five. It may be exciting for the people, but it's not good for the future.' That's why he brought in Big Ron Yeats at the beginning of his reign. He got that right, and then he developed his midfield with Ian St John, Roger Hunt and the two wingers, Ian Callaghan on one side and Peter Thompson on the other. That was the start of Liverpool's success, which they carried on for many years. Wenger had a solid defence in place at Highbury when he took over in 1996, and it was the basis for Arsenal's double-winning season in 1997/98, but they lost their way a bit when Adams, Dixon, Winterburn et al got older and Wenger was suddenly left short in defence, to Arsenal's cost and Manchester United's benefit.

Of all the current Premier League managers, Sir Alex Ferguson is the longest-serving and the most successful. And to think he could have been on his way out in 1990. Had United lost to Crystal Palace in the FA Cup final replay that year, he would probably have been sacked. A single goal, a solitary win, can either make or break a manager. Exactly the same thing happened with Howard Kendall at Everton: they were about to sack him but an own-goal in their favour during a crucial League encounter away from home saved him. From then on Everton went like a bomb, winning the FA Cup and the First Division title. That 1–0 win over Palace kickstarted a new era of success at Old Trafford.

A similar thing happened to our team in the 1962/63 season. Ours was a disastrous season in the League and we nearly went down, but then we turned it on in the FA Cup final against favourites Leicester City and that was it, the springboard to further success.

Just look at Alex's record at Aberdeen against the two big clubs in Scotland, Celtic and Rangers. While he was at Pittodrie he won something like nine trophies, including a European trophy. Aberdeen are a big club, but they're not in the same league as the other two where money's concerned. Still, Alex dominated football in Scotland in the face of those two giants, and to think that one bad result with Manchester United could have seen him on his way from Old Trafford with nothing but his P45 . . .

Fergie's qualities are very similar to those of Sir Matt, Shanks and Jock Stein. They all had that hunger. Every now and then all managers are accused of buying bad players, but more often than not they're simply players who don't slot in for some reason. The important ones are the good buys who go towards making a team, and the young players coming through the ranks. Busby put his faith and the future of the club in youth, but you have to be gentle with the youngsters because we all know if you have too many of them in your team you're going to struggle. You need to have a blend, and Fergie has been successful in bringing on his young players and mixing them with world-class players. He knows that to ensure the club's future the set-up behind the scenes is as important as the first team. We have seen a number of top-quality youngsters come through at United, more so than at any other club; the scouting system behind the scenes on the schoolboy side is clearly very good. And the club still has the wherewithal to go and buy players from around the world. When you have both sides working well like that, it makes the job easier, but you still have to maintain that balance between British players and foreign imports.

I see Alex quite often, and get on great with him – he's a good friend. He has a bad reputation with some of the media, but, to be fair, a manager's job today is extremely difficult. As well as dealing with the media on a daily basis he himself is under the spotlight all the time. There is only so much you can say, and then you have to keep time available to look after team and club affairs. That's what decides your future. He doesn't suffer fools gladly and he has a long memory for those who cross him, but, quite frankly, I don't blame him. I'd feel the same way myself. If somebody treats me badly, I'll react to it. At least Alex will say it out loud and not walk away.

I'm delighted at Alex's success because it was always going to be very difficult for anyone to take on the legacy of Sir Matt Busby. Ron Atkinson did quite well in his five years or so with the club, with a couple of FA Cup successes and an unfortunate season when the League looked to be a certainty until injuries crippled the side; he also made some excellent signings and his teams always played good football. But he found himself up against a Liverpool outfit that was the best at the time. Winning the League is a long, tough process, but invariably the best team does win, not like the FA Cup where the draw can be vital and the top teams can knock each other out. At that time, the problem with Liverpool winning at home was that they could also go on to compete in Europe's top competition. Their success hurt the United supporters and the club because they felt their team should be up there doing a similar thing. Getting into Europe these days is a lot easier. Now, the top four clubs go straight into the Champions League. Then, it was a knockout competition. The pressure was on, and if you blew it you were out, whereas now, as Newcastle showed, you can lose your first three games and still go through to the next round. On that basis, Ron would have taken United through every season because of their high finishes in the First Division, and how would that have changed the future of the club?

Winning the League may still look good on your CV, but it's not as important any more in the boardrooms at Liverpool, Newcastle, United, Arsenal and Chelsea as the Champions League. When you're in that competition, you can sit back and count the money coming in, at least while the television contracts remain so high. You can even be knocked out of the Champions League and still go in the UEFA Cup, which used to be as hard as the European Cup to win because it invariably contained most of the teams that had been chasing their domestic titles that season. You were playing top teams in Europe without the glamour of the European Cup. The Cup Winners' Cup was almost a special cup for the English clubs because it was only here that we took our domestic cup competition really seriously, and so we had a string of winners.

Playing in Europe is crucial for Sir Alex, and it's the lifeblood of a club like Manchester United. Television made a massive impact because it wasn't just Britain showing the games, it was the whole world. History counts, too. People from around the globe began to follow United's results out of a sort of morbid post-Munich interest, to see if a once-great team could rise from the ashes. Then, because United gained some success and played attractive football throughout the 1960s, interest grew. Now, the name of the club is all over the world. You can pick up a paper almost anywhere and there is the name of Manchester United in the sports page headlines. Even the Americans are beginning to take notice. United rival Real Madrid as the best-known team in the world; perhaps they even surpass them because Premier League matches are shown live in many countries. The Manchester United brand name is huge in much the same way as Coca-Cola and McDonald's, and everything has changed as a result: the stadium, the ground, the training and the medical facilities. Injuries could rule you out for ever in the blink of an eye a few years back, but now they have microsurgery and players are back playing ten days after a cartilage operation which would have kept us out for six weeks or more. Diet has changed radically too, because it's now big business. Even the pitch has changed. We used to train on it because there was nowhere else to go, and if it rained it was ruined, maybe for the entire season. I have played in games and I've seen games where the ground was so mucky the match should have been called off. I remember when they used to hold show-jumping events at Wembley. I couldn't believe it; the pitch wouldn't recover for several years. It was like taking cows to graze on a bowling green. Incredible. When you look at pitches now at the end of the season, they're still beautiful. If you can't play football on those surfaces, you can't play football anywhere. We had the best conditions for around six weeks, maybe two months at the most; once we were into November it was invariably muddy right through until April, by which time you only had grass in the corners.

Envious? Of course I am! I would have loved to play on such perfect pitches all season and earned the sort of money the boys are earning now. I know envy is one of the seven deadly sins, but look at great players like Stanley Matthews, Tom Finney and Johnny Haynes, earning a pittance in the 1950s, and you can understand why some of us old ones think wistfully about what might have been.

The business side of things continues to grow, and now that's what the game is about off the pitch: hospitality, entertainment, fundraising, merchandising, sponsorship, stock markets. Sometimes this is all seen to be to the detriment of the normal, average supporter, but maybe Roy Keane was a little over the top with his comments about the prawn-sandwich brigade because these are still the people who pay his wages. I suppose you could say he was right in some respects, especially when people who aren't really football people are invited, but that's the way the world has gone and corporate revenue plays a big part in the success of the club. And to be fair to Manchester United, they're still one of the cheapest clubs to watch in the Premier League, and

Old Trafford is a lovely stadium now. They've done it right. Everything about the place is right. It's just like a hotel in certain areas, absolutely beautiful and a million miles away from my playing days. We don't want to go back to the old days when the toilets were outside and you had to queue to get in. The punters were forced to line up and shuffle forward to go in one door and out the other. The only good thing about the old grounds was the meat pie and mug of hot Bovril, but even then you had to queue and maybe miss ten minutes of the second half. People went regularly to the cinema and were used to a bit of luxury with a nice seat and good toilet facilities, and then they would go to a football ground and it was chaos, fifty thousand people with three toilets between them. That's why the supporters peed down the terraces.

The one aspect I don't join the supporters in is the demand for a return to standing-room-only terraces. I can only believe these are people who did not live through the dark years when the game was almost wrecked by some of those who took advantage of the anonymity of the terraces to cause trouble and worse. I remember covering a game for the BBC when Aberdeen played Liverpool in one of the European competitions. Aberdeen was the first ground in Britain to have an all-seater stadium. Peter Jones and I were commentating on the game from the back of one of the stands, and every time Aberdeen attacked, the entire crowd in our stand stood up and we had to do our commentary standing on the seats at the back of the stadium. I know all-seaters can be annoying, but safety issues are paramount. I also recall watching the game between Brazil and Holland in Dallas during the 1994 World Cup. I was there with Jack Charlton and we were very relaxed because we weren't covering the game until the highlights later on in the evening. We had nice seats in the middle of the stand, but we had the Brazilian supporters in front of us and they never sat down the whole game. So after ten minutes in the second half I was so fed up I turned to Jack and told him I was going back to the studio because I could watch the game better there. We cannot go back to what it was, but maybe Barcelona have the right idea. At the Nou Camp they provide standing room in one corner at the back of the stand where the fans can't obstruct the view of anyone else.

The people who claim corporate hospitality and all-seater stadia are killing the game are talking rubbish; it was in the 1970s and 1980s that the game was in danger of dying because of hooliganism. Families weren't going, children, women and sensible men weren't going, and the lunatics were taking over the stadium. The entire scene changed after the awful events at Hillsborough during that semi-final between Liverpool and Nottingham Forest, and after the fire at Bradford. Things had to change, and fortunately they did.

It is actually incredible that grounds are still full despite the staggering amount of live football on television these days. At Manchester United, they even have their own television station, showing interviews, matches, reserve matches and youth football. I suppose for supporters it's interesting to see the second team playing, but I must confess I don't subscribe. Still, I don't see anything wrong with it. Manchester United, after all, is an industry. What I don't agree with, however, is the constant changing of kit, but then they have to do it because football is a business and it is run like a business. It's marketing, and they need it because it means extra revenue for the club, and big bucks are needed to run any club these days and to finance wages and transfer fees. That's why television is so important.

But these things can go too far. Look at the clubs that were plunged into trouble when the Granada deal folded. There were more than a few of them spending money they didn't have.

They were spending money on a promise, and that's dangerous whatever line you're in – and in this instance we're talking about an awful lot of money. Premier League clubs must have nightmares about Sky pulling the plug, but it won't happen because everything is based on their football coverage. They thought they were going to build the station around movies, but that didn't work. Take away the football and they would struggle. But when it comes to cashing in on football there has to be a ceiling; you can only ask the public for so much of their money. I noticed that when Italy and France went for pay-for-view, offering all the big games live, it was an absolute flop, and at the same time the Italian attendances began to drop. The Premier League, I am sure, will have taken careful note of those events to make sure they do not get their fingers burned. It was a failure because people were being asked to pay for stuff they had been receiving free to air, or had already been paying for as part of a package. It sounded like a good idea: four of you watching Manchester United versus Liverpool at £2.50 a head would surely have been easy to sell. Or so the moneymen thought. The only sports that have been successful on this basis in America are baseball and boxing. But title fights happen only every now and then, not every week. I don't know how it will go here, but the powers-that-be have obviously done their homework and a package can be as little as fifty pence a game.

Still, ITV's pay-for-football deal with the Football League collapsed because there weren't enough people willing to take up the option. The figures aren't huge in Britain – maybe a million will watch an average game – but it's not Britain that funds live televised football, it's the world market. Wherever you go on holiday – Mauritius, Barbados, Thailand, Malaysia, Australia, India – there is Premier League football live on the box, even in Europe where they boast their own top leagues. The English game is still the best to watch because it's end to end with lots of action and plenty of excitement.

One thing I've noticed that has changed here is that people are becoming selective with their viewing. In the old days when there was a live match on television, whatever the level, you would sit in an armchair and watch it, then tune in to the recorded highlights on *Match of the Day* on a Saturday, but now there is so much live football broadcast on the various channels that viewers can afford to pick and choose, watching only the games they want to watch. Even if you do fancy a game a night, how could you make your family suffer while you watch seven games a week? The divorce rate would go through the roof!

As for the future, I can see only Manchester United getting bigger and bigger, trading on its name. We have been wondering for many years now how smaller clubs are going to survive. When the television deal collapsed there were grim warnings of half of them going to the wall. They were in trouble, but the dire predictions haven't come true. Still, there have to be some large crumbs from the rich men's tables for the game to survive as we know and love it, in all its variety. Football has grown into an integral part of the British way of life, and I doubt it is going to change dramatically in the near future.

INDEX

NOTE: Main matches mentioned in the text are listed under names of clubs. Club managers are listed separately under their own names. Highlights of author's life are listed in chronological order under his name.